Student Voice Research

Student Voice Research

Theory, Methods, and Innovations from the Field

Edited by Marc Brasof and Joseph Levitan

Foreword by Susan Groundwater-Smith

TEACHERS COLLEGE PRESS

TEACHERS COLLEGE | COLUMBIA UNIVERSITY

NEW YORK AND LONDON

Published by Teachers College Press,® 1234 Amsterdam Avenue, New York, NY 10027

Copyright © 2022 by Teachers College, Columbia University

Front cover illustration and design by Vanessa Gold

Library of Congress Cataloging-in-Publication Data is available at loc.gov

ISBN 978-0-8077-6712-2 (paper)
ISBN 978-0-8077-6713-9 (hardcover)
ISBN 978-0-8077-8111-1 (ebook)

Printed on acid-free paper
Manufactured in the United States of America

Contents

Foreword

Tell all the Truth but tell it slant—
Success in Circuit lies
Too bright for our infirm Delight
The Truth's superb surprise

—Emily Dickinson

Consulting young people and having them participate in research intended to render schools as places in which authentic learning is available to all—teachers, administrators, and learners alike—is a means to reveal the "truth" of learning as a "superb surprise." The hint in Dickinson's poem is that the route to "truth" is a challenging and often convoluted one. This, for me, is one of the many strengths of *Student Voice Research: Theory, Methods, and Innovations From the Field* in that it acknowledges the stubborn resistance to consulting and engaging with students and, in the face of such intransigence, offers ways and means for building an irresistible way forward.

There is a clear acknowledgment, throughout the work, that this is no easy journey. The book is underpinned by "the positionality of youth as students who have agency and essential insights into improving schools, working towards social justice, and informing educational policy" (p. 46). In effect it recognizes students as the consequential stakeholders who bear the burden of decisions most often made by others; or in effect, as Lawrence Stenhouse put it many years ago, "The first claim of the school is that of its pupils for whose welfare the school exists" (Stenhouse, 1983, p. 153).

Writers have been making the case for working with students as the consequential stakeholders in educational practices for well over 2 decades, myself included (Groundwater-Smith, 2007). When arguing for a form of boundary spanning that would act to bridge relationships, I drew upon the notion of occupying a borderland, citing Gloria Anzaldúa who has written most evocatively upon the existence of those living on the frontiers between cultures and languages (Anzaldúa, 1987). Culturally determined roles are imposed from the outside and dictate *who* is acceptable and who is not; *what* is acceptable and what is not. Anzaldúa's borderlands are a metaphor for the political and psychological positioning of those denied power. Finding the means to negotiate power relationships is a core theme of this impressive collection and is embedded in the Student Voice Research Framework.

As practitioners saturated in the minutiae of that which is required of us in our current audit culture, we can be *opaque* to ourselves. To be engaged in our work as *praxis*, embedded in theory, reflection, and action, requires that we are alert to alternative voices that can cast another light beyond merely measurable achievements. To attain such insight requires reflexivity, another central theme of the book, whereby *inter-alia*, biases and assumptions are revealed, examined, and interpreted. Hexter (1972) a notable historian mused on reflexivity as "the second record" that impels the researcher:

> [T]hat is, the constellation of subjectivities that are held by the researcher at the time of collecting, analysing and interpreting information, and that cannot fail to influence the work, it is "indefinite in scope, and much of it personal, individual, ephemeral and not publicly accessible" [Hexter, 1972, p. 104]. (Groundwater-Smith, 2005, p. 330)

Hexter's argument is "not *whether* the second record should be drawn upon, but *how* and *how best* it might be utilized" (p. 181). In other words, rather than escaping from the influence of life's experiences, it would be wiser to acknowledge them and their impact upon ruminations and writings and make them available to both the self and the reader. Much of this is now acknowledged as critical to the notion of reflexivity that not only requires the capacity to reflect, but also to understand from whence ideas and constructs have come.

The focus on reflexivity, intersubjectivity, power dynamics, and context is featured throughout the book. Also included are a number of practical methods that researchers had used to stimulate conversational encounters. These range from photo-voice work to physically developing a web of reflection that illustrates the manifestation of power in a particular context.

Each chapter can be seen as contributing to our current understandings of student voice work. In this way the book is a resource that will both appeal to those already engaged with and committed to such endeavor as well as those who are looking for guidance to embark on the challenge of participatory inquiry with young people. It acts to push against the current tide of a particular form of empiricism that objectifies students as solely subjects of research. At the same time the collection extends the range of practices to their limits by simultaneously putting together and taking apart ideas and practices; each chapter requires a careful and critical reading. It is a thoroughly disruptive text that understands that this orientation to research is incomplete and evolving; in the words of Dickinson, it *tells its story slant.*

—Susan Groundwater-Smith

REFERENCES

Anzaldúa, G. (1987). *Borderlands/La frontera: The New mestiza*. Aunt Lute Books.

Groundwater-Smith, S. (2005). Painting the educational landscape with tea: Rereading *Becoming Critical*. *Educational Action Research*, *13*(3), 329–346. https://doi.org/10.1080/09650790500200295

Groundwater-Smith, S. (2007). Student voice: Essential testimony for intelligent schools. In A. Campbell & S. Groundwater-Smith (Eds.), *An ethical approach to practitioner research* (pp. 113–128). Routledge.

Hexter, J. (1972). *The history primer.* Allen Lane.

Stenhouse, L. (1983). *Authority, education and emancipation.* Heinemann Educational.

Introduction

Student Voice: Reframing School Change by Repositioning Educational Research

Marc Brasof and Joseph Levitan

The best educators meet students where they are.

—Old adage

Student voice, at its foundation, is the involvement of young people in school and community leadership to ensure that youth can inform, participate in, and/ or lead the decisions that impact them on a daily basis. When young people and adults work together, classrooms, schools, and communities can become more socially, intellectually, and academically engaged. A growing body of student voice research has uncovered myriad ways that young people's perspectives about themselves, peers, educators, school life, curriculum, policies, pedagogy, and their communities have engendered richer understandings of teaching, learning, and life.

As a field, student voice research has increased our understanding of young people's needs and challenges, as well as the important knowledge(s) and expertise students can contribute to schools. Learning about students' hopes, dreams, perspectives, and values—knowing where students "are"— makes schools more responsive to their realities and fosters a more just and vibrant educational space. Not to mention that engaging and collaborating with students in research can be a valuable and rich learning experience for both students and educators!

Findings from student voice research have given teachers, school leaders, and policymakers better insight into the root factors and phenomena of perennial educational issues: from behavioral challenges and student engagement in learning and school life, to social justice concerns and solutions within the school or broader community. These insights highlight the centrality of students' voices in educational improvement. At regional, national, and international levels, the work of student voice researchers and practitioners is helping to make youth part of civic and human capacity-building initiatives in order to finely (re)tune the attention of educational institutions and focus on the needs and experiences of youth in relation to society (Baumann, Millard, & Hamdorf, 2014; Conner, Ebby-Rosin, & Brown, 2015; Holquist, 2019; Levitan & Johnson, 2020). This has generated a growing body of evidence showing that genuine inclusion of youth in research uncovers new, better ways to think about and engage in school and classroom change (see Brasof & Mansfield, 2018; Czerniawski & Kidd, 2011; Ginwright, Noguera, & Cammarota, 2006; Rudduck & McIntyre, 2007).

Nonetheless, approaches to the study of (or research with) young people from their perspectives as students are still underutilized. The lack of engagement from the research, academic, practitioner, and policy communities is often due to misunderstandings and misinterpretations about the processes and underlying reasons to engage in student voice research, as well as assumptions or stereotypes about the capacities of students to engage in research and/or understand educational problems. Yet, student voice research processes have too much potential for supporting the aims of cultivating schools that are just, caring, engaging, and intellectually rigorous to be ignored. In this book, we offer a comprehensive discussion and "how to" of student voice research. Along with seminal figures within this burgeoning field, we discuss what student voice research is and the theories and methodologies that go into effective studies. We explore when and why student voice research might be a useful approach for classroom, school, policy, or community change initiatives, and how to engage in student voice research effectively.

WHY STUDENT VOICE RESEARCH IS IMPORTANT

Early in his research career, Marc engaged in an ethnographic study of youth leadership in an urban school called Madison High School (Brasof, 2015). At MHS, students were increasingly becoming more disengaged in their academics, and behavioral problems were becoming more common. After the first few meetings with the school's student government leaders and educators, it became clear that the adults in the building believed the issue could be sourced to the students' lack of school spirit—if leadership could get students to care more about their school and instill a sense of pride, then the academic and behavioral issues would dissipate.

Student leaders, seeing that this analysis was based on unproductive images of youth, were unconvinced, so they leaned into democracy to suss out the issues. They built and implemented a survey collecting data on students' and faculty's perceptions of school spirit and what they wished would change. Through the survey and by observing classroom spaces with an eye toward student engagement, students began building a much more complex understanding of the challenges the school faced. That is, framing school challenges as a "lack of school spirit" actually blamed students for deeper systemic issues happening in the school. The findings brought out new understandings of the true issue, namely that school leaders had conflicting visions, which impacted instructional practices, such as generating yearly shifts in class scheduling that reduced students' abilities to fully engage in the school's project-based learning curriculum, as well as a haphazardly designed and implemented discipline system. In other words, the educators were turning their attention away from their own individual and structural challenges and instead focusing on the symptoms of the school's root problems.

As a researcher, this was an a-ha moment for Marc. He saw students engaging in conversations with educators that were leading to meaningful organizational learning. Without this critical student-led data collection, analysis, and discussion, it is unlikely the school's leadership team would have been able to begin planning strategies that would effectively tackle the root causes of the student disengagement and misbehavior. And the school could have easily continued down its path of creating solutions to the wrong problems. From this experience, Marc began to truly see the necessity of student voice research in uncovering new understandings for the field, but also how integral these voices were for the betterment of the school. Marc was inspired that his research could actually make substantive differences in schools, that studying student voices could be a key approach to enriching our understanding of the data and bridge the scholar–practitioner gap (Czerniawski & Kidd, 2011).

Student voice researchers have spent the past few decades uncovering a variety of findings that were "hidden in plain sight" because leaders and researchers were unwilling or unable to fruitfully engage with students to learn about their experiences. Commonly, what student voice researchers discover are loosely coupled systems and policies creating incongruences between the needs of students and teachers and the mechanisms used to foster improvement within schools or other educational organizations. Such disconnects create unresponsive or ineffectively designed systems (Brasof, 2018) and resistance to policies that ultimately makes buy-in and follow-through less likely (Fowler, 2009). Investigating the perceptions and experiences of youth within and across educational settings is often the missing link in educational research and practice that is aimed at improving schools and, ultimately, cultivating high-quality, person-centered, and socially just learning communities (Fielding, 1999a).

This missing link is often a result of a culture that infantilizes and espouses unproductive images of youth (they cannot be trusted to be honest, mature, or insightful), which is then reinforced through alienating leader-ship and classroom structures in schooling (Costello et al., 1997; Rudduck, 2007; Rudduck & Demetriou, 2003). Omission of students' voices is also a result of the broader contexts that situate research and practice in school reform as creating "high-performance" organizations, which have more in common with market-driven ideology (Fielding, 2006) than the full de-velopment of human potential and advanced democracies (Woods, 2005). Such issues have resulted in educational change strategies that tinker with school structures and processes without making substantial improvements to student learning and well-being (Darling-Hammond, 2010; Fowler, 2009; Mitchell & Sackney, 2011).

Instead of upholding unproductive images and excluding youth from educational decision-making, centering students' voices into educational re-search facilitates more self-determined and responsive approaches to stu-dents' learning, engagement, and belongingness in schools (Mansfield, 2014a). Responsive organizations that consider how youth interpret and respond to change, what their lived experiences can illuminate about daily life in educational organizations, and to what extent they share the values, goals, and strategies of schooling, build stronger cultures and improve student en-gagement and learning. Thus, student voice is an intersection of research, pedagogy, professional development, and organizational learning, which can tighten couplings to support an organization's ability to adapt and change (Mitchell & Sackney, 2011).

THE POWER OF STUDENT VOICE RESEARCH

Since 2010, Joe has worked with students and community members from rural, Quechua-speaking (Indigenous) communities in the Peruvian Andes. Having worked as a social justice–oriented community educator, Joe was asked by a friend to support a community-based educational initiative in the Andes to improve access to schools and the quality of education.

Joe learned about the power of student voice research through collaborating with the community on his first visit. To understand the problems in order to overcome them, Joe was invited to observe classes. In the first class, he saw students dutifully taking notes on European history. The students had a book read to them about Amerigo Vespucci, celebrating his accomplishments. Although a cultural outsider, it was not difficult to see that the students were not engaged. When the teacher asked a question to check the students' understanding of the text, there was a deafening silence. The teacher then "cold-called" a student, who was unable to answer. The teacher asked another student. By the third student, the teacher helped along the answer. Clearly frustrated, the teacher admonished all of the students, saying that they had to work harder and pay attention.

Watching this scene, Joe saw a non-Indigenous Peruvian teacher telling students from Indigenous communities that they were "not working hard enough" and "not paying attention"—implying that these students were not intelligent and/or that they were lazy (which is how this teacher described the students to Joe later). He also interpreted the scene as the teacher using a text that was a severe oversimplification of a complex history and which seemed out of place with (and antithetical to) the values and realities of the students. He saw students writing with their heads down, unable to answer questions, clearly not engaged in the process of learning. In each classroom he visited, the dynamics were similar.

Instead of interpreting this dynamic as an issue with the students (as the teachers would tell him after the classes), it seemed clear that pedagogy and curricular content were not aligned with the students' interests, goals, or realities. Having read Indigenous scholars' critiques of formal education in colonized societies (e.g., Adichie, 2009; Faircloth & Tippeconnic, 2004; Mackey, 2018; Smith, 1999), Joe was worried that the educational practices he saw, which did not speak with and grow from the students' realities, were also causing epistemological harm to the students. The public school system's curriculum and learning materials were centered on knowledge from European communication practices, history, science, and mathematical principles. The rich and deep Quechua knowledgebase was being ignored or tokenized. Instead of being authentically engaged with, it was being erased from the school and erased from "what counts" as knowledge.

Joe, being an outsider and painfully aware of the "white savior complex," did not know or want to assume "what knowledge is of the most worth" (Pinar, 2011) in this context. "What knowledge is of the most worth?" is a foundational question for curriculum, so he did not want to assume that his perspective was correct. The experts on the issue of school engagement were the students themselves. They (along with parents and elders in the community) were best situated to know what knowledge is of the most worth for their values and goals. Since Joe did not want to cause any further epistemological harm, he walked carefully through this work and started by asking questions and having conversations—building positive, reciprocal relationships with community members through shared interests (like soccer) and a willingness to work side by side when there were community-work days.

After doing some homework, Joe shared the idea to engage in a collaborative inquiry project in which students led meetings to ask and answer the questions that seemed to be assumed in classrooms: What did they want to learn? Why were they getting an education in this school? And who do they want to be and become? Engaging in community-oriented demo-cratic processes, such as roundtable discussions, collaboratively creating and analyzing surveys, and students engaging in interviews with elders and parents, the students identified a series of important areas of learning, which, with the support of adults, we implemented in a few selected classroom spaces. When the learning spaces became more responsive to the students' identities and goals, they were able to be much more energetic and engaged in the learning process. The students transformed the education center from a space of fear and confusion into a lively space of engaged learning and collaboration. This also led to improvements in learning throughout the school (Levitan, 2015; Levitan & Johnson, 2020).

The youth-led curriculum design showed teachers, parents, and the students themselves that students were not lazy or disinterested (which was often implied or stated outright in conversations about problems in class-rooms), but that they were very capable of driving their own learning and engaging in advanced work. The students mobilized their power to trans-form the school, showing the leadership and teachers that thoughtful, engaged student voice research can make powerful changes to improve edu-cation. The adults who carried negative stereotypes about students (such as deficit views about their capacities for learning) missed the root of the issue: what students were being taught stifled their ability to learn. When students co-led research projects by engaging in data collection and analysis to enact and demonstrate their values and co-create rich learning spaces, they thrived. The loosely coupled school, in which curriculum content, pedagogy, and policy did not connect to the students' realities, was the core of the problem, and students—a vital source of leadership and information—were the only ones in a position to address it.

Both Marc's and Joe's stories present students' voices as counternarra-tives. Too often students are positioned as receivers in schools and subjects in research. Data collection is designed without considering students' per-spectives on methods or epistemology, and analysis is done without member checking with students, undermining its validity. Instead, including students more genuinely into the research process increases our ability to understand and create more human, person-centric institutions, ones in which the full potentiality of individuals and a community can be realized through self-actualization, an ethic of care, and democracy—features too often in short supply.

One of the greatest challenges of student voice research projects is that they are not just common inquiry methods (like interviewing and focus groups) performed with students; rather, they require specific epistemologi-cal orientations (thinking about what knowledge is and what "counts" as knowledge) and nuanced understandings of the role of relationships and power dynamics in the creation of knowledge. What knowledge is for stu-dents and how their knowledge can be enacted to improve schools is a key question and challenge for student voice researchers (Levitan, 2018; Levitan & Johnson, 2020).

THE CHALLENGES WITHIN STUDENT VOICE RESEARCH

Student voice research texts offer a mosaic of methodologies, all of which argue for different theoretical and normative understandings about what student voice research is (e.g., Cook-Sather, 2018a; Groundwater-Smith, Dockett, & Bottrell, 2014; Nelson, 2015). Diverse perspectives allow for researchers to choose the approach that matches the context, questions, and students they are working with, but they also can create confusion. To fruitfully engage in student voice inquiry, researchers need to understand both the challenge and the possibilities of engaging with students' voices in the process of research. This starts with an understanding of what student voice research is.

From its inception, the notion of student voice went beyond the sounds an individual makes to the collective wisdom and diverse perspectives of youth and the partnerships youth and adults can develop to foster reciprocal relationships and engender change within individuals, institutions, and communities (Cook-Sather, 2018b). How definitions of students' voices are leveraged in research projects will depend on the project's context, which in turn will delineate the range of possibilities for approaches to research question creation, project framing/process, data collection methods, analysis, and dissemination. For example, Fielding's (2001b) student-as-researcher framework focuses on the centrality of students' positionalities in the research process and how, by shifting those positions, research can create different forms of knowledge.

Fielding (2001b) offers a multidirectional continuum of student positions and engagement, demonstrating how positioning students as respondents, to positioning/collaborating with students as co-researchers, generates different information. For example, if students are framing the research questions (rather than adults) student perspectives are inherent in the project from the beginning. However, at times, adults may have a specific question for students, which might be best understood through engaging with students as respondents. So, project creation, researcher questions, data collection, and analysis would be more adult driven. For more radical and transformative approaches, youth–adult participatory frameworks are even more explicit of the critical, potentially transformative nature for those involved in the research process (Mirra, Garcia, & Morrell, 2015). These brief examples illustrate just a few ways of approaching student voice research—between research *on* students to a more participatory *with* student posture. Careful consideration and thoughtfulness on the adults' part is crucial (and challenging) for quality student voice work. These variations also illustrate how fundamental it is to interrogate the role of adult priorities in relation to the needs, desires, and experiences of young people.

Another challenge to student voice research is the multitude of methods available to researchers and teams. Surveys, tests, interviews, response to interventions, as well as arts-based, photo-based, action research, and activist-based participatory research, are just a few of the data collection approaches student voice research can take. Qualitative and quantitative methods are available, and there are no shortage of creative, rigorous ways to engage with students in data collection practices. This is an opportunity as well as a significant challenge, as some data collection approaches may be more appropriate than others, and researchers may need to expand their repertoires of data collection techniques to fit their work within the context, roles, and relationships of a student voice project.

STRUCTURE OF THE BOOK

So, how do researchers navigate these complex decisions and choices? To create both flexibility and clarity for the field, we have distilled the underlying assumptions and values within the literature and made them explicit in this book, creating a cohesive and flexible paradigm of student voice inquiry—the Student Voice Research Framework. Chapter 1 will introduce readers to this framework, which will be used throughout the book to conceptualize how to intentionally and productively engage with student voice work. The rest of the book consists of chapters that (a) offer philosophical and theoretical justification for the importance and role of student knowledge in educational research, leadership, and policymaking; (b) discuss the preparation and considerations necessary to engage in high-quality student voice research; and (c) offer step-by-step "nuts and bolts" examples of different student voice methods through reflexive case studies. After reading this book, readers will have the necessary foundation to fruitfully engage students' voices to transform (or simply improve) their classrooms, schools, or educational organizations for a more just and vibrant space.

This book is organized into three parts. In "Part I: The Student Voice Research Framework and Philosophical Underpinnings," we discuss the underlying ways of approaching student voice research that yields productive engagement dynamics with students, as well as the considerations of interpretation and understanding necessary to build useful knowledge with them. We cover the Student Voice Research Framework (SVRF) as an overarching paradigm of principles and processes for undertaking quality student voice research.

Chapter 1, "The Student Voice Research Framework," lays the foundation for the rest of the volume. The editors, Marc Brasof and Joseph Levitan, discuss the SVRF, describe the principles of the framework, and demonstrate how these principles underlie quality student voice research. Each chapter in the volume explicitly engages with at least one principle covered by the SVRF to show its efficacy in practice.

In Chapter 2, "Epistemological Issues in Student Voice Research," Levitan and Brasof discuss the epistemology, or philosophies, that underlie the SVRF. This chapter shows researchers the ways in which adults can think about and justify their approaches to student voice research—providing the epistemological arguments and frameworks to think through how to apply the SVRF to context, as well as showing the efficacy of student voice research.

"Part II: Preparing for Student Voice Work" discusses the pre–data collection activities that are necessary for undertaking quality student voice research: ethics, space and context, power dynamics, research questions, operational concepts, and the extent voice is accessed in research projects.

In Chapter 3, "The Ethics of Student Voice Research," William C. Frick discusses the ethical implications of student voice work, asking readers to consider the intersection of the SVRF principles and empathy, self-awareness, presence, and intellectual humility. Frick pushes readers to consider how our engagement and research is "right, true, good, and praiseworthy."

Chapter 4, "Considering Space and Time: Power Dynamics and Relationships Between Children and Adults," by Kate Wall, Claire Cassidy, Carol Robinson, Mhairi C. Beaton, Lorna Arnott, and Elaine Hall, considers how various modalities of voice, particularly with young children, are intertwined with space, activity, and time.

Lindsay Lyons, Ellen MacCannell, and Vanessa Gold, in Chapter 5, "Student Voice: Assessing Research in the Field," examine a large body of research to uncover common themes in student voice research methods, ultimately making the argument that the field is beginning to move toward a mature stage.

Chapter 6, "Reflection and Reflexion on Student Participation and System Change," by Pat Thomson, explores an ongoing pesky challenge of defining when and how to position students within the research process, especially when the aims are to tackle systemwide issues. She uses her deep history and experience with student voice research projects to instigate reflection of the difference between "voice" and "voiced" research. Questions and concerns of epistemic justice are front and center.

Part III: Student Voice Methods in Action offers particular research strategies that leading scholars are currently using in the field. Each method chapter covers one approach to student voice research and discusses ways in which the researchers' methods apply the SVRF in their work. These chapters make up a menu of methods that are aligned with the SVRF and include materials in the appendix to support implementation of the particular method. We aimed to highlight methods that are less commonly used, yet are powerful approaches to capturing and elevating students' voices.

Kayla M. Johnson kicks off Part III with Chapter 7, "Making Meaning and Planning Change with Students Using Photo-Cued Interviewing." Here Johnson illustrates the power of photos as a means for researchers' critical self-reflection and as a contextually considerate tool to elicit participants' stories and reflection with Indigenous students in Cusco, Peru.

In Chapter 8, "Participatory Visual Data Analysis: Tools for Empowering Students Toward Social Change," Lisa Starr takes readers through two youth participatory action research projects that use visual methodologies and participatory analysis to foster change and address pressing social and educational issues. The chapter focuses specifically on the process of engaging in the participatory process of analysis and important considerations for researchers interested in youth participatory action research methods.

In Chapter 9, "Listening to Relations of Power and Potential with Material Methods," Eve Mayes examines the entanglement of relations between participants and the researcher. Mayes focuses on the possibilities of using materials to collaboratively surface, name, and analyze the impact of power in student voice work and unpacks the process in two projects: the first in Sydney, Australia, and the second in Victoria, Australia.

Building from the work in Chapter 5, Lindsay Lyons discusses innovative student voice research practices in Chapter 10, "Balancing Breadth and Depth: Using Mixed Methods in Scale Development Research." Demonstrating how to approach research with students to create large-scale surveys that speak to students' realities and contexts—in New York City—Lyons takes readers through her process to scale up research projects in secondary schools using mixed methods.

Chapter 11, "Intersecting Voices: An Integrative Approach to Applying the Student Voice Research Framework in Teacher Education," illustrates the *sine qua non* of student voice praxis in which the research and practice of student voice informs the development of teacher education—where everyone involved is a student, educator, and researcher and thus an equal participant in the creation of knowledge. Alison Cook-Sather, Heather Curl, and Chanelle Wilson take readers through the iterative process of research, reflection, and action in two projects, in Philadelphia, Pennsylvania, that informed over 25 years of teacher development.

What we hope to make clear in this volume is that student voice is a powerful conduit to increasing the quality and impact of educational research and, ultimately, schools. The SVRF and subsequent innovative practices can support researcher introspection, planning, and praxis. Educational research would change dramatically if we were in constant conversation with students—as there would be more understanding about students and school life—and more collective action on critical underlying issues. In our field, education research often decenters students by talking about them (or talking about student outcomes based on principles set by adults), but not with them. As a result, we often miss the mark on what is most important. This leads to research that does not actually have a direct contribution to the lives of students. Student voice research as a field and practice, and the SVRF specifically, seeks to change that.

Part I

THE STUDENT VOICE RESEARCH FRAMEWORK AND PHILOSOPHICAL UNDERPINNINGS

CHAPTER 1

The Student Voice Research Framework

Marc Brasof and Joseph Levitan

Early in Marc's career, he engaged in a research study to examine how a teacher fostered evaluative thinking in a mixed-ability Advanced Placement (AP) U.S. government course in order to understand how equity-based policies might influence learning. This class was unique in the school, as any student could participate, regardless of how prepared they were for the rigors of a college-level AP course. This equity-driven policy created a predictably challenging environment. Marc believed that high expectations coupled with support would be the key to student success and knew this particular teacher excelled in inclusive and responsive pedagogy. However, as the study progressed, he observed, and students reported, a lack of critical thinking in course activities and assignments, which often focused on rote memorization and application. Marc then unknowingly came to the wrong conclusion, leading to a flawed analysis of the efficacy of classroom learning. Marc was beginning to conclude that critical thinking was in fact not being facilitated and that it was due to this particular teacher's pedagogy, not the equity-based policy. Turns out both claims were incorrect.

What is the difference between student voice work that offers accurate information and useful knowledge, and student voice work that does not? Over time, Marc realized the assumptions and design of the above study were flawed—insights that did not surface until a more reflective process on his own assumptions about the actions of the teacher and the context of instruction. Upon deeper interrogation, Marc realized that his understanding of what happens in AP courses was misguided. That is, this AP course, designed by a testing company, was never meant to cultivate evaluative thinking. The teacher would have risked low student performance on the national exam if he had strayed away from the rote memorization that drove the curriculum. In essence, AP is not the gold standard in curriculum, as so many people believe. Many AP courses facilitate rote memorization, application, and analysis and spend little to no time on fostering evaluative thinking—the latter being the concept that undergirded the design of Marc's study. The curriculum was not examined as a part of the study because AP, in Marc's K–12 experience as both a student and teacher, was rarely questioned. Furthermore, Marc's interviews with students confirmed suspicions about the efficacy of classroom instruction. Yet, interview protocols never opened up enough space for students to offer more global critiques, and terms like "critical thinking" and "equity-based policies" seemed to be confusing language to students.

Interviews became even more problematic because of the relationships built between the researcher and students prior to the study. Marc, a former teacher at the school, taught courses explicitly designed to be student-driven and engage in project-based learning, which engaged his mixed-ability classes. The project-based approach was the norm across the school. As a result, students and Marc held a mutual understanding on what "good instruction" looked like, and this AP class was not that. In other words, the power dynamics between researcher and participants was built within the context of this particular school's history and remained unexamined walking into the study. Those dynamics and history surfaced an important understanding of the mismatch between the school's curricular approach and an AP course. No one participating in the study, however, was raising those questions, and instead the focus of analysis was on classroom dynamics.

A reader might conclude that Marc's story is one of a novice researcher and that such mistakes can be mitigated with the better research design that comes with expertise and experience. We agree. But we also see researchers continuously come to conclusions about schooling environments without open and deep consultation with students, and often, student voice research surfaces opposing more nuanced narratives about young people and their lived experiences than other approaches to inquiry. In Marc's study, young people were positioned as respondents to prompts, giving them very little control over the insights they could possibly offer about mixed ability classrooms, evaluative thinking, their understanding of quality learning, or the curriculum itself.

Marc could have ensured that students had more agency in the development of research questions and design in the study. This would have resulted in a much broader and critical investigation of how the school facilitates evaluative thinking in all of their classes, and the policies, principles, and practices that undergird those designs with a particular idea of mixed-ability spaces. Students might even challenge the notion of the existence of a mixed-ability AP class as something unique and derived from narrow views of learning, and instead advanced that high-order learning was a norm in every classroom. Such collaborations would have provided an opportunity for Marc to develop new relational dynamics appropriate for research *with* students that would support the development of relevant inquiry and provide access to a network of respondents and information across the school (via student researchers) who could provide critical insights.

After decades of experience with studies such as these, as well as our numerous studies with other excellent researchers, teachers, and leaders who engage in student voice practices, we have developed the Student Voice Research Framework (SVRF), which offers principles that can be adapted to the many different contexts of research with youth. What we offer below are principles and ideas for understanding how to connect to where students "are at" from many different identities and in many different spaces to engage in meaningful, useful, and important research. The SVRF is steeped in ideas to prepare researchers for the iterative process of research with youth. We also consider more thoughtfully what it means to be researching youth in educational settings. The SVRF covers four interconnected principles: intersubjectivity, reflexivity, power dynamics, and context. These principles provide a framework for core considerations when planning and undertaking student voice research.

INTERSUBJECTIVITY

The goal of the SVRF is to ensure that researchers and youth build intersubjective understandings together. Intersubjectivity in student voice work comprises mutual understanding built between youth and adult researchers. Attaining intersubjectivity is the primary goal of social research for change. To get to productive, mutual understandings, adult and youth positionalities and assumptions need to be understood and thoughtfully considered.

Implicit assumptions of adults often make building intersubjective understandings difficult. Reflexive practices, along with transforming power dynamics and adjusting methods to context, are necessary to achieve intersubjectivity in student voice research. Achieving this is no easy feat, especially because we as researchers are often blinded by our own biases, have inequitable power dynamics between the researcher and the participants, and are not attuned to the context where we work. This is why explicit considerations of intersubjectivity with younger people are necessary.

The challenges in building intersubjective understandings are well exemplified in Alison Cook-Sather's (2009a) project designed to support future educators' development. Called Teaching and Learning Together (which is discussed in Chapter 11 by Cook-Sather, Curl, and Wilson), findings from her work offer poignant examples of the difficulty adults have when attempting to build intersubjectivity with youth. Cook-Sather had college students in a teacher education program engage in prolonged dialogue with high school students in order to foster more student-centered and responsive teacher dispositions. In the project, Cook-Sather's college students asked about and studied high school students' perspectives on the efficacy of classroom learning. Yet, this proved challenging, as Cook-Sather (2009b) observed:

> [T]eachers are not privy to the worlds of students because they occupy different positions, have different identities and roles within schools . . . Inviting students to see the world of teaching, and, conversely, affording teachers opportunities to glimpse the world of school from students' perspectives, and including both these newly valued angles of vision and voices in discussions of school reform, are all moves that have the potential to facilitate a change in ways of thinking about schooling and about positioning those who work within its established forms. (p. 224)

This meant that co-constructing shared understandings of teachers in the realities of students, and vice versa, required hours of dialogue, because teachers are socialized by education systems to be unresponsive to youth's needs and interests. Teachers are positioned mostly as the authoritative sage, which limits their understanding of why they should listen to students. As one college student reflected, "At the beginning I came into [the Teaching and Learning Together project]with the idea that [my high school student partner] could probably learn something from me, and I was so wrong. I learned SO MUCH from her" (quoted in Cook-Sather, 2007a). In this study, the teachers needed to understand that to build intersubjective understandings they needed to listen in order to learn.

It also turns out that the quality of the young people's participation in those dialogues and subsequent change depended largely on how serious their views were taken by teachers. In Cook-Sather's project, college students had more genuine and responsive relationships with young people when they investigated their own understandings and practices on not just how to listen to young people, but why. Dialogue that centered on the perspectives of youth created discourse that explored youth's perspectives of hurdles that inhibit flexible and responsive education systems, which helped to shift these college students' images of students as solely learners who are not able to or less interested in understanding and shifting the dynamics of how their learning environments are built. In essence, the socially constructed identities of an educator/adult and student/youth, with the power dynamics and assumed roles built from that socialization, facilitated college students' misunderstandings of students, but sustained dialogue informed by reflexive self-analysis helped those college students revise their understandings.

Exchanges between adults and youth, even outside the context of school change, illustrate how different positions in society create power dynamics, which leads to a greater probability of miscommunication and a lower chance of building intersubjective understandings. In another student voice project, Heshusius (1995) asked college students in a teacher preparation program to just hold an unplanned conversation with a young person. The college students were asked to simply get to know a young person, transcribe the conversation, and then write a paper reflecting on what the conversation illuminated about themselves. Heshusius's examination of her students' papers and transcripts found that the conversations turned to and remained on the concerns of their own identity as an adult or educator, which interfered with or dictated the direction of the exchange. The college students expected not to have much in common with the young people, so they turned the conversation into an interview due to their inability to maintain a dialogue and kept a psychological/emotional distance, making it harder for both parties to connect.

Heshusius's college students struggled to listen and build a dialogue with a young person. So, they missed an opportunity to reflect on those exchanges to learn more about themselves and their developing educator identity. The task of holding a conversation with a young person should not be so difficult, especially for aspiring educators. However, much of our cultural upbringing has socialized educators to think and behave in a way that positions students in a subordinate, infantilizing role, especially as they relate to educators and hierarchical structures built for learning (Costello et al., 1997). As Heshusius's and Cook-Sather's work help illuminate, power dynamics impact how educators and students relate to and build intersubjective understanding of each other.

Despite these challenges, building relationships that root out misunderstandings and build intersubjectivity is possible. Not all of Heshusius's students had these problematic outcomes. Some of the college students questioned why they were so surprised at the high level of knowledge the young people exhibited, realizing their expectations were set too low. One student reflected, "I was the one out of touch. . . . [The young person] was aware of more than I thought." Another wrote, "A child can bring to a conversation . . . a perspective that has never been considered" (p. 120). A few of Heshusius's students experienced a powerful lesson about their emerging educator identities by gaining a deeper appreciation of the self and how they relate to students. Even with such interrogations, though, misunderstandings abound, so it is imperative that we engage in specific practices and considerations if our aim is intersubjectivity.

Like teachers, researchers need to push themselves to listen more attentively to students so that their presuppositions do not block them from building intersubjective understandings. Researchers potentially know quite a bit about being young due to their own experiences growing up and through their educational research, but it is this very foundation of knowledge that can lead to exchanges with and/or the study of young people that end up advancing unproductive misunderstandings. Socially constructed identities that inform the self and our relationship with the other are baked into student–educator, youth–adult, and researcher–subject relationships, creating power dynamics that distort the meanings and expressions that youth may (mis)communicate. For example, young people may easily slip into the performative when dealing with adults, confirming researchers' perspectives using the words, symbols, and actions of adults instead of sharing genuine insights (Cammarota & Fine, 2008; Conner, 2015; Johnson, 2018a). Or, adult researchers may mischaracterize students' perspectives due to contextual sensitivities that carry with them different meanings, depending on the educational and/or broader community or cultural context (Czerniawski & Garlick, 2011); thus, careful consideration and reflexivity from the researcher is necessary to ensure research quality standards. Exchanges between youth and adults must be mined to root out these forces. We need tools to interrogate our positionalities at all stages of the research process to help us (a) create boundaries for mapping when we are inviting students into our world and when we cross into theirs, and (b) recognize how these exchanges influence our understanding of one another.

In response, we share strategies for building intersubjective understandings and strengthening the quality of findings in student voice endeavors.

1. Consider the kind of voice students are using when speaking with you. As a researcher, it is important to consider what kind of voice is engaged or being offered by the youth. We use Hadfield and Haw's work (2001) to support this identification. Some students use an *authoritative voice*, which may be intended to represent a specific group of youth. Youth's positionalities are unique and different from any other group, encompassing a multitude of identities as well as variations of emerging power, independence, responsibility, and knowledge, within and across heterogeneous groups and in relation to adults. It is crucial that researchers do not assume that shared perspectives represent the voice of all youth, even if common experiences are the focus. Contextual sensitivities press researchers to further consider how a specific group's or an individual's experiences in one setting might not mirror the experiences of the same or similar group in other spaces.

Another type of voice is *critical voice*, in which youth are challenging assumptions, policies, practices, and procedures driving organizational logic and the stereotypes people have of one another. Researchers engaging youth in critical work on ideas, systems, and people need to be reflexive in order to understand how biases, positionality, interests, and perspectives are communicated. Careful consideration of how intersubjective dynamics (such as verbal and nonverbal cues researchers communicate) influence criticism is also necessary. Whether youth are sharing their authoritative or critical voices, the role of socialization within and without educational settings that normalize biases (Harro, 2000) can impact youths' and adults' understanding of one another.

2. Consider if the space and data-collection activities created by the researcher are distorting the words and actions of students. The space a researcher creates to collect data requires careful investigation of the social forces inside and outside of the classroom. In other words, "what [students] say depends on what they are asked, how they are asked it, 'who' they are invited to [embody] in responding" (Bragg, 2007, p. 31). Without attention to such operating forces, research can obscure the meanings, words, and actions of youth by prioritizing a study's operational definitions and sample, leading to the under-investigation or misrepresentations of youth's experiences (like in Marc's story above).

Questions to consider when collecting data are: To what extent are the words and actions of youth being described or framed by youth? How do researchers ensure youth are sharing their most insightful/authentic voices, and to what extent do researchers need to further validate students' voices?

3. Check in with students to make sure your understandings are correct. Building intersubjective understandings includes paraphrasing students' words or summarizing their actions as you have them reflect to see if you are on the right track with your understanding. If you communicate your understanding of the students' conclusions, it offers students a chance to reflect themselves and make any adjustments to what they said so that they can better communicate. Communication is a tricky endeavor, and people often benefit from a chance to rethink and restate what they mean. Paraphrasing and/or summarizing and asking if that is correct offers participants a chance to do so. We suggest that researchers learn how to use silence to allow students to process questions, give students space and time to reconsider and/or change the meaning of what they say, and monitor the "feeling" in the room to make sure that students have an opportunity to uncover unspoken issues or ideas.

4. Learn students' language (but we do not suggest using the language yourself). Each generation of students makes their own contribution to popular culture through slang terms. Words that may have a certain denotation in the old use of a word often develop different connotations for youth, so it is important to recognize when, as a researcher, you might be saying the same words but meaning something different (e.g., Levitan & Johnson 2020). With this in mind, we recommend going back to your participants and clarifying what they said and meant with specific terms.

5. Be metacognitive about the research process (explain what you are doing and why). Making oneself and others aware of the thinking processes that go into the construction of research activities can surface and open up the possibility of interrogating assumptions and intentions. Laying out why one is researching a particular phenomenon and why a particular strategy was chosen while simultaneously offering genuine opportunity for input can produce opportunities to create feedback loops and empower young people to take more ownership over the conversation. Are our assumptions and intentions congruent with our and others' actions? What needs adjusting? As a continuous practice, metacognition can minimize problematic power dynamics inherent in the researcher-participant paradigm. It requires the participants to surface intentions and strategies for the purpose of opening up space to dialogue about these intentions and approaches when necessary.

These strategies, along with the principles outlined below, will help researchers and educators engage in valuable research to understand important educational phenomena through working with youth.

REFLEXIVITY

As we argue in intersubjectivity, researchers must be reflexive about their conceptions of youth and the influence of the researchers' own childhoods and schooling experiences on their interpretation of students' voices. Student voice researchers' past experiences, biases, and theoretical positions can romanticize or conjure negative images of young people, as adults are likely to feel that they have special insight into childhood, adolescence, schooling, and maturation, since they were once youth.

These possibilities raise the critical issue of to what extent researcher biases, power dynamics, and expectations are impacting youths' responses and researchers' interpretations in student voice studies. Researcher biases and power dynamics form the main subject for reflexion, or critical reflection of self and one's impact on the examined phenomenon, which is a necessary approach to understand the influence of researchers' biases on the conception of research projects and their positionality within them.

Reflexive student voice researchers probe their own professional and personal perceptions and ask questions such as: "Why do we [do] research [with] children? How would we characterize our childhood [and schooling]? What romantic or negative ideas of childhood [and school] do we hold? What characteristics do we represent (age, gender, race, class, ability, religion, nation)?" (Lahman, 2008, p. 292). Additionally, reflexive researchers will ask: Which youth are asked to respond, and does this represent a range of voices? How am I asking my questions and how do I respond to students from different identities and personalities? Other essential foci include (a) the consideration of one's assumptions about the values of youth, (b) how one should raise children, and (c) what constitutes a good life. These positions influence the researcher and the work they are engaged in and thus should be interrogated. A reflexive student voice researcher uses these or similar points of personal inquiry to critically reflect before, during, and after a study. The subsequent components of this framework provide additional insights into reflexivity.

In addition to reflexive work on personal histories, values, and biases, reflexivity also means becoming aware of the assumptions and underpinning ideologies/philosophies of the theoretical and methodological paradigms that inform and make up the data collection and analytical approaches researchers take on when performing student voice research. These paradigms are related to, but separate from, one's personal values and experiences, as research paradigms are selected from traditions of scholarship. Researchers have recognized that a single theoretical approach when working with students can actually work counter to the values and goals of the researcher(s) and the students themselves.

In a student voice project with female Indigenous students in the Peruvian Andes, Joe (e.g., Levitan, 2018) and colleagues engaged with students in seminar conversations about learning goals to improve the quality of education, with an aim to decolonize schooling. During these student-run seminars, all but one of the students shared that their main goal was to become a "professional." Here, it was tempting to take a development theoretical lens. This lens would imply that school improvement would align with neoliberal economic paradigms, where intensive tutoring, workshops with professionals, engagement with learning technology, and exposure to cutting-edge content based in Western paradigms to increase competitiveness on the job market would support the students' overarching goal to become professionals.

However, making this interpretation would have been a mistake. When the students and the educators engaged in deeper inquiry into what it meant to be a professional by coming up with hypothetical examples, engaging in student inquiry through speaking with family members, and engaging in further seminars, the students and adults realized that their conceptions of a professional were different. Students assumed that being a professional was "wearing a suit and earning a salary." They did not think they would have to give up their home cultures to do this. The adults thought that being a professional was any work for which an individual was paid. However, to get a paying job, thought the researchers, meant embracing a Western language and lifestyle, since most companies required Spanish language skills, European clothes, and U.S.-style customer service.

The discrepancy in understanding had important implications for the curriculum. Thinking through the students' words and how to meet their goals in educational practices and content, the team engaged specifically with feminist, critical, and post/decolonial theories as points of comparison with development theory interpretations to understand the educational implications of the students' ideas. The educators were able to develop a much more nuanced understanding of what values and norms students wished to retain, which allowed Joe and his colleagues to make curricular decisions that were more grounded in the values and meanings the students shared, supporting the students' goals and ultimately avoiding the potential severe harm that could have happened if they had only taught students the neoliberal vision of a professional (e.g., Levitan & Johnson, 2020). What was key for the adults was engaging with multiple theoretical perspectives to better interrogate how they understood the students, which helped Joe and his colleagues ask better and more open, engaged questions and have more open conversations with students. This process ultimately helped the researchers avoid making assumptions so that they could build intersubjective understandings.

In addition to misaligned assumptions about what certain words mean (like "professional" in the example above), the methodological approach of an adult researcher—like Joe—and how that researcher positions themselves in relation to students carries implicit theories about youth, what constitutes knowledge, and the goals of a research project. These implicit theories can inform and bias approaches to data collection, interpretation, and analysis. While researchers need theories to guide action and decision-making when doing research, engaging in reflexive practices allows researchers to understand explicitly the ideological underpinnings and assumptions of the theories they use and to address possible shortcomings or problematic contradictions within their chosen theories as they relate to the researcher's specific context and the students they work with. Whereas narrow framing might support focused analysis, explicitly engaging in reflexive analysis with multiple theories ensures that researchers do not re-create unjust and biased work that misrepresents students' voices. Along with reflexivity, the SVRF principles and strategies are meant to assist with selecting an appropriate orientation, method, and interpretive approach applied to the researcher's context when performing student voice work.

Reflexivity is a practice—before, during, and after the project—so here are five strategies to engage in reflexivity.

1. Identify your many identities and think about how these identities might influence students' behaviors around you. Educators' and students' overlapping and intersecting identities impact meaning-making and relationship building (Levitan & Carr-Chellman, 2018). Understanding your own identities and how those identities influence your values, reactions, and interpretations in various contexts and relationships can support greater insight into how you relate with students and how students relate with you (Levitan, Mahfouz, & Schulsser, 2018). To understand your identities, it can be helpful to note the different types of identities you have, such as the roles you take on, the personal preferences you have, and the groups you belong to. This is in addition to the identity markers of ethnicity, race, class, language, (dis)ability, gender, and sexual orientation you might identify. Understanding the subtle identities you embody, and where those identities might pop up in different circumstances, will help you to better understand the influence of identities in daily interactions. It may also help you find points of commonality with students. For example, if you and students both like similar music or a sport, that shared identity can build a bridge and open up communication. In addition to different types of identity, thinking about the importance of your identities to you can help you recognize when students' identities might be important to them. This might help you think through how to interact in ways that allow for shared understanding and appreciation/valuing of difference (see, e.g., Levitan & Carr-Chellman, 2018; Levitan et al., 2018 for more information on identifying your own and students' identities).

2. Identify your assumptions about youth (e.g., what youth value, why youth act in certain ways, and the goals youth have), your own values, and the ways you think youth should be brought up, as well as what you think constitutes a good life so that you do not let your personal values unduly influence how you interact with youth. Without consciously reflecting on and identifying our values and assumptions, researchers and educators may let personal opinions (such as the kinds of foods people should eat, the aesthetic of art or clothing a person likes, body art, or the way youth spend their time, among many other examples) influence how they treat students. While implicit biases about race, class, gender, orientation, are widely discussed (e.g., Gullo, Capatosto, & Staats, 2018), subtler values and markers of identity also play significant roles in treating students in a way that fosters positive, clear, and productive communication. Reflecting on your own values, biases, and assumptions will allow you to identify and become aware of when you may react to students who embody behaviors or values different from your own, without being fully conscious of your reaction. Asking simple questions like "What do I think are the right ways to raise children?" and "What does a good life consist of?" will allow you to become more aware of your assumptions and better able to respond rather than react to students.

3. Identify unspoken values of the organizations you are working with. Members of organizations like schools are socialized to certain attitudes and behaviors, which impact how youth and adults behave and communicate, and what is deemed to be "acceptable." Hidden values might affect the information you are able to gather. Organizations are powerful in shaping members' attitudes and behaviors. It is important to remember this when proposing and implementing research projects so that when researchers engage in analysis, they do not blame students and ignore problematic institutional or other societal dynamics. That is, the researcher must be careful to understand that youth behavior is nested within an organization. This is important to remember when youth appear to be thinking and acting in ways that seem detrimental to their own education. Costello et al. (1997) provide an analysis on the intersection of student voice and the origins and evolution of the socializing effects of mass education. This reflective work can surface the ways in which youth are viewed and treated in organizations that are supposed to be designed to support them. To uncover the hidden curriculum

(Giroux & Purple, 1983) and socialization process, Brasof (2015, 2018) models the double loop learning dialogical process that directs reflection on organizational norms and assumptions. This analysis helps identify (in)congruences between what individuals and organizations espouse and believe versus what actually occurs.

4. Think about who (which students with which identities) you are asking to respond and if there are voices and positionalities that might be left out. Goodman (2011) charts the dominant-subordinate identity continuum for racism, sexism, heterosexism, transgender oppression, classism, ableism, ageism, religious oppression, and xenophobism (p. 7). This chart and Goodman's subsequent analysis of intersectionality can support reflection on social identity categories. But as Cook-Sather (2007a) points out, educational researchers have "the potential to reinforce rather than disrupt existing social conditions and dominant arrangements of power and participation" (p. 2). One of Cook-Sather's concerns is making generalizations about a particular group as oppressed without considering the specificity of people's lives. Identity can be a starting point in sample selection or data collection, but Cook-Sather recommends investigating the experiences and perspectives of youth being labeled or owning a particular label: "Creat[ing] opportunities for students to gain critical distance on their experiences and invit[ing] them to analyze those experiences with an eye toward changing them are key components of student voice work as well" (p. 11). Citing Orner (1992, p. 76), Cook-Sather offers the following reflective questions:

> What must the "oppressed" speak? For whose benefit do we/they speak? How is the speaking received, controlled, limited, disciplined, and stylized by the speakers, the listeners, the historical moment, the context? What is made of the "people's voice" after it is heard? (pp. 10–11)

5. Think about engaging in analysis from multiple theoretical perspectives to not mistakenly (mis)interpret students' ideas. Like metaphor, theory helps to illuminate and obscure facets of a phenomenon to provide analytical focus. Thus, using a singular theory creates analytical limitations (Levitan, 2018). Interdisciplinary, multi-theory study can bring new perspectives to light and support the development of theory and alternative theories that might better align with students' meanings and make for more accurate understandings of the issues. To understand how to engage in multi-theory analysis, Earle and Kruse (1999) provide various theoretical perspectives for understanding organizational values, structures, behaviors, and outcomes. Two other useful texts for examining organizational life and students' voices from various perspectives are G. Morgan (2011) and Levitan (2018). Ultimately, looking at any phenomenon from multiple perspectives will provide richer and more nuanced understandings.

POWER DYNAMICS

Reflexivity allows for deeper and more insightful considerations of the relationships and power dynamics between youth and adults. Understanding and transforming power dynamics is necessary to break through walls of misunderstanding and build positive relationships, which then fosters intersubjective understanding. So, in order to overcome the challenges of building intersubjectivity, as mentioned above, it is important for students and adults to have fair, trusting, equitable, and socially just relationships, which in turn means special attention and responsiveness to power dynamics (Mansfield et al., 2012).

As indicated above, not acknowledging and attending to power dynamics can have the unintended effects of inhibiting or silencing students' truths or voices, leading to inauthentic performativity (Johnson, 2020). We define power here as multifaceted, including but not limited to factors such as (a) youth and adult identity intersectionalities, including race, ethnicity, gender, orientation, religion, and class; (b) the ability to make decisions for oneself; and (c) the ability to not only be heard (audibly) but to be listened to (considered deeply) when engaging in a wide range of social exchanges. For example, adults too often do not adequately consider or attend to the influence of age and hierarchy in social life, including holding the positionality of researcher, policymaker, or teacher (Cammarota & Fine, 2008; Conner, 2016; Johnson, 2018a). The influence of these personal and/or bureaucratic characteristics in which adults have obtained knowledge and abilities perceived as superior can result in an expert–layperson dynamic that creates relational distance between researcher and participant (Reeder, 1972). Attention to such power dynamics goes beyond the foundational respect for persons as inherently autonomous agents able to make their own decisions (Department of Health, Education, and Welfare, 1979) and into the realm of considerations about the possibility of creating spaces for students to claim power so that they can make decisions within and beyond a given student voice research project.

Within student–researcher dynamics lie the possibilities of the more powerful to hold power over the less powerful, for both parties to share power (power with), or one or more people to hold power to accomplish something (power to) (Berger, 2005). Power over, with, or to can run through all relationships in terms of who has decision-making facility, who is listened to, and what happens. For student voice research, power dynamics can specifically relate to the framing of a research project; for example, who controls the decisions about research questions, orientations, and participant selection (such as in the example at the beginning of this chapter—Marc had the power over the research questions and methods), as well as whether the relationships between parties are trusting, open, and authentic (Cook-Sather, 2015).

Furthermore, power dynamics also determine what can be discussed and what the expectations are, including the language that students are expected to use (Levitan, 2019b). In essence, relational power dynamics include issues of appropriateness and norms of behavior as well as what mediums and dialogical styles (technology mediated discussions, slang, humor, etc.) can be engaged in to share experiences (Mansfield et al., 2012).

Negotiating for time and space to build relationships and create opportunities for students to claim power in research projects can help build the conditions for rapport (trusting and socially just relationships) with young people, especially when adults may have specific or perceived established roles in institutions replete with rules and norms (Lahman, 2008)—such as how students are expected to present themselves and speak to adults. Researchers often enter into and have little control over institutions with preestablished expected behaviors for youth and adults. Nonetheless, addressing such conditions is foundational for quality student voice work and moves beyond reminding participants of the nature of the study. Participants need to feel safe and able to share authentic insights. How students feel is often a result of what youth are being asked to share, where sharing happens (privacy, comfort, etc.), who is being asked, and the nature of youth–adult relationships in the organization (Lahman, 2008; Mansfield, 2014b). Thus, intentional time and space to negotiate rules and norms facilitates the development of a social environment helpful for co-constructing meaning. In other words, researchers must take into consideration the impact of youth's contexts on power dynamics in research.

Quality student voice research is considerate of, and responsive to, the relational dynamic with students, with a particular concern for power dynamics between people and within educational contexts—ensuring that the researcher does not eclipse or repress the insights of students due to implicit and subtle micro-actions that suppress students from claiming their voices and asserting their knowledge and power. Making these considerations explicit in the design and write-up of student voice research is important because it carries significant implications for how student voice researchers can interpret the data and how confident readers can be in the conclusions of a research project (Levitan, 2018; Mansfield, 2014a).

Following are four strategies to create equitable power dynamics.

1. Identify existing power dynamics within the study. Power discrepancies can easily be understood through positionalities of participants and the researcher. *The Belmont Report*'s (Department of Health, Education, and Welfare, 1979) principles of ethical research—respect for person, beneficence, and justice—are an important starting point for any research project. Those principles require researchers to treat individuals as autonomous people who can make their own decisions. With that said, existing power dynamics that lie beyond *The Belmont Report* influence student voice research. It is important to identify the more subtle existing dynamics within the study to have trustworthy findings. For example, issues such as language can create an imbalance in power. If the researcher uses too much jargon that students may not know, then there is an implicit power dynamics imbalance, with the researcher claiming a certain kind of power of knowledge, potentially affecting how students respond and the kind of voice they use. So, jargon needs to be edited out of explanations, spoken, as well as delivered in written form, to participants.

Identifying power dynamics also requires thinking through who bears the burden and benefits of this research. Often participants do not receive any immediate or long-term benefit due to the researcher-practitioner divide in student voice research (Czerniawski & Kidd, 2011). Power also has to do with whether students feel compelled or forced to engage in the research project, even if they don't want to. A good practice is to remind youth at every interaction that they should not feel coerced into participating and that they can withdraw at any moment before, during, or after the study. Youth should also be reminded that while the use of recording devices is incredibly important for capturing data, at any time they may request to have a conversation continue off record or request exclusion of something said while being recorded. Certainly, these rules might hamper the goals of a research project, but considering the power dynamics inherent in the researcher–participant relationship, it must become part of a researchers' routine to ensure that youth feel and have a sense of control over their choices and perspectives. Additionally, participants' positionality in the research process can be reimagined or shifted (see discussion below on Fielding's [2001b] students-as-researchers framework). There will likely be ways to change those dynamics by structuring the study differently.

2. Think about who is being heard and listened to and who is not, and the ways in which race, ethnicity, gender, orientation, class, and language might influence power dynamics. Plan to address imbalances. As suggested in the section on reflexivity, each social identity can be understood as situated on a contextually bound dominant–subordinate continuum. Social identities create even more complex manifestations of power and oppression when those identities intersect. It is useful to think about the ways in which identity intersects when power is exercised in an organization. How do social identities, like race and gender, impact who speaks, who is listened to, and who is "taken seriously"? Are there people whose ideas are considered more deeply, more often, and do those people have similar identities (historically, white and male; Mcintosh, 1988)? In student voice research, who are the students who dominate the dialogue and discussion (traditionally middle-class, high-achieving, white students)? If patterns are identified in a student voice project, the researcher might need to think about strategies to address the imbalance (which is discussed in Chapter 9 by Mayes). Imbalance is common, as people from certain identities often coalesce around shared tasks and goals and use those alliances to influence the control of (a) formal authority; (b) resources; (c) organizational structure, rules, and regulations; (d) decision processes; and (e) knowledge and information (P. L. Morgan, 2006). In contrast, in-group conflict is also normal in which the aims and strategies of a particular movement are not always agreed upon, causing tensions (Jakobsen, 1995). These differences often originate from the various positionalities and intersectionalities that emerge from diverse social, economic, political, and cultural experiences.

3. Identify the ways you, as the researcher, might have power you do not know about (such as framing the questions)—would that power be better distributed among the participants, or not? In what ways does your role as the researcher endow you with power to make certain decisions? In initiating a research study, the questions, issues to be addressed, methodological approach, and interpretive orientations you decide on and bring to the research space are forms of power. Are there other forms of power that you bring to the space that you might not be aware of? While having power as a researcher and a professional is not inherently a problem, it is important to be cognizant of how that power is enacted. Decision-making and using power that causes harm (even inadvertently) is obviously a problem, so with your power comes responsibility.

As part of your personal reflection, it is important to ask yourself questions and work to uncover the power that you have. In what ways do you have power over choices or decisions? What are the ways that you can make things happen? Those are forms of power. Are there professional relationships that allow you to have access to certain resources or goods? Those are also forms of power. Again, although having power in itself is not a problem, to help ensure that power is not enacted inappropriately it is good to identify the forms of power you come with. Even the most subtle forms of power, like deciding on the wording of questions, might make a difference in terms of whose voices are present. As the researcher, some power is necessary and important to have and use, but it is also helpful to ask yourself and others if there are ways to distribute that power to be more productive and open new possibilities when working with students.

4. Identify the kind of power you are enacting (over, with, to), when engaging in research. What kind of power do you enact when working with students? Berger (2005) defines "power over" as enacting a form of domination in which the interest of the researcher may not be in the same interest as that of the students, but through forms of convincing (rewards) and coercion the researcher gets students to agree to or comply with their wishes. "Power with" relations look to shared decision-making, in which the power is distributed between the students and the researcher. "Power with" values include dialogue, cooperation, and open reasoning, rather than enacting authority to make decisions. "Power to" relations are focused on resisting dominant or hegemonic norms—questioning current realities and creating alliances to address problems within the school or organization. "Power to" relationships focus on critical engagement and thinking for liberation or change. Each power dynamic will create different relationships with the students and foster different kinds of information. Multiple kinds of power (over, with, to) will be enacted in any given study, so thoughtfulness in terms of the context in which you are enacting these different forms of power will help.

CONTEXT

Researchers must select strategies congruent with the students' and the study's contexts: the cultures, experiences, perspectives, and knowledge that the research project is seeking to access/understand. The variety of methodologies available to student voice researchers is immense, and therefore, selecting strategies should be aligned with research questions; principles of ethics, justice, and equity; and the likelihood that such approaches work with the population engaging in the study. The challenge is for researchers to ensure that the methods or strategies to access or understand students' knowledge and experiences are aligned with their spaces, cultures, experiences, and perspectives—paying particular attention to power dynamics and relationships. Considering how to position youth in the research process is an important first step.

Student voice researchers have engaged with youth on a continuum of levels of student decision-making power, ranging from students as respondents to students as research leaders to better access youth culture, experiences, and perspectives and/or create changes. Fielding's (2001a,) student-as-researchers typology establishes youth and adult positions during the research process. Students can be a source of data, active respondents, co-researchers, or researchers. In this continuum, students provide data, interpret data created by others, develop new data and/or new interpretations with adults, or lead the inquiries. Likewise, Mitra (2007a) points out that youth can take on the roles of respondents, act as a facilitator, or take on leadership responsibilities in the research process. Such a range of options for collaborative inquiry can leverage students' knowledge, skills, dispositions, and networks in different ways to better understand their experiences, goals, needs, successes, and the challenges they confront on a daily basis within particular contexts. (See Table 1.1 for an elaboration of student levels of involvement and common research methods.)

Table 1.1. A Continuum of Student Voice Research

Student Participation Level (lowest to highest)	Youth Position	Common Method Options
1. Students-as-data-source	Involvement is passive because youth are seen as data via testing and other survey instruments.	Surveys, interviews, tests, (pre-post or summative tests), randomized controlled trials, focus groups, response to intervention studies
2. Students-as-respondents	Youth examine data created by researchers to support the interpretation of results, but researchers are leading all aspects of the project.	Interviews, photo-based interviews, arts-based projects, focus groups, surveys, activity-based research, with students providing feedback
3. Students-as-consultants	Youth provide critical insights into the research project as it is being conceived and constructed.	Informal individual and/or conversations with students, receiving feedback on research instruments (like surveys, interview protocols, activity/arts-based/photo-based protocols, etc.), formal and informal feedback on research questions
4. Students-as-co-researchers	Youth and researchers work together to build the entire research process. All aspects of this work is shared.	Interviews, photo-based interviews, arts-based projects, focus groups, surveys, scientific investigations, mapping, co-construction of materials, desk research (i.e., looking up information/ideas on the Internet), social psychology experiments, etc.
5. Students-as-researchers	Youth lead the entire research process with support from researchers.	Interviews, photo-based interviews, arts-based projects, focus groups, surveys, scientific investigations, mapping, co-construction of materials, desk research (i.e., looking up information/ideas on the Internet), social psychology experiments, policy evaluations, performance-based research

(continued)

Table 1.1. A Continuum of Student Voice Research (*continued*)

Student Participation Level (lowest to highest)	Youth Position	Common Method Options
6. Students-as-leaders	Youth engage in action research, initiate, and lead the research process.	Action research is built from a shared experience of a problem and is an iterative process of planning: inquiry, intervention, observing the intervention in action, and adjusting that intervention based on data analysis and reflection.

In addition to this range of involvement, students might take on more than research when engaging with adults in a project. Youth-Led Participatory Action Research (YPAR) (Cammarota & Fine, 2008; Mirra et al., 2015) is a youth-centered, youth-led process of engaging in action research projects—the goal of which is to directly change or transform some aspect of social life for the better. YPAR takes participatory research with students-as-leaders and adds engagement in transformative practices. Instead of presenting findings to leadership or arguing for changes to policy or pedagogy, YPAR takes active steps to see the change take place, and then evaluates that change for iterative improvements. Adults in YPAR can take on the role of advocates or implement change processes themselves while doing research to transform schools and/or society. Adults may play the role of supportive sounding board, thought partner, cheerleader, or connections broker (facilitating access to those in power) as students engage in their own action research. This approach is built upon principles of social justice that include ensuring that youth are driving the process to identify the issues that matter to them the most and working to ensure that the knowledge they gather is put into practice. "Nothing about us without us" is the motto here.

How one might decide where to center research methods on the continuum of student engagement can be determined by the youth, the relationships a researcher has with the individuals in a research space, as well as the history, current situation, issues, or questions to be addressed and institutional norms at the sites of study. Students taking the lead on their own projects, with the researcher as a facilitator, can create an open and trusting relational dynamic where students are able to assert themselves and explore topics that are important to them. However, it can also dissuade students from future activism and create a cynical disposition about democracy if their leadership is not taken seriously by adults (Wisby, 2011). In this case, a researcher can support students' research initiatives instead of taking the lead.

As co-researchers, students and adults may be very motivated to address a problem that they together have noticed in the school, where they form their own teams and approaches to, for example, improving some facets of a curriculum or adding a new offering in schools that students think is missing (Levitan, 2018). This approach leverages the social and intellectual capital of adults and young people with the aim of generating new knowledge that will have an influence on the institution. Though there are various position-alities within the research process, collaborative inquiry can be a means to not only reshape youth–adult power dynamics inherent in research and school improvement, but also fine-tune research questions, methods, and analyses to increase impact within the contexts under investigation. It is also a means to help evaluate congruencies between student and adult re-searchers' understanding of authoritative and critical voices and realities of the organization.

However, student voice research does not have to have students leading inquiries to foster congruences between questions, methods, respondents, and place. It could be the case that students are not particularly worried about an issue under inquiry, so their leadership may not be forthcoming. However, a lack of leadership interest or silence does not necessarily mean that inves-tigation into youth's experiences is not warranted. If a researcher wants to understand how a school could be more responsive to students' identities, for example, then students can be respondents via interviews, photo-voice, focus groups, surveys, and arts-based projects—just some of the options available. Such engagement needs to be further interrogated to understand congruence between methods, respondents, contexts, and power dynamics (see Figure 1.1). Ensuring that the strategies and methods are aligned with students' contexts and cultures requires consideration and engagement with the student voice research framework.

Here are three strategies to help you align methods with context.

1. Get to know the context and social dynamics in the space where you will work before planning too much. Making decisions about students' roles in research requires careful consideration prior to initiating a project. Understanding the context will support better decision-making. Knowing the spectrum of op-tions for youth engagement in student voice research, along with knowing the context and dynamics, will allow you to create more effective projects.

For student-voice-as-YPAR, there is often already some energy around an issue that students may be keen to explore and address but cannot because they do not have the institutional power to have time and resources devoted to the research and change of their cause. An adult who is sensitive to the context will be able to work with students to facilitate opportunities for them and share tips and knowledge to support their work (Cammarota & Fine, 2008; Shosh, 2019).

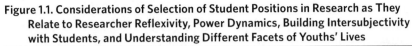

Figure 1.1. Considerations of Selection of Student Positions in Research as They Relate to Researcher Reflexivity, Power Dynamics, Building Intersubjectivity with Students, and Understanding Different Facets of Youths' Lives

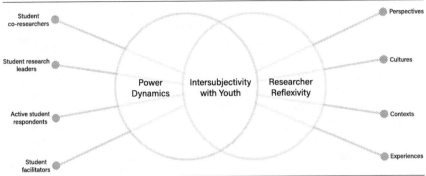

To engage in a students-as-researchers project, educators and students will need to be able to build a shared understanding of the project's goals, strategies, and outcomes. Students should also feel that not only does their participation matter and is supported, but that their engagement will result in educators taking their recommendations seriously and, when possible, lead to actionable changes (Fielding & Bragg, 2003, p. 25). Ultimately, if there is not a climate of trust and respect, it will be challenging to engage in collective inquiry and rebound when mistakes or missteps occur. One way to begin assessing and building shared understandings of the context is to involve students in the preliminary stages of the research. Thomson and Gunter (2006) narrate one example of what that process might look like, starting from a broad examination of a school's policies and practices and peer relationships to survey item development. Thomson and Gunter were careful to ensure the school's leadership was well informed about the project and enlisted their support early on. Here are some questions that will support assessment of how welcoming and valued students' voices are:

- Are students encouraged to share their perspectives?
- Do educators listen and respond to students' perspectives?
- Do students feel a sense of belonging?
- What are some collective problems that the school is trying to address, and how might student participation in research support those aims?
- Is there a sense that school issues are collective problems?

On a different end of the participation spectrum, to engage in a students-as-respondents approach, it is important to learn, understand, and honor students as epistemic subjects (see Thomson, Chapter 6, this volume), as well as understand the context and social dynamics within the spaces you may be working. Sometimes social dynamics and or institutional norms may prohibit students from engaging fully in a project (due to the question, issue, time commitment, and/or inclusion issues). It is good to know to what degree participation is feasible as soon as possible. It is also possible that students may not be interested in (or able to engage in) in-depth participation. However, that does not make a student voice study inherently invalid or problematic. It does lead to different questions of epistemic justice, which Thomson also discusses in Chapter 6.

For a students-as-respondents approach, researchers should think through the context and goals of their study in relation to methods to ensure the voices of students are understood and heard as they are, instead of being misappropriated for adult use. A common example of misappropriation is when adults use one students' comments to confirm adults' presumptions about a given issue, even if there is confounding evidence from other students. So, thinking through the epistemic justice of a method (how questions are phrased, who students are asked to embody in their responses, the analytical approaches, the search for rival theories to explain phenomena, and to what ends/whose interests the study is being used) is important for students-as-respondents approaches. Understanding the social dynamics of the space of research is important to guard against misappropriation. To ensure epistemic justice, some consultation with students for feedback on methods, even if implementation does not include students, might be warranted. There are risks with this approach, but there are also instances where this approach is contextually appropriate.

2. Think about the options of students' levels of engagement to build coherence between research questions, data collection strategies, analytical validation and reliability, and reporting strategies with the needs and goals of the sites you are engaged with. Students can be a source of data, active respondents, co-researchers, researchers, leaders, and activists. When students are a source of data, educators are interested in acquiring information about students' prior learning in order to improve pedagogy or policy. Educators collect data on student performance and other indicators measuring teaching and learning. Students listen to reports about performance produced from adult-created, evidence-collecting instruments. At this level, students are not partners in creating and discussing data. This traditional form of inquiry tends to assess curricular outcomes and disseminate information to students and the community.

When there is a need to engage students to deepen understanding of teaching, learning, and school environments or social issues, researchers might consider students taking on the role of active respondents. In this form, research is meant to create new forms of student data and to ask students to discuss their learning experiences. At the classroom level, students and educators might discuss and co-author learning objectives and examine the evaluation of student work together. This level of research is discussion-oriented; students, educators, and researchers are deliberating on what might work best and explaining results.

When students and educators become co-researchers, collaboration is about leveraging the capacities of students and educators to create a collective inquiry process. Here, youth and adults agree on and implement research projects with the hope of generating new knowledge. Conversation is dialogic, but researcher-led. By combining the social and intellectual capital of students and educators, there is a higher likelihood of uncovering the problems and possibilities of teaching and learning. And collaborations can provide opportunities for the researcher to discuss the research process more explicitly with students to examine the (in)congruences of goals, strategies, and data analysis. Additionally, students' networks can increase levels of participation in data collection. And, including students in the design and implementation of research produces more context-specific changes to pedagogical practices by sensitizing educators to the needs and concerns of students. A useful starting point here is to consider what kinds of data students might offer or have access to that researchers and professionals have not been able to acquire.

A students-as-researchers approach develops when students initiate, design, and direct research. With this approach, students control all aspects of the research project. Students form the research questions and design data collection. Conversations are led by students, and educators contribute by listening and supporting all stages of the research process. Educator support is fundamental to the success of the project. Educators help ensure not only that respectful relationships are maintained, but also that differences between and within groups are explored, valued, and thus contribute to a more nuanced understanding of individual and collective needs. Educator support is also there to help students navigate institutional hurdles that might emerge that stymie investigations and reporting of findings. Fielding and Bragg (2003) outline essential steps for doing this level of research (pp. 27–35):

- involving students (which students to include? are they invited or did they volunteer?);
- choosing topics to research (who decides? where is the real chance of change?);
- establishing staff roles (how much will they lead and how much follow students' lead?);
- matching inquiry strategies to the topic (what are appropriate ways to find answers to the research questions posed?);
- setting a time scale and distributing tasks among those involved;
- analyzing and writing up data (keeping records, identifying patterns, drawing conclusions, etc.);

- sharing the findings (format? audience? purpose?);
- celebrating it; and
- responding to it.

Of all the approaches described, students-as-researchers and YPAR have the most transformative potential for students themselves as both aim to redistribute power to youth for liberatory purposes. And by identifying the contexts in which there is real receptivity for the research project, there is greater likelihood that research can lead to wider changes.

3. Understand the context to understand appropriate methods. Depending on the level of student participation in a student voice project, there are many different methods that can be used. Methods include interviews, photo-based interviewing, manipulables (see Mayes's discussion of using a ball of yarn in Chapter 9), surveys, focus groups, work activities, arts-based projects, games-based projects, activist projects, scientific research projects, performance projects, and narrative projects (among others). In order to find the appropriate methods, we must know the context. Age, cultural norms, interpersonal dynamics, and time are all factors that need to be considered. We have found, for example, art-based and performance projects to be quite effective with young children, who can struggle at first finding the right words. Depending on the dynamics between students, focus groups with secondary students have resulted in powerful dialogues about school, but also illuminated social tensions between students that were quite relevant to understanding the phenomenon under study (Brasof, 2015). Learning about the context and social dynamics of the group you are working with will help you decide.

CONCLUSION

In this chapter we introduced the Student Voice Research Framework (SVRF), which lays out four principles for decision-making in student voice research necessary to ensure that a project more accurately reflects the experiences of youth and can support the development of a more responsive and vibrant educational space. Educational institutions are unique in that way—their purpose is to serve youth, and educational research can advance that aim by ensuring students are well understood.

The four SVRF principles are as follows:

1. an explicit conception of *intersubjectivity* with younger people
2. *reflexivity* about the researchers' conceptions of youth, the influence of the researchers' own childhoods and schooling experiences, and theoretical choices on their interpretation of students' voices

3. considerations of the *power dynamics* between youth and adult researchers
4. selection of strategies congruent with students' *contexts*, that includes their cultures, experiences, organizational membership, perspectives, and knowledge that researchers are seeking to access/understand

Performing quality student voice research to understand and improve schools and students' learning, experiences, and well-being is a complex task. Getting closer to attaining intersubjectivity requires genuine self-reflection and careful consideration of one's positionality in the research process. An examination of the intersection of power and identity is critical to get closer to intersubjectivity, whether that is the researcher thinking about the socio-cultural contexts in which any study is conducted and how those contexts impact youth, or the ways in which youth–adult relationships and/or strategies can hinder productive dialogue. This is not a one-and-done process. Researchers must continue to engage in this analysis before, during, after, and long after a project occurs. In this way, the SVRF is an iterative process of reflection and action but done so with an eye toward the positionalities of youth as students and for improving education.

In the following chapters, contributors write about past or current student voice research projects and how they have engaged in the methodological issues mentioned within the Student Voice Research Framework, using specific examples (of things that went well, and things that did not go so well) to provide future student voice researchers with a guide to student voice methods that are impactful, socially just, and transformative for schools and students.

CHAPTER 2

Epistemological Issues in Student Voice Research

Joseph Levitan and Marc Brasof

Although ideas, values, and principles about young people contributing to social life and social change have been discussed around the world for millennia, student voice research as a field is relatively young (Lyons, this volume; Rudduck & Fielding, 2006). Paradigms to support youths' contributions to knowledge were not discussed directly in the context of formal schooling until more recently. So, student voice research as a defined field of inquiry, with its constituent, specific principles for ethics, epistemology, and methodologies, is still emerging, and it is growing rapidly (e.g., Lyons, this volume; Lyons, MacCannell, & Gold, this volume; Rudduck & Fielding, 2006). With growth comes new understandings and exciting new initiatives and possibilities for the liveliness and democratic nature of schools and learning. Growth and popularity also bring about conceptual challenges and tensions that lead to questions about what student voice research is. What makes student voice research different from "traditional" research methods or fields? Is it actually its own field? Do you need to have specific knowledge or skills to do student voice research?

In this chapter, we discuss responses to these three questions. We begin the chapter with foundational philosophical definitions of the difference between "student voice," "student voice research," and "student voice activism," as well as the definitions of "student," "youth," and "adult" to engage in a discussion about student voice as a unique field. Using these definitions as a foundation, we then present arguments for why student voice research is its own field to address the second question. To answer the third question, we discuss often implicit arguments about the nature of research, what constitutes knowledge in different fields (epistemology), and epistemological considerations of student voice research. We end by exploring epistemological issues that adults need to consider when performing student voice research—demonstrating the need for the Student Voice Research Framework (SVRF). We argue that because of contextual considerations, interpreting student voice research from the epistemological paradigm of classical research is flawed.

Student voice research walks a unique line between declarative knowledge and procedural knowledge because of its contextual nature. Critical and transformative engagement of declarative and procedural knowledge requires student voice researchers to have specific conceptual and practical skills, which is why this is a field that requires its own paradigms and the SVRF.

WHAT MAKES STUDENT VOICE RESEARCH DIFFERENT FROM "TRADITIONAL" RESEARCH METHODS OR FIELDS?

Student voice research is different from traditional fields in that it positions students uniquely as agents and knowledge holders in the process of research and school (or social) change. It also engages with context and knowledge generation differently from traditional research. Before discussing these arguments, however, we begin by defining key terms and ideas so that the arguments that follow have a clear conceptual foundation.

Defining key terms helps to build mutual understanding—which is also called intersubjectivity, one of the principles of the SVRF. Intersubjectivity is especially important when engaging in complex work such as research or philosophical analysis. Defining concepts well, however, is difficult. What is often missed in defining ideas is that both the denotations (or the explicit definitions) as well as the connotations (or the implicit, often culturally, subjectively, or contextually understood implications of the term) need to be understood. Sometimes, the connotations of a word can create serious misunderstandings, such as in the story about the meaning of "professional" in Chapter 1. Below we discuss how some scholars define key words and concepts related to student voice research, thinking through the denotations and the connotations of these terms. These foundational understandings and distinctions will help foster intersubjective understandings (or at least diminish misunderstanding) about the framework for the epistemological and philosophical arguments that follow.

Distinctions and Definitions

The definitions in this chapter are not a comprehensive survey of all the definitions scholars use in student voice research. Instead, they serve as a way to start "on the same page" to delve into the arguments presented in this chapter. Making explicit the denotations and connotations of possible definitions for important terms serves the purpose of uncovering assumptions and thinking through implicit meanings that are sometimes hidden in plain sight when doing research. Unearthing assumptions allows for more open and constructive critique, development of better understandings moving forward, and collaboration, as student voice research is a lived inquiry process for an applied field.

Foundational Understandings of Student Voice. "Student voice" as a general concept is fluid and contested, and it consists of a range of practices. Among other denotative definitions, student voice itself is usually understood as discussion, consultation, democratic participation, equitable relationships, and engaged agency of youth in schools—students having a say in the decisions that affect them (Brasof & Levitan, this volume; Cook-Sather, 2018; Fielding, 2001a; Mitra, 2004; Rudduck & Fielding, 2006). Contrary to some connotations, a denotative definition of student voice does not necessitate research or activism. Teachers can engage student voice practices informally by simply speaking with students about decisions in the classroom. School leaders can create student advisory councils that have real power in decision-making, among other practices. This kind of student voice engagement has been occurring for centuries.

Documented formal cases of student voice in the English-speaking West began in the 1800s with Maria Montessori (in 1909), John Dewey (in 1902), and the Bedales School in 1890 (Rudduck & Fielding, 2006), among others. Rabindranath Tagore's school in India is a documented case further East (O'Connell, 2007). Teachers often intuitively engage in student voice practices, and specific educators have likely engaged in this work since formal schooling began (Levitan & Johnson, 2020). In leadership and policy discussion, however, student voice is less prevalent, as it requires values, relationships, systems, and organization within schools that are often missing (Brasof, 2015). As schools are complex systems, incorporating student voice within organizational leadership requires a different kind of student participation, one that usually necessitates more formal processes, and at times, research.

Student Voice Research. Distinguishing itself from student voice, the concept and practice of student voice research is best defined by the engagement with or consultation of students within formal research projects. Student voice research has mostly developed since the 1960s and 1970s (Rudduck & Fielding, 2006; Thomson, this volume). There are various definitions within the literature about student voice research and the roles that students are meant to play in research for it to be considered "real" (e.g., Cook-Sather, 2018; Fielding, 2001a; Mirra et al., 2018; Mitra, 2007a; Thomson, this volume). From students as respondents of an adult-created question, to students as leaders of the full research process, student voice research as a field positions students in different roles depending on the topic, issue, methods, and practicality of the project.

The positioning of students in research is an area of significant ethical and moral concern. In Chapter 6, Pat Thomson considers the ways in which students are engaged in "voice" and "voiced" research, as well as questions about epistemic justice (how knowledge from students is understood and used for their benefit and based on students' understandings of that benefit). Student voice research as a paradigm pushes back on antiquated assumptions about the contributions students can make on shaping the world. Many adults hold assumptions, and some may argue outright, that young people are too inexperienced, immature, and without the knowledge or tools to make significant or valuable changes to policies or practices (Dewey, 2008; Mansfield, 2014a; Montessori, 1982). Student voice researchers, through their work and scholarship, reject this argument. They show that students are not only capable of important contributions, but in many cases are in fact in the best positions to contribute knowledge for making schools and society better (Mansfield, 2014). Student voice researchers also developed their practices in response to the problematic nature of speaking about others and for others—working toward an ethic of speaking *with*, especially with those who are not often heard (Fielding, 2004).

Of course, there are things that youth are unaware of and may not be able to contribute to, and it is possible for young people to not take student voice research seriously or engage in it thoughtfully. Many student voice researchers carry an assumption, or argue outright, that it is the social construction of power and unjust/oppressive socialization that is the primary problem to be addressed when students do not meaningfully or seriously engage in student voice work (e.g., Montessori, 2009/1936; Wall et al., this volume).

There are also problematic assumptions in many narratives within the field that students always are unheard, oppressed, or marginalized. Conceptualizing the complexity and nuance of how some students' voices are heard "more" and given unmerited weight over others' voices is a constant issue in student voice work. This is why student voice research requires specific epistemological orientations and understandings of power dynamics and intersubjectivity—which is what we developed in the SVRF. When these skills and orientations are applied, study after study have shown that student voice research offers important and otherwise hidden insights into schooling, social justice, and society (Brasof, 2015; Mansfield, 2014a; Mitra, 2004).

Students often present novel ideas in quality student voice research and have new visions of what society could be. The positionality of youth as the most closely concerned about educational practices, and as newcomers and inheritors of a society, allows them to have fresh perspectives that others do not have access to. Student voice research relies on the argument that students' positionality is unique, and so their experiences, values, concerns, challenges, and insights can only be learned through engaging *with* them (to avoid problematic power dynamics). Students also often have the energy, time, and opportunities (when not marginalized, limited, or oppressed) to seek changes in society—especially when engaging with meaningful information—which is why student voice activism has been a major force for change throughout recent history.

Student Voice Activism. Student voice activism is the practice of individuals who have the position of students to actively seek changes in the world. While student voice research is focused on gathering, analyzing, and disseminating information, which ideally and hopefully is used to improve practice and policy, student voice activism is about mobilizing voices to make or push for specific defined changes, rather than seeking information to answer a research question (Lincoln, 1995). Student voice activism may include student voice research, such as in Youth-Led Participatory Action Research (Cammarota & Fine, 2008; Morell, 2008), and also may include student voice practices in the classroom or in whole schools. But the ultimate goal and outcome of student voice activism is a specific change to policy or practice through students presenting ideas and arguments for something different. Student voice activism can take on the form of student groups self-organizing and marching for change, creating petitions, creating street art, or participating in boycotts, sit-ins, or strikes. Student voice activism can also entail speaking before governing boards, creating public service announcements, or testifying before high-ranking policymakers. Student voice activism is usually (but not always) initiated by the students themselves (Altbach, 1966). Sometimes adults support the organization and messaging of students' demands or requests, but the leadership is generally members of a student community. Student voice activism often pushes the boundaries to (ideally) make fairer and more socially just societies, and for many, the goal of student voice research is to do the foundational work to support student voice activities so that students can change the world for the better. While we distinguish between research and activism, there are some paradigms such as Youth-Led Participatory Action Research (YPAR) that engage in both research and activism simultaneously. YPAR has its own paradigm within the field of action research when it comes to epistemology.

While student voice, student voice research, and student voice activism often overlap in practice, understanding their distinguishing characteristics helps us to identify the specific issues and tensions within the subject of this book: student voice research. Even though many underlying principles about students' positionalities, contributions to policy and practice, and social justice work overlap, each activity requires different approaches to the way adults think about and engage with students, and the roles that students take on within each of these activities. Here, we focus specifically on student voice research and the ways in which we can gain important and valuable knowledge when engaging with students.

Definitions of Students, Youth, and Adults. The definitions and considerations of student voice activities raise several questions: Who are students? How do we define "student" in the paradigm of student voice research? What are the denotations and connotations of this word? Scholarly debate about the positionality and definition of "students" is a foundational philosophical issue in student voice research, and it has been explored by educational philosophers to build out their pedagogical approaches (e.g., Dewey, 1902; Greene, 1977; Lee, 2006; Montessori, 1912). How student voice researchers conceptualize and define who students are, or the ontological nature of being a student, can impact and influence how adults engage with youth in student voice research projects. In the SVRF, how adults conceptualize who students are—beyond the denotative definition of student—will impact and influence their ability to build intersubjective understandings and will play a role in the analysis and methods they choose. So, thinking through "who students are" is fundamental work in student voice research.

One of the challenges of considering who students are is that the denotative definition is straightforward and mostly assumed. The common definition for "student" is a person who is learning about a subject or topic in a formal program of education, whether state-run or private (Cambridge, 2021). However, this simple definition belies the ambiguity and complexity of the word. The term "student" implies that there is a "teacher"—it is a relational word—connoting a relationship where there is a knower or body of knowledge who/which the student is learning from/about. There is a knower and/or knowledge instructing and a not-knower who is learning.

People with absolutist assumptions may see the connotation of the term "student" as meaning someone who is devoid of knowledge and who needs to have knowledge imparted on them by the knowing teacher—connoting a completely hierarchical power dynamic (Freire, 2000). Philosophies of student voice research productively question this connotation to reimagine the ways in which historically hierarchical relationships are remade into more democratic and just relationships of mutual consideration, sharing of knowledge, and honoring of perspective and identity. A fundamental premise of student voice research is that everyone is both student and teacher in different contexts. Even very young children have knowledge that they can impart, and that can inform adults—especially adults concerned with pedagogy, educational policy, social justice, and democracy—as well as with other students, and schools generally.

Thinking through the relational dynamic of student-teacher—and potentially breaking out of that binary—is important for engaging in productive student voice research. It is also important to consider how students can become teachers, as well as how teachers can be students in different moments. Breaking out of absolutist or rigid conceptualizations of the teacher–student dynamic can free up researchers to build productive relational spaces and make for insightful student voice research projects. But adults need to do reflexive work to uncover their assumptions about students, since adults usually come into a situation with more socially recognized power to organize the classroom and/or the research project.

While student voice researchers may or may not be teachers, because of social norms and cultural hierarchical norms researchers inherently take on a "knower" position in the research process as they relate to students. So, researchers need to explore and question reflexively how they do in fact relate with students in terms of decision-making power. In student voice work, most researchers are considered adults and students are usually considered youth—but that does not necessarily need to be the case. In addition to the ambiguity of the roles and identities of the participants, there are a number of other connotations that the word "student" holds that require exploration as well.

For example, there is no determined age range in the common definition of student. People as old as 96 have been known to be students in higher education, and people as young as a few months old can be enrolled in preschools (Guinness, 2021). Much of the student voice research literature, however, is focused on students in the upper primary, secondary, and undergraduate levels, which implies that student voice research is inquiry that includes youth and children (Rudduck & Fielding, 2006). Definitions of children vary, but it is typically understood that they range in age from 0 to 18 years (United Nations, 1989). Youth is generally understood to be people aged 15–22 or even up to age 35 (UNESCO Youth Programme, 2021). In fact, there is a lot of debate about the definition of "youth," as the term's meaning has changed over time.

Because the general definition of the term "student" is young people, this book engages with scholars who generally work with youth in the 6–23 age range. Being young adds a layer to the positionality of the students in student voice research, with different implications for the possible contributions and possibilities of student voice work at different ages—which often mean different positionalities and socially constructed possibilities for decision-making power. As the field grows, consideration of the connotations of student voice research may explore whether students must be young people, or if the role of "student," such as a graduate student, is included in the defining features of the field. *Prima facie,* it seems that the connotation in this field is that students must be youth (though the definition and age range is ambiguous). So, researchers engaging in student voice work need to think through how they conceptualize what age means in terms of positionality, and think through how age is not synonymous with experience or knowledge. They may also wish to reflect carefully about their assumptions of students' identities, abilities, and attitudes, and the meanings of their behaviors and words, which is why student voice researchers need to engage in specific forms of reflexivity related to student voice research.

Age and experience are not the only factors to think about reflexively. The roles, responsibilities, positionalities, and identities of students, regardless of age, are varied and diverse. As is a common refrain, students are not a monolith. A common connotation of the word "student" is that students are in a position of being cared for and that they are being educated, so they do not have the same responsibilities as adults or professionals. However, some students already have significant responsibilities and roles in their communities. Many students, especially those who are from nondominant backgrounds, take on essential caretaking, earning, and financial responsibilities outside the walls of a school. Older students may also be parents, leaders, and professionals. As a field, student voice researchers have not yet explored in enough detail and depth the particular roles, identities, and implications of working with students from various backgrounds to perform student voice research and activism. While the definition of the outside roles of students does not need to be a fixed concept, ensuring that students from various positionalities and identities can productively contribute to projects would help the field be fully aligned with its value of democratizing schooling.

Reflexive student voice researchers will also need to explore the role of the adult in student voice research projects, as adults' roles are contextual. For example, many student voice projects in K–12 schools are undertaken by graduate students in doctoral programs. So, these adults are also students, but in the context of a K–12 school-based student voice project—as most projects occur within primary and secondary schools—they are adults and researchers. So, the connotations of the term "student" are not well defined (nor should they be).

Nonetheless, though the age range and outside roles of a student are not well defined, there are some consistent positionalities and roles that students do play. They are usually in a space because they are required to, or want to, formally learn. This means that their positionality of power is inherently lower than the instructor for whatever topic or subject is being taught, as they are seen as knowing less than a teacher—at least for that subject. Generally, assumptions and connotations of being a student are that they are much less powerful than the instructor, whether that is because of age difference or difference in expertise. Thinking through power dynamics to build a more democratic, equitable, and socially just dynamic is necessary and critical. Philosophical reflection allows for the nuance and detail of diverse identities, experiences, and perspectives to be meaningfully understood.

Understanding the definitions and considerations necessary to engage fruitfully as a researcher with students, youth, and adults relates directly to all four of the SVRF practices of intersubjectivity, reflexivity, power dynamics, and contextualization. When following these principles, student voice research projects can ensure that there is epistemic justice, which will hopefully build toward better schooling experiences for students. With these definitions outlined, it is now easier to turn to the second and third guiding questions of this chapter.

IS STUDENT VOICE ACTUALLY ITS OWN FIELD?

One of the core arguments throughout this book is that student voice research is its own field. The fundamental difference between student voice research and other fields is that there are unique dynamics between youth as students, and their necessary positionality as students, and adult researchers as nonstudents. While other fields might work collaboratively with young people or adults, student voice research is focused specifically on the positionality of youth as students who have agency and essential insights into improving schools, working toward social justice, and informing educational policy. This foundational assumption about students—as agents of change, equipped with the necessary attributes to do school and social improvement work, and who are not only capable but also the best positioned to inform decision-making—is a radical shift from past, traditional paradigms of educational research. Student voice research requires its own paradigms and epistemologies, which makes it a unique field. It does not see students as passive subjects of clinical research without their own agency but as genuine agents in knowledge generation and change processes.

Because student voice research positions students as the agents of research differently than any other field, it also requires unique conceptualizations of what "counts" as knowledge and what kinds of knowledge are of value. Traditional educational research often does research on or about students to find generalizable knowledge, whereas student voice research engages *with* students to find contextually sound knowledge that can improve learning, and ultimately, lives. This engagement entails new epistemologies—the study of knowledge. Student knowledge may not fit into a traditional scientific paradigm, but in student voice research it is considered to be essential and important knowledge. Student voice research also engages in a unique approach to thinking about context, and the ways in which knowledge of context is interpreted and understood—generalizability is not as important in student voice research as contextually grounded knowledge, which is often what students are in the best position to offer. We discuss why below. Because of this difference, there are implications for the methodological and philosophical orientations student voice researchers need to take into account, along with the knowledge and skills that student voice researchers need.

DO YOU NEED TO HAVE SPECIFIC KNOWLEDGE OR SKILLS TO DO STUDENT VOICE RESEARCH?

Yes. Like any other field of inquiry, student voice research requires specific knowledge and abilities. This is why we developed the Student Voice Research Framework (SVRF). Over years of engaging in student voice research projects and reflecting on our processes, we realized that, like demography, intervention studies, psychological research, and historical research, student voice research has its own paradigm and values, as well as a range of specific methodologies. The four interrelated principles that we shared in Chapter 1—intersubjectivity, reflexivity, equitable power dynamics, and matching methods to context—are considerations and strategies that we found were necessary throughout all of our many studies, even if the specifics of each study were quite different. While many of the specific methods are similar to other qualitative research, the special considerations of student voice research and its applied, contextual, and ethical stances for working with youth require specific skills and experiential knowledge about how to relate well and justly with young people—skills that require specific attention to develop.

In addition to experiential knowledge, a few philosophical arguments undergird the Student Voice Research Framework. In developing this framework, we also thought deeply about important philosophical and practical questions about research, such as (a) what "counts" as knowledge?, (b) who decides what knowledge is?, (c) what is knowledge good for?, (d) how does knowledge influence people's lives?, (e) how do we know what we know?, and (f) is there a way to be sure in our knowledge? We also thought deeply about important philosophical questions in terms of what it means to be a student and what it means to be an educator—questions such as (a) what is the purpose of education?, (b) who decides on the aims of education?, (c) what is social justice, and how do we work toward it?, and (d) how do we engage in practices to improve education? To address these deeper questions, below are some considerations, specifically about the epistemological skills and orientations necessary for good student voice work.

Epistemology and Student Voice Research

When engaging in student voice work, it is important to understand the process of social research and some of the key issues of working with youth to improve schools. The foundation of all research is the epistemological orientation that a researcher takes in their practice. Epistemology, or the study of knowledge, is rooted in the questions "what is knowledge?," "can I really know anything?," "how does my knowledge relate to others' knowledge?," and "how do we come to know?" Epistemology examines the ways in which human beings understand information, sense experiences (like seeing or hearing), phenomenon, other people, and skills. Epistemology also covers questions directly related to research, such as what constitutes a justified finding in inquiry. Scholars of epistemology have uncovered a number of important challenges and questions necessary for researchers to address to ensure that their work can be used productively (Steup, 2020).

In social research, like student voice inquiry, the two most important questions related to epistemology are (a) whether a researcher can really "know" the perspectives or experiences of others, and (b) whether people can understand each other well enough to improve the lives and experiences of themselves and those around them. In response to the first question, many schools of thought, from neopositivist to postmodern, have different arguments about the possibility of truly "knowing" what another person really means based on what they are saying (Avramides, 2020; Besteman, 2020; Levitan & Johnson, 2020), or based on data about them (through observation, tests, or clinical evaluation, for example). There are strong arguments in social science research for why we cannot fully understand another person's experiences (Comesaña & Klein, 2019; Popkin, 2013). And with so much of the universe and the human condition still unknown, it is questionable if we fully understand our own personal journey and experiences (James, 2007; Levitan & Carr-Chellman, 2018; Schussler, 2006). However, in response to the second question, scholars and practitioners alike agree that we *can* build understandings between each other to carry out tasks, evoke emotions, and share common knowledge to improve experiences (James, 2007). This is known as an *intersubjective understanding* and forms a key facet of the SVRF and student voice research.

There are many challenges that epistemological scholarship has brought to the attention of researchers when it comes to understanding others. First, while it is possible to understand each other in day-to-day conversations, there is an increased level of difficulty, and the prospects for misunderstanding are higher, when working with others to change organizations, such as with educational practices and policies. Embedded in the work of school improvement is the acquisition of vital information, understanding the source of problems, and challenging norms and assumptions while aligning the design and enactment of change to address that understanding (Argyris & Schon, 1974; Brasof, 2015, 2018). This is more difficult than it sounds. Misunderstanding is a common phenomenon in day-to-day interactions and even more common when engaging in complex work.

One reason that misunderstanding occurs is that individuals make assumptions about what people mean. This happens when people do not think about how their own biases affect how they interpret others' words. Said another way, they do not engage reflexively with the people they interact with (Delpit, 2006; Demerath, 2002; Levitan, Carr-Chellman, & Carr-Chellman, 2020), leading to different understandings of the connation of words. The SVRF includes reflexivity for this reason.

Another common reason for miscommunication is that the power dynamics between individuals is rarely equal, and there are times when those who are in positions of less power feel less able to speak forthrightly and share all of their ideas (Johnson, 2020; Spivak, 1988). In social research, if an individual does not feel able to share all of the (considered) ideas that they are thinking, then it may not be possible to gather the necessary knowledge to make productive decisions—that is, the epistemological validity is compromised. So, student voice educators and researchers need to particularly be on the lookout to shift power dynamics so that students feel able to say everything they are (considerately) thinking. Especially in student voice work, when there is an adult who is a teacher and/or a researcher working with youth who are students, the age and position differences are two embedded facets of power dynamics that can potentially skew what students are saying (Levitan, 2018; van Manen, 2016). This is why considerations and work toward making more equitable power dynamics is a facet of the SVRF. These skills and abilities are unique in student voice research.

Finally, another epistemological challenge is that knowledge is only useful if it is congruent with the context in which it is used or enacted. Context is the values, people, places, events, time, policies, practices, and histories that situate the phenomena under study. As parents with teenagers know, context can completely change the meaning of words and the subsequent reactions of others when using the same words in different situations. For example, the word "floss" could mean (a) to clean one's teeth with a piece of waxed string, (b) to show off expensive clothes or jewelry, or (c) to do a dance.

Similarly, our knowledge and approaches to research projects may actually foster misunderstanding and trigger unwanted power dynamics when researchers (and teachers or school leadership) ignore context. For example, students will either know more or have different information about playground dynamics during recess than a parent, teacher, or researcher, and if a fight breaks out on the playground, teachers are often unaware of the context in which it started or why it happened. They usually see only the latest action, analyzing the situation incorrectly and often blaming the wrong student for the disruption. Students, on the other hand, saw what was happening in class just before recess that precipitated the fight, and they also saw the argument the day before on the bus (and perhaps some mistreatment by an older sibling). The students might know, too, that the fight was something that resolved tension between the two students, improving their interpersonal dynamic rather than harming it. Teachers or researchers might make things worse by imposing improper interventions. In situations such as these (and there are many examples in schools and personal experiences to pull from), the knowledge students have allows them to understand the root cause and resolve the conflict in a more transformative way—aiding an adult who listens to students to understand that context.

When considering questions of context in student voice research projects, it is important to take into account (1) who is posing the question, (2) how are others asked, (3) when they are asked, and (4) in what space are they asked. The answers will depend on the context and questions. Researchers need to be sensitive to the context to skillfully engage in appropriate methods and questions to ensure that intersubjective understandings are formed in alignment with the realities in the spaces of their student voice inquiry projects. Combined with the other three principles, student voice researchers need different levels and types of skills when engaging with students to uncover the important and useful knowledge, and these skills are qualitatively different than those for other researchers.

Different kinds of knowledge are useful for different contexts. Some knowledge is transcontextual (which means it can be applied to multiple—but not all—contexts), or transferable, such as principles and certain practices, and some knowledge is contextually embedded (meaning that it can be useful in only one instance or setting, where people have a specific history of engagement with each other in an institution that is situated in a unique community history). This is one reason why scaling up successful reforms in one context, based on rigorous study, still becomes problematic when inserted into settings with dramatically different sociocultural dynamics (contexts). As transferability relates to student voice research, we argue that the SVRF is transcontextual, but that in order to gain useful, actionable, and practicable knowledge in a certain space, the student voice researcher needs to be able to attune the methods and knowledge-gathering approaches to match the context in which they are working. This is why context is the final facet of the SVRF.

Although this may seem complex, in practice it can be fairly simple and straightforward. "Getting it" when students talk and asking the right questions can cut through this complexity, but "getting it" when speaking with youth requires experience, thoughtful theoretical engagement, or both. To add to this, for student voice researchers there are other kinds of knowledge as well. For example, there is declarative knowledge and procedural knowledge. These different kinds of knowledge are also important to consider in student voice research because a lot of the challenges in this field involve learning about the procedure to do the research in order to make change.

The challenges mentioned here are present in any research process. However, in student voice research specific and unique issues arise when working with students to understand and enact change. Adding to this challenge are considerations about the types of knowledge that might come about through student voice research. Some research is focused on declarative knowledge, but student voice research walks a line between declarative knowledge and procedural knowledge because of its contextual nature.

Declarative Knowledge and Procedural Knowledge

One of the core purposes of modern research is to contribute to the world's knowledge. Assumed in this understanding of knowledge (the epistemological assumption) is that the world's knowledge is knowledge *that*. In other words, knowledge *that* DNA is the building block of the cell. Or knowledge *that* the United States is getting more diverse demographically. This is called *declarative knowledge*. Declarative knowledge is a well-justified statement about some set facet of the world, whether that be the physical world, the social world, or the theoretical world of scholarship. To say *that* John

Dewey was the founder of the progressive movement in education and an American pragmatist in his philosophical orientation is a declarative statement about a theoretical world of educational philosophy. Generally, in research, the more people can use the knowledge that the researcher argues they have found, discovered, or invented, the more influential and more prestigious the research is.

Another kind of knowledge, *procedural knowledge*, is the knowledge of *how* to do something. Usually procedural knowledge is not seen as coming about through research, because procedural knowledge usually needs to be practiced, or put into work and the world. To read a book about how to perform brain surgery does not mean that you will be able to perform brain surgery successfully right away, for example. It is necessary to read the book, but it is not sufficient to *only* read the book, as surgery requires practice. So, procedural knowledge comes with more complexity and requires more facets of human capacity. Nonetheless, the development of brain surgery techniques was developed through research—usually through research of trial and error, clinical attempts.

In applied fields like medicine and education, practitioners need both declarative knowledge and procedural knowledge. Not only does a surgeon need to be able to perform the movements with the scalpel, but they also need to know which region of the brain and which kinds of movements are necessary for a particular case. Similarly, teachers, school leaders, and educators in general will need to know not only the information necessary to do their job (content knowledge, students' phases of development, structures of the school and the curriculum), but also how to teach, how to treat others respectfully and appropriately, and how to manage learning. Some of a teacher's knowledge is very specialized—knowing that Pat has a debilitating fear of spiders is declarative knowledge that can inform procedural knowledge about how and when to do a lesson on arachnids and the advisability of bringing in live spiders without particular preparation for Pat. This knowledge can be acquired through observation, discussion (interviewing), and experimentation (seeing what happens if a small spider makes its way into the class)—all of which are methods used in research. Of course, writing about Pat's fear of spiders and possible adaptations for Pat in a 5th-grade classroom will not likely be a particularly influential or prestigious article. The people concerned with Pat are generally Pat's family, friends, classmates, and teachers. So, a publication writing up the justification of the empirically supported belief that Pat has a debilitating fear of spiders is probably not going to be cited very often. However, the way in which the teacher might have figured out how Pat has this particular fear may prove to be important for other teachers to learn about, if for example, Pat was too embarrassed to talk about it, or if no one knew except for one teacher. The procedural knowledge of learning about how a young person might be prevented from fully engaging in the classroom because of a serious issue is important and might have a wider reach. If that knowledge is developed through a process that is adaptable and contextually transferable, then the case study of Pat might be a helpful example to others as well.

The knowledge gained in much student voice research is usually declarative and focused on a specific context. Schools might learn that students have a serious problem with the way the history curriculum is organized, or how a discipline program is or is not working. Students may also have ideas and generally agree on how to make the situation better. However, understanding the nuance and complexity of how students think and feel about a particular issue in schools is complicated, because students are not monolithic—they do not speak with one voice and they do not all have the same concerns. What works for one group of students may not work for another—making wide and broad outreach and engagement with students incredibly important and challenging. It also means that student voice researchers need to use specific research methodologies—methodologies that other researchers use, but the findings from which may not specifically be relevant to other schools or spaces. This means that the research scope and influence will likely be smaller than the influence of the discovery of messenger ribonucleic acid (mRNA). Nonetheless, a lot of student voice research also gains important procedural knowledge, as well as knowledge about how to change and positively impact the lives of specific people.

So, rethinking the epistemological orientation and value of student voice research is important. Studies published by scholars, and books like this one, offer greater procedural knowledge as well as some declarative knowledge. This means, however, that because of contextual considerations, interpreting student voice research from the epistemological paradigm of classical research is flawed. Emerging student voice researchers would benefit from thinking about the ways in which they communicate their research—with greater focus on how the knowledge gained in the research process is used to improve the context itself—and they must be very clear on the procedural knowledge gained about the process and the successes and failures of that process. This kind of knowledge is important and valuable to student voice research.

CONCLUSION

Student voice research is a unique field due to its epistemological orientations. The strength and some of the confusion with this field is this specific positioning and orientation to what knowledge is and what counts as knowledge. The Student Voice Research Framework offers guidance on the ways in which to engage in the multiplicity of methods and analytical frameworks within the field. Using this framework can support researchers in building the procedural knowledge for making sure that the declarative knowledge gathered with students is valuable and useful. The ways in which student voice researchers approach their work with students to uncover, create, or understand information can liberate new, enriching educational practices and policies.

Part II

PREPARING FOR STUDENT VOICE WORK

CHAPTER 3

The Ethics of Student Voice Research

William C. Frick

Research that involves human participants should be designed and carried out in ways that result in maximum benefits for society while causing minimal risk for participants. Fundamentally, respect, beneficence, and justice (as a principle) serve as the ethical anchors for the development and conduct of research projects (Department of Health, Education, and Welfare, 1979). Essentially, these assurances have assisted in protecting human participants and enabling research to go well. But mere compliance with higher education and oversight agency standards and institutional rules does not necessarily mean someone is being an ethical researcher. The fact is, we must all think critically about what it means to be an ethical researcher and carry that out in our formal inquiry work (Practical Ethics Center, 2003). Carefully attending to this premise moves us well beyond getting a study through institutional review board (IRB) approval and on to normative ideals that are historically grounded within communities (Christians, 2018).

The Student Voice Research Framework (SVRF) provides a way for us to contemplate and carry out a set of normative ideals when engaging in discovery work with students. These normative ideals can be derived from the four discrete but interrelated components for engaging with children and youth voice through research: intersubjectivity, reflexivity, relational dynamics, and context. Normative ideals are derived from a process of social valuation, or a belief of value, and constitute what is understood within moral philosophy as axiology (Sheehan & Johnson, 2012), or often referred to more specifically as value theory. Extending this notion further, Biedenbach and Jacobsson (2016) argue that axiology is the basis for understanding the purposes of research and the morality of carrying it out, in addition to strengthening its legitimacy. Central to the morality of carrying out student voice research are the virtues and character of the researcher themselves, whether that be formed habits, motivations, and/or broader forms of moral literacy such as sensitivity and reason (Tuana, 2007). This chapter will be organized by these important ethical considerations.

CHILDREN AS A SPECIAL CLASS

Students, for the purposes of this book, are children and youth. Children and youth hold special status as research participants (in line with naturalistic social science and the aims and objectives of the SVRF, the use of the term "subjects" is unsuitable when referring to students who are involved in voice research in multiple ways). Children under the age of 18 in most state jurisdictions of the United States (and under the age of the majority in other countries of the world) are considered vulnerable research participants because of age-related limited intellectual capacities and the possibility of being coerced into participation. Student vulnerability is intimated within the research methods guidance of the SVRF and should be made explicit here.

In the United States, there are regulations derived from the Federal Policy for the Protection of Human Subjects (also known as the "Common Rule") regarding research involving children (i.e., Department of Health and Human Services, 45 CFR 46 Subpart D §46.402 (a), 2018). Additional protections are afforded children involved in research because of their recognized vulnerability. Part of the Common Rule states by way of definition that "children are persons who have not attained the legal age for consent to treatments or procedures involved in the research, under the applicable law of the jurisdiction in which the research will be conducted" (Department of Health and Human Services, 45 CFR 46 Subpart D §46.402 (a), 2018). Who qualifies as a "child" depends on laws of localities whether in the United States or abroad. U.S. federal regulations classify permissible research involving children into four categories described in relation to "minimal risk."

For the purposes of student voice research, a large majority of study topics and designs within education and the social sciences would not involve greater than minimal risk to students. Although this may be the case, a careful review of potential risk is necessary prior to conducting any study. Under studies deemed "minimal risk," there is a minimum requirement for research with students: (1) permission from at least one parent/guardian, and (2) assent of the child (if the child is 7 years of age or older) (i.e., CFR 46 Subpart D §46.408).

Parental or guardian permission is acquired through an informed consent process and is required. To the greatest extent possible, based on age, the child or youth is required to give "assent." Assent means that the participant agrees to participate in the study under question. Failure to object is not equivalent to assent. In other words, due to students' circumstances and vulnerable positionality, they may consent to participate in a study involuntarily due to several reasons, including social pressure, anticipation of some benefit, or perception of expectations that can influence a decision concerning assent.

Vulnerability can be reduced by the processes and procedures of IRBs, where board membership is represented by relevant persons of the study population and/or advocates for the population to be researched. Responsible and responsive research takes vulnerability seriously, regardless of the more complicated process of caregiver consent and child assent. To this end, as we increasingly come to understand and appreciate the sociological and educationally implicated realities of child and youth culture, in its multiple and unique variants there is reasonable expectation that researchers may carefully consider obtaining group consent as well. As Hopson (2009) explains, this level of careful sensitivity can result in "reclaiming of knowledge at the margins" (p. 429).

ACCESSING AND STUDYING STUDENT VOICE

The ethical dimensions of student voice activities have been previously explored whether in relation to social science research specifically or broader engagement in youth activity (Mitra, Frick, & Crawford, 2011; Parker, 2020). Strengthening the connection between research on student voice and ethics can provide "a deeper, richer, knowledge of students' school experiences as well as their life experiences outside of school" (Mitra et al., 2011, p. 375). How? If we are to seriously consider the "deep underlying structures and taken-for-granted ways of organizing, conducting, and disseminating research" (Smith, 2005, p. 88) endemic to the academy, think tanks, philanthropical foundations, and other agencies and institutions of knowledge production, we invariably realize that "research is not just a highly moral and civilized search for knowledge; it is a set of very human activities that reproduce particular social relations of power" (p. 88). It is up to individual researchers and their practice communities to call for critical self-reflexivity that questions their own positionality as hegemonic experts who define commonsense norms and manufacture consent (e.g., Gramsci, 1947, 1973). Additionally, the interrogation of our own claims and motives implies the practices of deep listening to, and mutual learning with, students (Parker, 2020).

To access and study student voice with trustworthiness, or "goodness" (Lincoln & Guba, 1985), requires praxis. By committing to and engaging in praxis, the four interrelated components of the SVRF are more readily evidenced in research plans, procedures, and outcomes. Praxis is not a technical research maneuver based in specialized craft knowledge focused on production. Rather, praxis is practical activity related to the "conduct of one's life and affairs as a member of society. It is about doing the right thing and doing it well in interactions with fellow humans" (Schwandt, 2015, p. 249). The end or aim of praxis as activity is realized in the very doing of the activity itself (i.e., being a good human being, or teacher, or physician, or social science researcher). Therefore, you cannot take your leave of praxis and set it aside at will as you can a productive activity, such as taking a break from conducting a long, involved research project. Praxis is wide-awake engagement with communally shared values tied to the historical embeddedness of human experience. Practical activity calls forth practical knowledge (wisdom), and this way of knowing is different from strict technical or scientistic capacity. Wisdom is "bound up with the kind of person that one is and is becoming. This kind of practical-moral knowledge characterizes a person who knows how to live well; it is acquired and deployed in one's actions with one's fellow human beings . . . , demanding a disposition toward right living and the pursuit of human good" (Schwandt, 2015, p. 250).

There are three prominent ways of knowing and dealing with the world—*theoria* (abstract, contemplative thinking about a phenomenon), *techne* (the concrete practice of doing something), and praxis. Praxis is moral action in the political context of purposeful human conduct. Praxis is informed behavior guided by virtuous character, intentions, motives, normative morality, shared understandings and values, emotions, and developing literacies of the human condition (Hodgkinson, 1991).

A praxis for carrying out student voice research, then, would involve "the application of theory plus action plus critical self-reflection—in a continuous feedback loop" (Parker, 2020, p. 56). Stated in the most direct terms, all the social scientific research methods in the world, understood as technical specialization, cannot address and account for all unique persons as participants and their contingent situations; practical-moral judgment is required of the researcher in any investigative endeavor.

RESEARCH ETHICS AND THE FRAMEWORK COMPONENTS

As mentioned earlier, the SVRF supplies researchers with principles/strategies and constitutive methods for engaging in thoughtful focused inquiry. The SVRF, at its heart, is value-laden, and this section will expand upon the four interrelated dimensions of (a) intersubjectivity, (b) reflexivity, (c) power dynamics, and (d) context with research ethics in mind. These ethics should apply to any relevant form of student voice research whether carried out as an observer, surveyor, co-participant, facilitator, interviewer, or any combination thereof. The principles/strategies call for moral imagination—a blend of affective and cognitive activity that together contribute to discernment about oneself and one's actions as potentially helpful or harmful. The imaginative process is a "blend[ing] of reason and emotion through attending to what is taken for granted, what is left out of a situation, [and] how possibilities could be otherwise envisioned" (Tuana, 2007, pp. 374–375).

Reflexivity

Researcher bias and field reactivity can be enormous challenges for the student voice researcher. Reflexivity can address some, but not all of this. Reflexivity is not the same as being reflective or engaging in critical reflection, although these skills are needed for reflexivity. Reflexivity, rather, "is an act of self-reference where examination or action 'bends back on,' refers to, and affects the entity instigating the action or examination" ("Reflexivity (social theory)," n.d.). In the most general terms, "reflexivity is considered to occur when the observations or actions of observers in the social system affect the very situations they are observing" ("Reflexivity (social theory)," n.d.). Being self-referential requires the capacity to become aware of oneself, to be self-conscious about the entirety of your work as a researcher, and to understand deeply that by the very act of planning and carrying out research both the investigator and those being investigated are altered. In this sense, we may refer to reflexivity as demanding critical self-reflection that is multidirectional.

Falsely held assumptions and the way in which research is conceptualized and carried out can result in student voice misrepresentation. There are technical moves within methods that can help to attenuate the risks that are ever present (e.g., Patton, 1990), but methods cannot replace the attitude and disposition of self-inspection by researchers themselves. Through self-inspection, we become aware that no realist tale (Gullion, 2016) can be captured by any student voice methods variant. Ultimately, a researcher must recognize themself as being "inextricably part of the phenomena studied" (Maxwell, 1996, p. 67).

An attitude and disposition of self-inspection is much more than "salutary" (Schwandt, 2015, p. 268). Working to identify bias within oneself and field reactivity to one's presence or instrumentation, seeking to address it, and attempting to account for it takes on moral properties. How is reflexivity imbued with moral significance? What is of the researcher that is right, true, good, and praiseworthy with relation to reflexivity? A virtue candidate to put forward is humility, and more specifically, intellectual humility.

Bias can be unconscious and unrecognizable, and ignorance can lead to imperceptibility of participant affect. In this respect, education, mindfulness, and socialization are required. But false pride can likely play some role, especially if one knows better about research threats. And if one knows better, they are not honoring their mind as a deliberative critical thinker. Being intellectually humble can be understood as involving the awareness and owning of one's cognitive limitations, recognizing one's intellectual indebtedness to others, and possessing a low concern for domination and status. Of central importance is the quality of "withholding attributing knowledge to yourself and questioning whether you know" (Hazlett, 2015, p. 76). A cluster of character traits coalesce in the intellectually humble researcher such as open-mindedness, a sense of one's fallibility, and being responsive to counterarguments and alternative reasons. A variety of mental states follow from the character quality, including acknowledging cognitive mistakes, being receptive to evidence, being balanced skeptically and anti-dogmatic, attenuating belief to specific and credible evidence, and being aware of tendencies toward bias (Lynch et al., 2016).

Intersubjectivity

A researcher's positionality is always a challenge because they inevitably hold a privileged status within the research process by occupying a significant role in producing and reifying knowledge. The very real threat here is monolithically objectifying children and youth, limiting their agency through the conduct of research, and misrepresenting their voice and how it's used (Parson, 2019). This is taking participants for granted and not seeking to ensure youth are sharing their most insightful and authentic voices. An intentional focus on aspiring to intersubjectivity (coming to know participants on their own terms) can address some, but not all of this. Social location, identity categories, lived experience, worldview, institutional context, and other properties of one's locality and person that unavoidably reside within the research process can limit or broaden one's awareness and understanding of others. This is simply a fact. There is an outsider and there is an insider. Becoming aware and seeking to understand participants resides along a continuum, but mutual understanding should be built between youth and researchers.

Intersubjectivity is both a space and an occurrence "between or among (or accessible to) two or more separate subjects or conscious minds" (Schwandt, 2015, p. 161). Intersubjective agreement is our way of making meaning of experience through the social constitution of self, and within the study context, a means by which the researcher comes to know and feel the lifeworld of participants. This process is essentially dialogic and constitutes a form of "listening to the claims of others" requiring "position-taking from the perspective of the participant" (Call-Cummings & Ross, 2019, p. 5). Additionally, intersubjective dynamics include verbal and nonverbal cues along with varieties of language and code. Within this dynamic are contextual and setting forces as well that require awareness and sensitivity. From this account it becomes more apparent that intersubjectivity carries within it moral properties. How is intersubjectivity imbued with moral significance? What is of the researcher that is right, true, good, and praiseworthy with relation to intersubjectivity? A virtue candidate to put forward is empathy.

Empathy involves being aware of, identifying with, and wanting to understand another's situation, feelings, and motives. Seeking to understand and acquiring awareness by taking another's point of view is, as Taylor (2010) suggests, "a core competency for twenty-first century citizens" (p. 16), let alone academics who are professional researchers. Taylor (2010) reminds us that valuing empathy and developing it within ourselves works against unconscious bias, indifference, disparagement, indignation, or worse. Empathy helps us "to have a relationship to our own reactions rather than be captive to them" (Kegan, 2001, p. 199) to "resist our tendencies to make 'right' or 'true' that which is merely familiar and 'wrong' or 'false' that which is only strange" (Kegan, 1994, p. 302). Empathic capacity is required to appreciate and insightfully respond to the claims of others. The foundations of this capacity are nurtured in infancy and early childhood through a developing social sense, but empathy needs to mature over a lifetime where consciousness and intentionality are directed toward "reasons and opportunities to appreciate similarities and respect differences" (Taylor, 2010, p. 18).

Possessing empathy and its related strengths of holding self-interest in check through an altruistic commitment to reciprocity and relationships yields a "felt connection and identification in some way to the persons or group whose welfare [is of] concern" (Peterson & Seligman, 2004, p. 373; see also Eisenberg, 1986). And although empathy is biased toward the proximate encounters of those who are like oneself, compassion, empathy, and social responsibility can be developed and made integral to one's identity if exercised in action. Perspective taking is critical. To "imaginatively place yourself in the proverbial shoes of another" (Peterson & Seligman, 2004, p. 403) is foundational for moral deliberation, and more specifically, the source for what "drives us to act on the principle of universalism" (Taylor, 2010, p. 15). This intrapersonal capacity of empathy melds the cognitive (evaluation of a person's general position, situation, and obligations) and the affective (attending to the particularity of a person's perspective, experience, and projects), bringing about fuller knowledge of others and their standing (Peterson & Seligman, 2004).

Power Dynamics

Carrying out student voice research implicates relational power dynamics. Recognizing power as an issue in the inquiry process is a first step. "Power is everywhere . . . it is the name that one attributes to a complex strategical situation" (Foucault, 1976/1978, p. 93). And strategy certainly plays a role when accessing student voices. The risk of not being strategic can lead to silencing, inauthentic performativity, and relational distance—all, of course, corrupting the very purposes and intent of voice research. Therefore, "power is a big problem" (Comer, 2005, para. 28).

The goal of interrogating the nature of relational power dynamics within the research context is to promote a joint experience for adult researchers and students that is trusting, safe, equitable, authentic, and even-handed. The continuum of power over, power with, and power to is an important consideration here and goes beyond fundamental respect for persons as autonomous agents. Some method variants are more susceptible to concentrated researcher decision-making and control throughout the research process than others, and this is a result of the very nature of the methods per se. Being aware of the power dynamics issue as realized within various methods can help a student voice researcher rethink or reaffirm the nature and purpose of a study, its design, and how knowledge is reported. Pressing this issue further, a researcher should consider ways of researching *with* students rather than *on* or *for* them (Alderson, 1995, 2000). This of course can lead us too far afield into the politics of research. Needless to say, power is a self-interest value ordered as the ability of a person to affect the behavior of another (Fowler, 2004) and, as such, needs to be closely examined within the research process.

How is relational power imbued with moral significance? What is of the researcher that is right, true, good, and praiseworthy with relation to power dynamics? Fowler (2004) indicates that "using power ethically requires considerable maturity, self-awareness, and effort" (p. 49). Again, a characterological disposition of personhood is implicated. A virtue candidate to put forward is justice (as virtue), or justness. With respect to power dynamics, this character strength is sometimes referred to as a socialized power motive. Constructive by nature, the quality has been defined as an unconscious motive to satisfy power needs in ways that are socially desirable for the betterment of others rather than self (House & Howell, 1992).

Justness is the quality of being fair irrespective of the symmetrical or asymmetrical context of power dynamics or how that power may be deployed, either distributively or facilitatively (Fowler, 2004). Justice as a trait regards moral issues having to do with distributions of those things deemed of value. Decisions made arbitrarily and capriciously are antithetical to justness. Justness has been described as a continual development of a literacy in rightful and unprejudiced sharing practices (Widlok, 2018).

> Self-interest accounts for the possibility of our being motivated to act as the virtue of justice requires, and both the utility and the agreeableness, both to ourselves and others, of a resulting social order, leads to [an] approbation of that motivation as a virtue. (LeBar, 2020, 1.2)

Moving beyond giving oneself and everyone else their due, and advancing ideas about justice as virtue further, acting justly, from a motivation of justness, involves "striving to reduce and remove inequalities in people's capabilities to function in ways that are elemental to life . . . [a] striving to reduce and remove shortfalls in well-being" derived through freedom (Drydyk 2012, p. 31). As a researcher you cannot outright trade the welfare, agency, and "capabilities to function" of students for your own welfare, agency, and "capabilities to function." Power must operate symmetrically and facilitatively within the research process.

Context

Congruency to setting in social scientific research is a serious matter. Without congruency a study becomes disjointed, forced, and inauthentic. Methodological congruence is important "due to the need for careful planning of coherence and purpose among parts of research studies" (Thurston et al., 2008, p.14). From the worldview and paradigmatic stance of the researcher (e.g., one's ontology, epistemology, axiology, etc.), to the topics deemed important, to the problems and issues identified for inquiry, to the questions that are developed and refined, all should follow with coherence to the selection and use of carefully aligned research methods. These methods should concern appropriately selected/involved participants or respondents, within specific spaces, settings, and localities that are known and appreciated. Of particular importance to the SVRF is the thorough problematization of mis/match between methods and students' existential lifeworld (consciousness and meaning-making within the context of lived experience). The broad diversity of research method variants makes coherence particularly important in carrying out student voice research. From researcher-driven survey studies to facilitative student-led co-research projects, methods and their signature characteristics must be thoroughly considered as a backdrop to careful discernment of correspondence to student context.

The existential realities of students are dynamic and highly varied. Assuming an understanding of the different facets of youth's lives without appreciating that shared student perspectives do not necessarily represent the voice of all youth can dramatically undermine both the research itself and the possibility for socially transformative outcomes beyond a given study. Contextual sensitivity must push researchers to further consider how a specific group's or individual's experience in one setting might not mirror the experiences of the same or similar differently situated. How is existential congruency suffused with moral significance? What is of the researcher that is right, true, good, and praiseworthy with relation to existential congruency? A virtue candidate to put forward is presence.

There is a lot to "presence" as a character strength. Presence implies attentiveness, consideration, alertness, discerning prudence, concentration, and being mindful and engaged. As Starratt (2004) explains, "being fully present means being wide awake to what's in front of you" (p. 86). Presence is required for being responsible and authentic. This is particularly the case because presence "requires us to remove ourselves from the center of the universe. It requires a certain self-displacement, letting [others] enter our space" (p. 90). Part of presence involves sensitivity to the signals, events, settings, values, aspirations, and histories of others. In this sense, being present is knowing and seeing people and situations intricately. This knowing is not simply curiosity but rather based on who the researcher is as a person and the roles they perform while excluding wishful thinking about what should be.

As being present is a form of knowing, there is a corresponding cognitive skill involved in fully realizing the virtue as part of one's character. Critical reasoning is required. A careful discernment of student contexts requires assessing both relevant and uncertain facts to best understand a setting or situation as much as possible. A careful discernment of methods requires assessing the suitability of those methods and their related procedures considering student contexts. What's required is a robust, rich understanding of the interconnected relational issue of setting and methods so that sound inferences can be developed (Tuana, 2007). This is being present as a student voice researcher.

CONCLUSION

As has likely become apparent by now, this chapter has drawn specific attention to an ethical virtue approach to student voice research. The virtues of intellectual humility, empathy, justice, and presence focus on the character of the researcher as a basis for ethical research rather than the prescription of standards of conduct, the proposal of rules and principles, an assessment of utilitarian outcomes, or other means by which moral determinations can be made regarding research conduct. Not discounting the viability and dynamic nature of an ethically pluralistic approach to living (Hinman, 2013), the SVRF and its associated principles provide an important entrée for thinking about the ethics of research in relation to the dispositions, character strengths, and moral nature of the researcher from the inside out.

Intersubjectivity requires empathy. The positionality of a researcher is always a challenge because one inevitably holds a privileged status within the research process and with that separation becomes a very real threat of uniformly objectifying children and youth and limiting their agency. By feeling connection and identification, perspective taking can take hold through imaginatively placing oneself in the position of another. One pursues research with an intentional open heart.

Reflexivity requires intellectual humility. Honestly seeking to identify bias within oneself and field reactivity to one's presence or instrumentation, striving to the fullest extent to address it, and attempting to account for it through carefully designed methods cannot be achieved unless a researcher is genuinely open-minded, acknowledges cognitive limitations, and willingly questions whether or not they know. One pursues research as an unprejudiced learner unguarded about themself and others.

Power dynamics require justice. The problem of power is the differential that exists between persons regarding resources, decision making, situational control, and the free pursuit of projects. Justness works as an unconscious counterweight for the betterment of the collective rather than for personal self-interest. One pursues research characterized by power *with* students that aspires to symmetrical and facilitative standing.

Congruency of the context and methods requires presence. Correspondence between methods and the lifeworld of participants means that researchers must plan for and carry out methods that honor and that are sensitive to the existential realities of students. Every potential participant and research setting is unique. Presence is required so that alertness supports robust critical knowing about what is important: the signals, events, settings, values, aspirations, and histories of others. One pursues research open-eyed.

By drawing together a relationship between the SVRF principles and connected virtues, the guidance presented here and insights from the entire book can offer ways for research methods to be impactful, socially just, and transformative for students and schools. Doing this work necessarily means striving for excellence, and this cannot be achieved unless researchers are integrated persons who are motivated to become increasingly equipped with the necessary virtues to do not only good work, but work that is good.

CHAPTER 4

Considering Space and Time

Power Dynamics and Relationships Between Children and Adults

Kate Wall, Claire Cassidy, Carol Robinson,
Mhairi C. Beaton, Lorna Arnott, and Elaine Hall

In this chapter, we will focus on how space and time influence voice in early childhood. Voice is one factor of eight that arose from the Look Who's Talking project[1] that ran in Scotland during 2017 (Arnott & Wall, 2021; Wall et al., 2019). The eight factors that we identified to support eliciting voice with young children from birth to 8 years old are *definition, power, inclusivity, listening, time and space, approaches, processes,* and *purposes* (Wall et al., 2019). These eight factors can be seen to align with the Student Voice Research Framework (SVRF) with regard to intersubjectivity (definition, listening, and purpose), power dynamics (power and inclusivity), and context (time and space, approaches, and processes), with reflexivity reflected in our intent for these factors to be used as part of our praxis. This reflexivity will be exemplified through the process undertaken by the authors in generating the eight factors, and also in the discussion of particular practices from early childhood settings.

Voice research and practice in early childhood (from birth to 8 years old) is an often-overlooked component of the wider voice community (Clark, 2005; Smith, 2016; Wall, 2017). There are a range of reasons for this oversight, and they primarily pertain to the lack of status of young children and those who work with them. These examples include that (a) young children learn through, and associated practitioners work with, the formal education system; (b) contexts vary widely; (c) the practitioner community lacks professional recognition and a voice of their own (despite, we will argue, leading in innovative practice); and, probably most significantly, (d) adults hold negative assumptions about young children and their abilities (Bucknall, 2014; Komulainen, 2007; Roberts, 2000). However, our youngest children have, under Article 12 of the United Nations Convention on the Rights of the Child (UNCRC) (United Nations, 1989), the same right to express their views as those who are older, though with reference to the due weight according to children's views in Article 12, the issue of capacity remains fraught with challenges (Lundy, 2007). To address the need to take account of young children's voice, a growing group of researchers is working in this area (e.g., Clark, 2005; Harcourt et al., 2011; Wall et al., 2019). The practices of those working in early childhood education also offer a series of rich, creative, and diverse practices that facilitate young children's voice. This research and practice holds much for those working with older children and young people (Cook-Sather, 2006c).

In an educational setting, there are undoubtedly challenges when working to elicit voice with a group of children that includes those who are non-verbal, pre-verbal, and emergent verbal. While we use the term "voice" throughout this chapter, it is important to note that we are not assuming that all children share the same voice. As a starting point, one cannot rely on a definition of voice that is dominated by the spoken word. In this context, the adult needs to attune to the "100 languages of the child" (Malaguzzi, 1996, and applied to the field of voice by Clark, 2007), and then be a translator; both are different roles from those adopted when working with older children. There is, of course, a significant issue around power in this dynamic that must be considered. In addition, the methods used need to be context specific and pedagogically appropriate to the maturity and capabilities of the children involved (Blaisdell et al., 2018). Yet if these aspects are foregrounded, then the perspectives shared by these young children can be rich and insightful, are worthy of inclusion alongside their older counterparts, and should carry influence in the decisions that affect them (Wall, 2017).

DEFINING VOICE

The Look Who's Talking project created opportunities for dialogue among those working to support children's voice in the early years. The international team included academics, researchers, practitioners, and third-sector partners, all of whom, in their own contexts, were interested in promoting the voice of children from birth to 8 years. The project was established and continues to move debate forward, develop guidelines and provocations for practice, and advance understanding in relation to the affordances and constraints of the implementation of Article 12 of the UNCRC with young children.

In the earliest stages of the project, it quickly became apparent through the reflexive process, as articulated within the SVRF, that there was significant diversity within early childhood contexts with respect to what might constitute voice for children in compulsory schooling in comparison to toddlers and babies. For example, working with practitioners in rooms dedicated to babies in the nursery, it is clear that their daily lives are structured around interpreting meaning from action, which requires continual and re-sponsive reflexivity to evaluate the authenticity of their interpretation of the child's meaning. This raised questions about how we might advance tradi-tional, and at times limiting, definitions of voice that privilege the verbal. We know, for example, that there are challenges with a simplistic definition of voice, particularly for marginalized individuals of all ages, not just very young children (Komulainen, 2007). As a result, and quite fundamentally, the term "voice" was seen as particularly challenging and needed to be ad-dressed directly. There was a view that "voice" was often indicative of ver-bal orientation and that this was a mistaken view that could be attributed to dominant work with older age groups, although we would argue that this is also limited in its view of the potential of voice. To situate the work within the wider field of student voice, the team determined to retain the term but agreed that it required definition. In generating our definition, it was agreed that voice is context specific. We went on to assert that "voice is considered to be more than verbal utterances; it allows us to express who we are. Voice, therefore, includes, but is not limited to: words; behavior; actions; pauses in action; silences; body language; glances; movement; and artistic expression" (Wall, 2020, p. 2).

As the definition might variously be interpreted across different contexts, it became the first of eight factors to support practitioners thinking about eliciting young children's voice. As with most research and practice, concep-tualizing and unpicking definitions and terms underpins the remainder of the discussion and decision-making, so it made sense that defining voice was the focus of the initial activity. The remaining factors are *power*, *inclusivity*, *listening*, *time and space*, *approaches*, *processes*, and *purposes* (Wall et al., 2019). Central to the presentation of these factors is a stance that does not presume any single factor would provide an answer or a key to the issue of eliciting voice in early childhood. Rather, they could be explored individu-ally or in combination relevant to a particular context. This framing fa-cilitates an understanding of voice on a trajectory that will never complete, involving the adults and children in an ongoing range of dialogues where the factors and associated questions provide scaffolding to focus and challenge assumptions. Each factor, therefore, becomes a heading, an umbrella term, that might be usefully considered in order to advance practice, without pre-dicting or stipulating requirements.

This chapter will focus on one factor from the eight: *time and space*. In considering the notion of time and space, we will explore some of the key conceptual and practical issues associated with time and space in the context of early childhood education. The "modes of language" that young children employ require space—an environment and culture that facilitates opportu-nities of expression—but they also require time to evolve, to be articulated, to be sought and to be understood. Only in affording time and space for the evolution, articulation, and recognition of voice can it be understood and advanced to have influence. We will argue that building an environment in which time and space support eliciting voice is more aligned to the building of dens than major urban planning. It should be acknowledged that the eight factors are interdependent and that ideas relating to time and space have connections with the other eight factors presented. As such, we may draw on some of these factors to elucidate the discussion.

THINKING ABOUT SPACE AND TIME

Space and time are aligned in several ways, and both have an important role to play in facilitating young children's voice in practice and research. It is, however, important to note that in early childhood the distinction between research and practice is problematic due to a close relationship between the way research and practice are conducted with strong influences from dominant pedagogies and methodologies having common roots (Arnott & Wall, 2021).

Although "time" and "space" can be treated separately, they are more often complementary or interconnected (see Figure 4.1). Both may manifest themselves physically, such as the space and place occupied by a specific building or setting and the ways in which the building/setting is divided into rooms or areas. Time is physical when one thinks of timetables or schedules that govern day-to-day activities. At the same time, however, space and time may be viewed as more abstract concepts. For example, one may speak of space and time, particularly with respect to children's voice, as opportunity; that is, practitioners can create time and space—opportunities for children to express themselves.

Space is generally spoken about as occupied or empty. Certainly, children occupy physical space in, for example, their homes, and in our streets, parks, and educational settings. It is hard to ignore their physical being. It is easier, however, to ignore their voice, particularly in spaces where children can be considered as not belonging, due to these spaces being dominated by adults. Children attend school and preschool settings and it is here, aside from the home, where they learn what it means to have a voice and how to use it (or not). Educational settings belong to children, though they are shared by adults. These settings are occupied, with children both seen and heard. Though they may be heard in the sense that their laughter, shouts, and conversations resonate around the place, they may not be listened to by adults or have influence over what happens within the setting or space.

Physically occupying a space does not ensure that voices are heard. In some respects, simply having children occupy spaces does not guarantee any commitment to ensuring that their voice has any degree of influence on what happens in those spaces. This is true for educational spaces and for spaces in wider society. In this respect, space may seem to be empty, devoid of substance, and what emanates from children is noise rather than voice. If space is considered more metaphorically, as opportunity, children's voices can carry some weight. Opportunities are required for children to express themselves, and their expression needs to have meaning for themselves and for those around them. These spaces are more difficult to manufacture because they can be unpredictable. Or, at least, what happens in these spaces is unpredictable because in creating these spaces and opportunities for children's voice, adults must relinquish some control. The SVRF speaks to this issue with the concept of power dynamics.

It is worth acknowledging that children will also create their own spaces. They may occupy or appropriate a space physically by putting themselves and their belongings in that space. In so doing, they may also begin to occupy the metaphorical space. They may express themselves, use their voice, to say what they think or express how they feel, thereby shifting the balance of power within that space.

Time, too, may be captured by children who, ironically, are determined by time. The passing of time sees children progress through the years toward adulthood. This element of time is less easy to control, though some adults try by behaving toward children in particular ways that diminish their opportunities for participation. However, children capture time in the ways in which they choose to use it. Time might be viewed as either linear or cyclical. In noting that children progress toward adulthood, time is linear, with an inevitable conclusion or endpoint. This may be an overly negative view of children, as it leads to behavior that treats children for what they will become, rather than as they are. A linear approach suggests preconceived developmental stages through which children progress and that determine, often limiting, their (perceived) abilities (Cassidy, 2007; Donaldson, 1987; Matthews, 1994). Adopting this linear view of time in relation to children limits the scope for their voice, both in terms of ensuring space is created and that time is given to voice. It diminishes the weight young children's voice carry.

Seeing time as cyclical may be a more helpful way of supporting children's voice (Kohan, 2020; Murris, 2020). It enables one to think of childhood as a particular period in one's life, as part of the life cycle. It is one of several cycles through which we change rather than progress, with the cycles connecting in a spiral. Recognizing childhood as one cycle in the life course connected to the other cycles in one's life allows us to recognize children's voice as children's voice alone; they are not juxtaposed against adults' voices that are valued more, but are the expressions of children as they are in relation to themselves. Further, if time is cyclical, it suggests that there is no end point. In creating opportunities for children's voice, it means that the ideas or self-expression shared by children can be revisited; they are not completed on articulation and never considered again. This sense of time recognizes that voice requires practice and that such practice will refine one's voice and one's sense of identity. However, it will also provide time (opportunity) for others to listen to what is being said and for voice to have influence on the space (physical and metaphorical) that has been made for it. Consequently, the ways in which practitioners or researchers work with and in time and space becomes important in the facilitation of children's voice.

There are many ways in which practitioners or researchers might engage with time and space in the early years setting. To exemplify the ways in which time and space may varyingly offer opportunities or constraints to children's voice, we turn to three apparently binary notions of time and space: as open and closed, as formal and informal, and as inside and outside. In so doing, we refer to three different practices common in early childhood settings. We will discuss each notion in turn and relate each to one of the practices, but the reader will quickly see that there are crossovers and intersectional relationships across both concept and practice. It is complex and the opportunities for voice are fluid and need to be treated flexibly.

Open and Closed Space and Time

There are clear tensions between time and space in relation to these being open and/or closed with respect to facilitating young children's voice. However, it is not simply a case of open time and space(s) providing opportunities for children's voice to flourish and closed time and space(s) being unreceptive to facilitating their voice. This will be true regardless of whether voice is viewed through the lens of research, practice, or both.

One may assume, because space is open, available, and accessible to all, that it is easy to support voice and that all will be heard. Certainly, an open, available, and accessible approach that promotes an environment in which children are encouraged to express their voice is to be welcomed. However, in some open spaces a melee may ensue where there is competition to be heard; it may be that louder voices are privileged or dominate that particular space. The quiet child, or the child whose cultural capital (Bourdieu, 1977) does not align with that of the school, or for whom the language of the setting is not the same as that used in the home, may struggle to articulate what they wish to say. Where a child's voice is only one voice among many, and where they fail to attract the attention of other children or the adults in the setting with whom they are trying to communicate, their voice may, in effect, be silenced. By "voice," one should remember that in the context of this chapter, it is understood as an expression of self that does not rest solely with the verbal; rather, it refers to whatever way the child chooses to communicate.

With regard to open and closed time, time may be set aside formally, as a part of the day, where children can express themselves to one another or to the practitioner or researcher. This may be, for example, during a particular activity. While this time is "closed" from the perspective that it is bounded by a timetable, it can also be seen as "open" because it is a guaranteed period of time set aside for the purpose of listening to all. An example of an activity in which time and space has both open and closed elements is that of story time. During story time, a specific, boundaried space and a set duration of time are set aside for the sharing of a story with a group of children. The children may choose the story, but the voice that reads the story aloud to the group, particularly in the early years setting, tends to be the adult. During this time, unless the children are asked a question, the space is dominated by the adult voice. This does not mean that the children are passive, as they are engaged in the story with the adult. At the end of the reading of the story, the children may have the opportunity to discuss with one another, and with the adult, their views in relation to the story. Thus, the space becomes open in the sense that it welcomes a range of perspectives and contributions from children, with children's voice becoming more dominant within the space, and time is given over to their meaning-making.

Regardless of whether time and/or space is open or closed, for young children's voice to be facilitated those listening need to be receptive to those voices. Being receptive suggests that attention is paid to "'active listening" (Fielding, 2004); that is, to creating an ethos where adults listen to children, where children listen to adults, and where all are encouraged to listen to one another. Attending requires a particular disposition that must be fostered. The concept of reflexivity in the SVRF supports the creation of those dispositions. Adults need to model behaviors that attend to voice, and a conscious effort has to be made to furnish children with the skills to share their voice and be receptive to the voice of others. Creating "safe spaces" (Lundy, 2007), where adults conspicuously listen and in which the climate is marked by trust and openness (Rudduck & Fielding, 2006), will support children to feel comfortable to express their voice, regardless of how diverse these may be.

Boundaries are important considerations in the promotion of voice with respect to time and space. They may act as barriers and may be represented by the philosophy of education adopted in the setting. For example, when children are assigned to groups at a set time for a specific activity, such as to eat a snack or lunch, there may be no opportunity for children to leave their group to sit with friends of their choice. In such circumstances, children's choice, and therefore voice, becomes restricted through the boundaries imposed by adults. Conversely, within the context of free play, boundaries of space and time may be set by the children themselves. Children may determine who they invite, or even allow, to engage in the activity, thereby excluding some of their peers. A very clear boundary is, therefore, established that allows the dominant voices—for example, those children playing in the sandbox—to choose who is to play in the sandbox with them. Children have taken over the space that is the sandbox and have either excluded or included other children from this space, thereby demonstrating that children are able to control and manipulate boundaries with respect to the spaces they occupy and the time spent within them.

In seeing space and time in a more abstract, rather than physical sense—as opportunity—we can recognize when these opportunities may be more open or closed, and the resulting tensions that emerge between the openness or closed nature of that time and space. As seen in the story time example above, the physical time and space is both open and closed at different points in the activity. In the same way, opportunities for voice are both open and closed. There is limited opportunity for children's voice during the reading of the story, though the adult may stop along the way to present and discuss the illustrations, but this will always be time-bounded because the adult wishes to get to the end of the story. So, while children are encouraged to read along with the adult, the adult is in control of the timing/pace of the activity and determines when the children might speak. At the end of the story, there are greater opportunities for voice. The adult generally opens the floor for responses to the story, and though there will be turn-taking so that individuals are not speaking over one another, what is important is that voice at this point in the activity revolves around the opportunities to share a range of views. The adult is more open to, receptive of, whatever the children wish to say.

Note that the audience in the story time discussion need not be the adult but that the children should be encouraged to speak and listen to the others participating in the activity. This goes some way to ensuring a more open discourse, as when children direct their comments to the adult it is more closed and suggests that the children need not attend to what is being said by their peers. Such an example illustrates the tensions that may arise in creating more or less formal/informal space and time within the early years setting.

Formal and Informal Space and Time

For those new to early years settings, it may appear initially as if the activity taking place, both in terms of space and time, tends toward the informal. The predominant activity would appear to be children engaging in play that flows freely throughout the setting. However, once more detailed observation is undertaken, children's experiences fluctuate between formal to informal encounters that underpin the dynamic nature of children's voice across time and space. We say dynamic because in some cases, depending on the children's experience at various points in their day, voice may flourish, be silenced, or be disregarded, depending on how they move through and interact with others in a range of ways through formal and informal space and time.

Lundy (2007) highlights that voice refers not only to adults listening to children, but also to children having a listening audience in order to have the opportunity to influence. Within practice settings, voice involves a complex power-laden relationship between adults and children, or even between children. This relationship is framed by the informal or formal social and cultural contexts within which the dialogue and communication (in a broad and not always verbal sense) occurs. From this perspective, listening and voice can become cultural processes as part of everyday early childhood practice, which encompasses relational social pedagogy (Petrie, 2011). This becomes particularly challenging to describe because in many cases voice can be seen through this lens as an intangible dynamic, which, while realized through multiple actions, in practice is not something that is easily pinpointed or quantified.

When exploring informal and formal space for voice, understanding how space can be described or structured is particularly helpful. If space is understood not just as physical space but as metaphorical space, it can be helpful, particularly when we explore the embodied or dynamic ways that children embrace opportunities to articulate their voice. Through the lens of Claxton and Carr's (2004) framework of learning spaces and the associated concepts of prohibiting, affording, inviting, or potentiating, it might be assumed that children's voice is more apparent and facilitated in spaces classified as potentiating. Rogoff et al. (1993) define these spaces as "(powerful) environments: those that not only invite the expression of certain dispositions, but actively 'stretch' them, and thus develop them" (p. 533). This might include the informal moments as children arrive at the setting and engage in dialogue with adults and their peers, or more formal activities, such as when an activity has been planned by the practitioner or researcher with more specific goals.

Role play is one such shared activity often offered to young children. It is common for an area within a setting to be assigned to role play, for example, a home corner or a dressing-up box. This gives the activity a formal role within the space, but how that space is used and the time spent there by adult and child, and the relative formality or informality of the experience, can afford voice or not. The adult may initially adopt a guiding role for role play through their choice of artifacts offered to the children. These decisions may demonstrate a clear intent by the adults to guide the direction of the role play with an invitation to the children to explore particular roles. For example, a dressing-up box including uniforms such as those worn by firefighters, police officers, and nurses may signify an invitation for the children to explore their understanding of professional roles. In this scenario, if the adult tightly controls the role play as it unfolds, this could result in the voice of the children being limited. Alternatively, if they view role play as affording the children the opportunity to express themselves and direct their own play using the provided artifacts in ways that are meaningful to them, then the process and outcome might be different; the nurse becomes a superhero who develops superpowers. An individual child may determine the direction of the role play, or it may be that a group of children develop the story line collaboratively—with or without intervention from the adult—as the superhero nurse saves the child from a burning building. The key factor is whether the children have, or do not have, the space or opportunity to expand the story line, take it in a new and unexpected direction, and make it meaningful to themselves. The boundaries of formality or informality all influence the potential for voice within the time and space marked out by the role play activity.

The practitioner or researcher needs to be aware of sharing the decisions around the boundaries of space and time within the role play activity, allowing the opportunity for the children's voice to flourish. As with free play, this can lead to some individual children dominating the activity, directing the storyline, or determining who adopts specific roles. In this instance, an individual child's voice may be limited by their peers. The adults must then make the challenging decision as to whether their involvement will be an intervention or interference, a decision that is context-dependent and relies on the skill of the adult to facilitate in an inclusive manner that enhances the opportunity for all the children in the setting. This means the stance taken by the practitioner or researcher in relation to voice is key in formalizing, or not, the space and/or time.

On a simplistic level, the decision around the boundaries of time in the example of role play may also be shared between the adult and child as the practitioner or researcher may allow or encourage the role play to develop over an extended period, although this places them in a position of power. However, an individual child can also determine when a story line begins or a group of children may collaboratively determine when a story line has ceased to be of interest. However, returning to a cyclical understanding of time, role play may also permit the children to return multiple times to particular story lines, adding new ideas and complexity to the original role play. An important element of voice with young children is the opportunity to revisit previous ideas and concepts and understanding how to refine, clarify, and expand original articulations. The extent to which formality, or otherwise, is understood by all participants in the role play activity becomes crucial.

When children take the opportunity to direct their role play activity, they demonstrate yet again that they can control and manipulate the boundaries of what is possible within what might be thought of as formal elements of early years practice. Indeed, role play may be an ideal exemplar of the definition of voice within early years settings as it so obviously encompasses the full range of what is understood as voice, not just the verbal but also embodied voice in the form of gestures, actions and silence. Within role play, therefore, the adult must be attuned to the multiple modes employed by children in articulating their position and expression of the roles adopted within their role play.

Building on this conceptualization of what voice might look like in what may be considered traditional activities or space in early years settings, open and enabling opportunities for voice also arise within informal spaces in practice. The in-between moments of fleeting insight into the child's perspective or agenda are often manifest through, for example, children's questions or dialogue as they move between activities as much as they are during immersion in intersubjective play (Goncu, 1998), between children or between adults and children. Here we see the "mutual understanding" (intersubjectivity) described in the SVRF materializing in observable moments and relational encounters that can be gathered as part of research with young children and through pedagogical documentation from practitioners in early childhood settings. In these spaces and times, we may also encounter and deepen our understanding of the child when we move beyond the verbal. Reaching beyond the verbal allows us to reflect on another dimension of voice—voice that is inside and outside time and space.

Inside and Outside Space and Time

In early years settings, the focus on children's holistic learning is generally intertwined with the provision of inside and outside space to facilitate different ways of engaging with the world. Early years practitioners and researchers value the physical and tactile alongside the verbal and cognitive, considering the transmodal possibilities for learning. With regard to most early years settings, then, there are multiple dimensions to a consideration of inside and outside with respect to voice, especially when considering notions of time and space, across elements such as

- the day,
- the building,
- the attributed and free spaces, and
- the self and others.

When considering any of these dimensions, it is useful to be aware of not only the intended use of space or time (for example, story time), but also the way it is experienced by the different participants, both adults and children. Additionally, these spaces or times can be considered with respect to what occurred, the expectations that influence the occurrence, and the perceptions of the individuals involved concerning their experience of participation. Each element will vary depending on whether we consider the self or the group in relation to the voice being/as manifest. So, for example, a practitioner or researcher might plan for free play and observe the children busy in the moment in a variety of freely chosen activities. The experience of the children might be one of a more tightly framed activity with rules, both explicit and implicit in the space and time, that influence the extent to which it is "free." In addition, adults and children might perceive those experiences in the moment differently and can be impacted upon by the nature of who engaged with whom, the activities of others in relation to their own expressed opinions and choices, and satisfaction (or not) with affective outcomes.

If voice is something that can be intended, with more or less successful outcomes as experienced by children, then issues of power and inclusivity become significant. A consideration of inside and outside in the early years foregrounds how the dimensions of different space and time can be more or less conducive to voice, although rarely universally experienced in the same way. As a result, a range of types of activity, environment, and social grouping is essential to meet this range of needs and outcomes. Thus, consideration should also be made in relation to the perception of the insider and the outsider regarding whether voice has been successfully achieved. Only the individual can know whether they feel they have a voice, and this will vary across time and space and with respect to the extent to which they feel like an insider or outsider to the activity in which they are engaged. However, others from the position of being outside will be able to assess, rightly or wrongly, the extent to which they think that voice has been achieved (or not). What is critical is the importance of a range of intentions and experiences to suit different learners and outcomes.

In this, there is both an expansive view that critical learning experiences could take place in multiple spaces and at multiple times. There is also an acceptance that we do not and cannot know what takes place in the consciousness of another person, despite the potential to consider observable behaviors, although this is not a widely used theoretical lens in early childhood settings in the United Kingdom and should arguably never be relied on with young children. As a result, we can only consider our intention and the myriad other possibilities and weigh our responses. It is important to recognize not only the practitioner's experiences, expectations, and perceptions, but the extent to which these adjoin or overlap with each child's experiences, expectations, and perceptions.

The following scenarios of individual children participating in the same activity, free play, where voice and choice could be perceived as central to the time and space, are useful in advancing the point that inside and outside considerations of space and time are important:

- Ali has chosen to play cooperatively with a group using small toy animals in the wet and dry sand, and we know this because she is demonstrating all the impacts intended during this time: the play is sustained using a familiar narrative structure of loss, search, and reunion; there is relational engagement, including turn-taking, and both verbal and nonverbal dialogue that extends the play; her positioning in relation to the task and other children is eager;

there are facial expressions that read as positive; and she appears immersed in the group activity.

- Nat is engaged in building block play—at least, that is what we (think we) observe. She is playing "nicely" with the other children—not snatching or guarding blocks—and her gaze follows the activity of the group. She has built her own structure and appears to be inside the collective experience of the activity, aligning her structure with others and moving small vehicles around the collaborative space. She laughs along with others at a comic moment when a tower totters but is caught just in time. She does not offer any verbal comments, though her gaze follows other children when they speak.

- Bo is not really engaged (we deduce) in any particular activity, since she is physically restless and her gaze wanders, often away from the other children to other groups or beyond, out of the window, or up to the ceiling. Her activity is also intermittent, and she often roams the room, though mainly moving between the group in the sand and the group building with blocks. When Bo is with the builders, she laughs at a different moment to the rest of the group and tells a story apparently unrelated to the wobbly structure, though possibly to do with something that happened to the elephants in the sand. The other children are not able to follow Bo's story and do not respond.

There are several ways inside and outside could be considered in relation to these three children and their experience of voice within this specific time and space. Fundamentally, free play is considered as a time when adults take a conscious step back and children can make decisions about the activity they wish to participate in and who they would like to interact with. Nevertheless, adults tend to impose their own judgments of the quality of these play activities based on overt pedagogic intent or tacit social constructs of appropriateness. The success (or not) for each individual child is nuanced and personal and tied to their expectations and experiences within the time (free play) and the space (or spaces) they choose to inhabit during that time.

Yet, as early childhood practitioners and researchers we are concerned that children have high-quality experiences and as much opportunity as possible for voice in its many forms. Thus, in trying to understand what we (think we) see, we constantly need to be conscious of the distinction between how each child might perceive their engagement within the activity and how it might be observed by peers and adults. There are socially accepted assumptions about the rules of play: following the rules of the classroom means effective voice (Ali), silence is not a (or not a strong) form of voice (Nat), and different ways of engaging are not necessarily voice (Bo). These rules are strongly enforced by children and adults (from outside) and Ali, Nat, and

Bo may navigate these by consciously or unconsciously aligning or opposing their behavior on the outside. However, we cannot say with any certainty if the alignment or opposition observed reflects the inside experience:

- Is Ali replaying with friends the animal story they all know and/or is she working through her own narrative?
- Is Nat pretending to be compliant while imagining other worlds or quietly enjoying the game we see?
- Does Bo not understand the conventions of "pick an activity and stick to it," does she not have theory of mind awareness that the block builders haven't seen the elephants, or does she understand both those things but today she just doesn't care about them as much as the desire to roam and make her own connections?

If each observation has limited accuracy as a tool for assessing a child's capacity for voice, practitioners and researchers can fall back on forms of validation in past, present, and future focused discussions: (a) asking children to reflect on their play using photos and video, (b) inviting them to "think aloud" in the midst of play, and (c) encouraging them to make explicit to other children how they plan to engage with activities. These have value in extending the adults' perspectives of what constitutes meaningful play and signaling a genuine desire to know more about children's experience. However, they cannot assuage our anxiety to know what is going on inside, and they can potentially and ironically curtail the time and space available to the children to engage in free play, replacing it with another dialogue driven by an adult agenda, a dialogue in which, inevitably, certain sociocultural forms of voice will dominate.

CONCLUSION

In considering the dynamics and relationships of young children and adults in early childhood, we have shown time and space to be central to the facilitation of voice. While on the surface these related concepts may appear simple, closer inspection reveals them to be simultaneously complex with many nuances. We have demonstrated that although a critical awareness of these complexities produces difficulties for practitioners and researchers, it can also offer creative perspectives that facilitate a broader understanding of what voice is and can be. We assert that time could be more helpfully conceptualized as a spiral, where the linear and cyclical intersect. The physical and metaphorical nature of space, too, demands consideration. Aspects of these perspectives on space and time have been exemplified throughout this chapter with reference to the continua shown in Figure 4.1, but no single example could possibly encapsulate all aspects. This is especially so because

Figure 4.1. Illustrating Time and Space and Associated Continuums of Practice

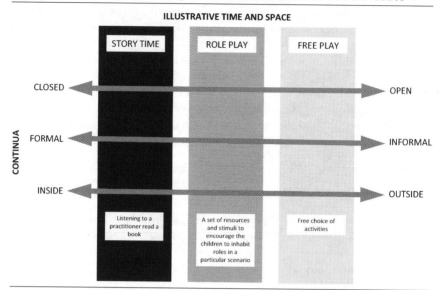

there is variation in what is expected and experienced, and what is taken forward by different participants. This should be considered to be a feature, not as a problem to be removed.

This chapter has shown that the lines blur between different aspects of voice in early childhood space and time as children's meaning requires interpretation and critical reflection by both researchers and practitioners. We need to reimagine the continua of closed and open, inside and outside, and formal and informal as intertwined and messy, where voice can be represented at either end of each continuum for different individuals. Rather than being characterized as sitting at one end or the other of any continuum, voice is flexible and fluid, and can be moved up and down the scale depending on how the participants envision and enact that space and time.

This means there are important conceptual, practical, and psychological aspects for practitioners and researchers to consider in relation to time and space, multiplied by the range of participants who all have different expectations and experiences of participating. Flexibility is needed, and the continua presented here start to show how voice might be considered. Bearing in mind that what is shared here is only one from eight factors of voice we consider important, then the dynamics and dilemmas inherent in eliciting voice are multiple. Yet, we would argue that these are productive knots to consider, and while exemplified in this chapter in early childhood, much potential can be seen for them to be considered in relation to those belonging to those who are older. There would be merit in practitioners and researchers working with other age groups to consider decisions made about how space and time might more effectively enhance voice for all; for example, how the continua of open and closed, formal and informal, and inside and outside, reflects the time and space other age groups inhabit, and how the practice exemplification we have used from early childhood enables a broadening of the lens for voice more generally. Therefore, in the same way that we would emphasize the point that *all* children have the same right to voice, then the practices and thinking we have outlined also apply equally to older children and young people.

NOTE

1. More information on the project and free download of the talking point posters can be found on the project website: https://www.voicebirthtoseven.co.uk.

CHAPTER 5

Student Voice

Assessing Research in the Field

Lindsay Lyons, Ellen MacCannell, and Vanessa Gold

Student voice is generally accepted as an assortment of activities through which students can influence decisions that affect their lives (Fielding, 2001). The degree of student involvement in these decisions can be understood through various typologies and frameworks. The purpose of this chapter is to identify current knowledge and the existing gaps in student voice research (SVR). We then lay the groundwork for future frameworks and research methods that better involve students. In order to frame this discussion, we use an existing typology: the student voice pyramid (Mitra & Gross, 2009). This typology was chosen so as to categorize and understand various levels of student involvement and as a means to advocate for the SVR field to move from youth as sources of data (Level 1) and into youth leading and influencing (Level 3) their worlds through research. This is done with the aim of moving SVR toward radical collegiality, the "expectation that teacher learning is both enabled and enhanced by dialogic encounters with their students in which the interdependent nature of teaching and learning and the shared responsibility for its success is made explicit" (Fielding, 2001, p. 130) and intersectional justice for education's most important stakeholder: students.

We chose the pyramid typology based on its fit to the objectives of this chapter. Our examination of SVR frameworks found a variety of options—including discrete categories of student involvement (e.g., Treseder, 1997), a matrix of student engagement (Lodge, 2005; Mitra & Kirshner, 2012), a ladder of methodologies (Fielding, 2011; Hart, 1992), and a pathway of student leadership divided into stages (Shier, 2001)—as well as the pyramid (Mitra, 2006; Wong et al., 2010), which revealed the varieties of conceptualizations about student involvement in SVR. The majority of these typologies highlight the role of the youth in the process of research (e.g., Hart, 1992; Shier, 2001; Wong et al., 2010). A few feature the concept of youth development (Mitra, 2006; Wong et al., 2010) as a goal. One of these frameworks contrasts the goal of youth development with the goal of addressing injustice (Mitra & Kirshner, 2012). Some typologies also address whether student voice is used instrumentally or relationally (Fielding, 2011; Lodge, 2005). Some emphasize the stages of commitment to shared decision-making, highlighting the importance of educator readiness and sustainable commitment (Shier, 2001) as well as educator mindset (Mitra, 2006). Finally, Mitra and Kirshner (2012) identify the locus of control as existing in the school, a community-based organization, or a blend of both.

These typologies demonstrate the variety of ways to conceptualize SVR, and the need for the field to develop a framework to understand the different contexts in which these typologies might apply. The Student Voice Research Framework (SVRF) offers the relevant considerations for understanding how to apply typologies to the context, as well as the reflexivity necessary.

THEORETICAL APPARATUS AND METHODOLOGY

For this chapter, we draw on Mitra and Gross's Student Voice Pyramid (2009) to frame our discussion of student involvement in educational research as each of the three levels are appropriate to analyze practices in both educational contexts and in the process of conducting research. This typology was chosen because it is frequently referenced in SVR work and its emphasis is on student involvement in the research process. Additional benefits of this typology include its concision, its use of the pyramid metaphor to represent how common each type is practiced, and finally, its inclusion of turbulence theory and the degree to which each type of voice impacts organizational change. This typology categorizes student involvement according to three distinct levels: at the base is (1) being heard, in the middle is (2) collaborating with adults, and at the zenith, (3) building capacity for leadership (2009). The first level, being heard, asks students to share ideas, which are then interpreted by adults. Data collection strategies may include focus groups, surveys, interviews, and shadowing students. The second level, collaborating with adults, offers youth more influence on issues that matter to them by taking action in partnership with adults in a way that simultaneously strengthens students' relationships with the adults and other students with whom they collaborate. The third level, building capacity for student leadership, requires students to have opportunities to practice being in leadership roles and developing their capacity to lead projects in which adults take on a support role. By conducting this general review of the state of research designs in the field, we found that the majority of research targets only the first level, which indicates an important target area for growth in student voice research. As such, this chapter will focus on how SVR—as it relates to typology and methods—needs more attention in the authentic collaboration and building leadership capacity spaces.

This chapter is not a systematic literature review nor a meta-analysis but rather a discussion of the SVR field as it stands so as to envision areas of potential growth in student involvement in research. As such, we speak generally about studies, summarizing salient points. We focus on broad concepts and large trends. As all three of the authors are native English speakers, we have not included the plethora of existing studies that have been published in languages other than English. Despite these limitations, we believe the trends we have identified and the implications for us as researchers serve as a powerful call to action that will enable the future of our field to advance radical collegiality (Fielding, 2001) and intersectional justice for all students.

In order to discover large trends in the field, we reviewed approximately 200 peer-reviewed articles from 17 online databases (such as JSTOR, Sage Publications, Taylor & Francis Online, and Wiley Online Library). The search period for articles related to student voice studies was set to any/all time and not limited to any specific geographic location. The scope of our initial search was also narrowed to peer-reviewed studies and dissertations, articles written in English, and articles with "student voice" or "pupil voice" in the title. Information according to seven categories was extracted, organized, and made accessible on a shared document. These categories included Purpose/ Research Questions; Quantitative/Qualitative/Mixed Method Research; Role of Students; More Methods Info; Geographic Location; Sample (representativeness); and Other. This systematic approach to reviewing the SVR field was necessary at the outset due to the large variance in how student voice/ involvement is framed. In order to discuss patterns, broad concepts, and large trends, we needed to clearly define our categories of comparison. This, in turn, allowed us the space to define what we believe the path for future SVR may be.

This broad exploration of the current state of SVR will follow the subsequent structure: First, we will provide an overview of the key findings of our survey of the field. We will then explore in depth the most prevalent types of research questions utilized in SVR. This will be followed by a review of the common research methods, sample populations, and the role of students in SVR. The chapter will conclude with a discussion of our vision for the future of SVR, including how researchers may begin to move the field forward.

SUMMARY OF KEY FINDINGS

We found that the majority of student voice research is qualitative and features common data collection methods such as interviews, observations, and document analysis. In their article on methodological fit, Edmondson and McManus (2007) argue prior work in a field of research should inform a study's methodological approach. The student voice field of research consists of predominantly qualitative studies addressing novel "how" and "why" questions, which fits with Edmondson and McManus's recommendations for the nascent stage. It is important to note, that in Edmondson and McManus's model, the nascent stage is positioned on a continuum along with intermediate and mature stages. The mature stage requires "precise models, supported by extensive research on a set of related questions in varied settings" (p. 1158). Indeed, mature stage research is supposed to be "elegant, complex, and logically rigorous, addressing issues that other researchers would agree from the outset are worthy of study" (p. 1159). It is our belief that this positivistic framing of research may not always be in alignment with the goal of involving students in research. As such, we do not posit mature stage research as an objective for all SVR to meet but rather as an important component of a robust field.

As it currently stands, the majority of SVR consists of case studies of student voice initiatives in single schools or youth community organizations. Typically, papers reporting case studies are a single case (e.g., Biddle, 2015; Møller, 2006; Yonezawa & Jones, 2007), but many use a multiple-case study design. When it comes to research questions, the majority of research designs employ Level 1 (or "Being Heard," Mitra & Gross, 2009) research questions that specifically seek the input (views, opinions, perspectives) of students. A general formula can be used to understand these questions: Research Question = YOUTH [input] OF [school(ing)] (see Table 5.1). As such, students are most frequently positioned as a source of data only. In other words, researchers collected students' reflections, opinions, and input through interviews, focus groups, surveys, drawings, and poems and then interpreted those inputs without further student involvement.

Other important areas to note about this research are that the majority of the research reviewed came from English-speaking countries, primarily the United States, the United Kingdom, Australia, and New Zealand, with some coming out of Latin America. Furthermore, studies using mixed methods are relatively rare, and rarer still are quantitative research designs. There is a growing trend of using nontraditional data collection methods in the field, many of which invite students to share their ideas through art (e.g., Enright & O'Sullivan, 2013; Maxwell, 2006; Sclater & Lally, 2013). While

Table 5.1. Frequently Used Terms for Level 1 Research Question Formula

Input	Assessment; Conception; Definition; Depiction; Description; Experience; Ideas; Opinions; Perception; Perspective; Reflection; Self-conception; Views
School(ing)	Adult perception; Adult practice; Behavior; Challenges; Change; Classroom management; Class size; Content; Enjoyable learning conditions; Experience; Ideal Learning; Initiative; Intervention; Learning; Own behavior; Pedagogy; Phenomenon; Practice; School(ing); Strategy; Tool; Teaching and learning

Table 5.2. Summary of Mitra and Gross's Pyramid vs. RQ Categories

Levels of Mitra and Gross's (2009) Pyramid	Level 1: Being heard	Level 2: Collaborating with adults	Level 3: Building capacity for leadership
RQ Category	Student Voice Youth Input Adult Lens	Youth–Adult Partnership (YAP)	Voice-Fostering Mechanisms (VFM)

this broadens students' entry points through multiple means of representation, students often remain seen as sources of data rather than collaborators, partners, or even leaders in the research. Less common to student voice research is employing Level 2 ("collaborating with adults") and Level 3 ("building capacity for leadership") (Mitra & Gross, 2009) research questions. Level 2 questions generally mention or imply active youth participation with adults (practitioners/researchers). Least common, Level 3 research questions explicitly state capacity building as a goal of the research itself. Level 3 and Level 3 questions tend to mention voice-fostering mechanisms or structures (i.e., student council) and/or youth–adult partnerships (see Table 5.2). By understanding the past and current scope of the field as well as the research designs of student voice studies, we hope to increase awareness of and opportunities for student voice that engage students at higher levels of collaboration and capacity building.

FIVE CATEGORIES OF RESEARCH QUESTIONS IN STUDENT VOICE RESEARCH

Constructing a research question is a notoriously difficult task—especially in a field that advocates for the meaningful involvement of students in educational change processes. Delicate relational power dynamics inherent in research with students can influence the authenticity of student participation and compromise validity (e.g., Cook-Sather, 2015; Johnson, 2020; Levitan, 2019b). Therefore, framing a research project with a question that values and positions students on equal footing is critical (Fielding, 2001). In order to review research questions currently utilized in the field, an adapted form of constant comparison method was used to analyze specifically *purpose/ research questions* and to generate categories of questions being asked in the empirical SVR here reviewed. Five major categories that emerged from our analysis include research questions that investigate (a) student voice, (b) youth input, (c) adult lens, (d) youth–adult partnerships (YAP), and (e) voice-fostering mechanisms (VFM). Common trends and big takeaways according to each of these five themes are discussed in greater detail in the following sections.

Student Voice

The research questions in this category specifically explored or assessed diverse facets of student involvement, including benefits (Mansfield, 2014a), challenges (e.g., Czerniawski & Kidd, 2012), processes (e.g., Ashton, 2008), relationships (e.g., Czerniawski & Kidd, 2012; Mitra, Serriere, & Stoicovy, 2012), methods (e.g., Coronel & Pascual, 2013), and implementation (e.g., Robinson & Taylor, 2013). One-third of these questions were paired with participatory or arts-informed approaches (e.g., Youth-led Participatory Action Research (YPAR), student co-researchers, collage), whereas two-thirds employed common methods (questionnaires, interviews, focus groups, observations). Depending on the study, this type of research question is either Level 1 or Level 2 of Mitra and Gross's Student Voice Pyramid (2009). Level 2 is only attained when common research methods are paired with participatory approaches that involve youth; otherwise, the research only targets information *about* youth and not *with* youth. See Table 5.3 for examples.

Youth Input

The research questions in this category specifically sought the input (views, opinions, perspectives) of students. The majority of these research questions were paired with common methods. A minority employed the use of arts-based methods such as drawing (e.g., Maxwell, 2006); photography/film making (e.g., Sclater & Lally, 2013); scrapbooking (Enright & O'Sullivan, 2013); and performance poetry (Coates & Vickerman, 2008).

Although listening to students is important, implicit to *youth input* questions are adult (mis)interpretations of youth expression (Fielding, 2004), as the principle of reflexivity in the SVRF clarifies. Furthermore, seeking *youth input* positions students as passive sources of information (Lee & Zimmerman, 2001 in Mitra, 2006) akin to Level 1 of Mitra and Gross's pyramid. Designing a study that seeks *youth input* is a first step toward acknowledging and valuing youth as partners in research. Researchers may consider pairing *youth input* questions with participatory/arts-based methods to facilitate youth–adult partnerships and offer alternative forms of expression.

Adult Lens

For our purposes, "adult" refers generally to researchers and practitioners who are either posing or answering questions to satisfy their own curiosity/self-interest (or an organization's interests). Though similar, questions in this category are not as formulaic as Level 1 *Youth Input* research questions and tend to be more varied in structure. *Adult Lens* questions are not specifically seeking the input of youth but consist of an adult querying *about* them and then interpreting that information. Some of these questions draw from

Table 5.3. Summary of RQ Categories/Levels with Examples

RQ Category	STUDENT VOICE	YOUTH INPUT	ADULT LENS	YAP	VFM
RQ Purpose	Investigates a facet of student involvement/ student voice	Seeks youth input on an aspect of school(ing) RQ = YOUTH [input] OF [school(ing)] *see Table 5.1 for terms to fill brackets	Offers an adults interpretation of phenomena ABOUT or involving youth/ youth experiences of school(ing)	Positions youth as co-researchers and/or states collaborating WITH youth or seeks to understand YAPs	Supports or investigates youth building capacity for leadership through voice-fostering mechanisms
Examples of Level 1 RQs youth as passive sources of data	*What are the benefits/ challenges of using photography as a mode of expressing student voice?*	*How do students describe their experiences of a new classroom management practice?*	*What are teachers' conceptions of their work with students?*	Not applicable	Not applicable
Examples of Level 2 RQs youth as active collaborators/ participants	Elevating these three RQ categories to Level 2 requires incorporating an element of collaboration with youth. Level 1 Student Voice RQ example becomes Level 2: *What can we learn about [researcher interest] i.e., students' experiences of schooling when they choose to investigate [student-driven topic] i.e., student engagement using [student-selected method] i.e., photography as a mode of expressing student voice?*			*What can we learn, with students as co-researchers, about improving teaching practices?*	Voice-Fostering Mechanism RQs only reach Level 2 when youth are not equipped or positioned as leaders, but collaboration is mentioned.
Examples of Level 3 RQs youth as active leaders and decision makers	Elevating these three RQ categories to Level 3 involves major changes to the research design so that youth are not only provided with the capacity to develop the skills required to collaborate with adults, but also positioned as leaders of the research. In doing so, these questions become YAP or Voice-Fostering. *What happens when youth are equipped with skills to lead research?* *What can we learn, with students as co-researchers, about students' research priorities?*			Though rare, YAP RQs can become Level 3 if youth are equipped to lead the research.	*When youth and adult school stakeholders collaborate toward school improvement, what can we learn about how youth–adult partnerships inform the process of curriculum making?*

adult experiences/observations to understand phenomena. Other questions rely on adult interpretations about youth (i.e., behaviors, interest, response to pedagogy, etc.), other adults/themselves, schooling (i.e., dropout rate, assessment, classroom management, etc.), or evidence-based pathways/trends to investigate. Also, technically all publications here reviewed were written by and therefore interpreted through the lens of adults. When it comes to designing a study that is collaborative and/or builds capacity for leadership, researchers might consider avenues to offer students an active role in the production of academic content.

The following examples of *Adult Lens* studies demonstrate the nuance, crossover, and complexity of questions in this category. What is clear, however, is that adults take on a disproportionately greater role in student voice research designs than youth.

Researchers write about processes of collaboration with youth (Levitan, 2018; Yonezawa & Jones, 2007), reviews on student action research (Davies, Popescu, & Gunter, 2011; Rubin & Jones, 2007), reports on innovation in pedagogy (O'Grady, 2006), and analysis of student voice/parent involvement (Mitra, 2006), among others.

Practitioners write about their interpretation of student mentorship (Russell, 2007), the impact of a unit on student skills (Camangian, 2008), beliefs about student voice (Cody et al., 2012), and document responses to calls for change (Bertrand, 2014), among others.

In most of the studies reviewed, it is not only the adult who comes up with the question but also an adult who makes sense of participant responses. The small number of studies that position youth as collaborators/co-researchers with more active roles in research design are accounted for in the categories of Youth–Adult Partnership and Voice-Fostering Mechanism research questions. One way to elevate this kind of Level 1 question to Level 3 would be to empower students with the skills to participate in decision- and sense-making processes throughout the research design.

Youth–Adult Partnership (YAP)

The research questions in this category mention or imply active youth participation with adults (practitioners/researchers). Of these, about half explicitly position students as co-researchers and/or state collaborating *with* youth (Biddulph, 2012; Johnson & Levitan, 2021; Lee & Johnston-Wilder, 2013; Levitan & Johnson, 2020) while the rest investigate fostering, learning from, pathways to, effects of, or processes of YAPs. Of the questions in this category, only one study employed a participatory approach (Mitra, Lewis, & Sanders, 2013) while the rest were paired with common data collection methods (e.g., Brasof, 2019; Levy, 2016). Youth–adult relationships and collaboration are important to student voice research (e.g., Mansfield, 2014; Sherif, 2018) and are aligned to Level 2. Fostering YAPs can support collaboration (McNae, 2018) and the development of leadership skills (Sherif, 2018), though leadership capacity building may not have been the stated objective in the partnership.

Voice-Fostering Mechanisms (VFM)

Sorely lacking in this review are research questions that are explicitly framed to support or investigate building capacity for leadership (e.g., Biddulph, 2011, 2012) in line with Level 3 of the Pyramid of Student Voice. Research questions in this category explicitly mention the creation and sustaining of voice-fostering mechanisms such as student co-researchers (e.g., Levitan, 2018; Levitan & Johnson, 2020; Yonezawa & Jones, 2007), person-centered planning (e.g., Barnard-Dadds & Conn, 2018; Maxwell, 2006), model UN clubs (e.g., Levy, 2016), youth court (e.g., Brasof, 2019), and student council (e.g., Quinn & Owen, 2016). Most frequently, examples in this category include research questions seeking to understand processes of/building/fostering YAPs (e.g., Mitra et al., 2013; Zeldin et al., 2016) more in line with Levels 1 and 2. Of the questions in this category, one study employed a participatory approach (Mayes, 2019), one incorporated arts-informed approaches (Maxwell, 2006), while the rest were paired with common methods (e.g., Barnard-Dadds & Conn, 2018; Mitra, 2008b). Research studies in this category require youth research skill development to be built so as to foster student capacity to create and contribute meaningfully to the field of research in question. Once these foundational skills are established, adults and youth collaborate to co-create research questions, design, and knowledge mobilization.

However, not all voice-structuring mechanisms explicitly include youth–adult collaboration and leadership capacity building. Indeed, although voice-fostering structures, such as student councils, are colloquially associated with leadership, they can also often serve a performative, tokenistic, or consultative purpose (Quinn & Owen, 2016)—and in this case are more in line with Levels 1 and 2.

The five research question themes discussed in this section offer insights about the current approaches to SVR and potential directions to strengthen work being conducted in the field. Studies that use youth as a source of information, or *youth input* questions, are used most frequently, but they only meet Mitra and Gross's (2009) first level, in which student voice is relegated to just being listened to. Student voice researchers may instead want to consider composing research questions and designs that investigate/support collaboration and leadership capacity-building with youth. Though more difficult, designing a study with a question that attends to power dynamics positions students as active participants or, better yet, as leaders who help direct student voice research. So as to understand how researchers in the field may begin to achieve these goals, we must be familiar with current research approaches in SVR.

RESEARCH APPROACHES IN STUDENT VOICE RESEARCH

As a field, student voice research methodology is closest to the nascent stage (Edmondson & McManus, 2007) of research, as studies mostly seek to identify emergent themes from qualitative research. Nascent research is characterized by primarily qualitative studies that feature data collection methods such as interviews, observations, and document analysis. Several studies have moved the field toward the intermediate stage, in which research "presents provisional explanations of phenomena, often introducing a new construct and proposing relationships between it and established constructs . . . research questions may allow the development of testable hypotheses, [but] one or more of the constructs involved is often still tentative" (Edmondson & McManus, 2007, p. 1158).

These studies are typically a hybrid of qualitative and quantitative methods that conduct exploratory testing of a new construct or measure. Scale development studies such as Jones and Perkins's (2005) development of the Involvement and Interaction Rating Scale, which aimed to measure youth–adult relationships; Zeldin et al.'s (2014) development of an instrument to measure youth–adult partnerships in community-based organizations; and Lyons, Brasof, and Baron's (2020) development of the Student Leadership Capacity Building Scales are examples of studies that have entered the intermediate stage. Very few research studies have engaged in formal hypothesis testing with focused questions and primarily quantitative data collection, which are hallmarks of Edmondson and McManus's mature stage of research.

To ensure a student voice study has methodological fit, the choice of methods should be informed by the current stage of the field of research. Doing qualitative research in a mature field of research can be beneficial, as researchers can and should have opportunities to challenge existing theory. This is especially important for the field of student voice as described in the Student Voice Research Framework with tenants such as intersubjectivity and reflexivity, in which researchers must question their projects' impacts on schools and the images they wish to reinforce and challenge, and how such work is truly built from the perspectives and ideas of youth.

Qualitative

Looking back on the 15 years of student voice research between 2004 and 2019, the vast majority of studies are qualitative, most often case studies. Typically, papers reporting case studies are single (e.g., Biddle, 2015; Møller,

2006; Yonezawa & Jones, 2007), but many use a multiple-case study design. Some studies included a high number of schools in the same context, such as Mitra's (2007a) study of 13 high schools in the same geographic area. Other studies span school type, such as Parnell and Procter's (2011) study of two primary schools and two secondary schools.

Youth participatory action research has consistently made up a percentage of predominantly qualitative study design, and many of these feature students as co-researchers (in alignment with the context tenant of the Student Voice Research Framework and Level 3 of Mitra and Gross's pyramid). Examples of this include Bergmark and Kostenius's (2018) study in an Irish high school, Lee and Johnston-Wilder's (2013) study of student math ambassadors in the UK, and Rose and Shevlin's (2004) study, which trained and involved nine young people with dis/abilities as co-researchers. These studies differ from publications such as Mitra, Lewis, and Sanders's (2013), which examines youth engaging in participatory action research as a student voice initiative, but the authors used a multiple-case study design.

However, qualitative approaches, often informed by grounded theory, are time-intensive and, in a mature field of study, risk replicating existing findings rather than making novel contributions. For a field in the nascent stage such as SVR, Edmondson and McManus caution against moving too quickly into quantitative studies, as results may indicate relationships among novel constructs by pure chance, sending researchers on "fishing expeditions" (2007, p. 1171). At the same time, remaining in the qualitative realm may result in lost opportunities to "add specificity, new mechanisms, or new boundaries to existing theories" (p. 1160) that are critical to informing policy and practice solutions in various contexts.

Mixed Methods

Mixed-methods research is relatively rare, and many of these studies are scale development and are helping to move the field out of its nascent stage. One example is Lyons, Brasof, and Baron's (2020) study to develop an instrument to measure student leadership opportunities in school, which aligns to Level 3 of Mitra and Gross's pyramid. That study will be discussed at length in Chapter 10. Mixed-methods studies that were not designed to develop a scale use predominantly qualitative approaches with some minor quantitative elements. Smith and Haslett's (2017) study of primary school children is one example. For this study, students were asked to draw what they liked and did not like about their school and explain their drawings when possible—an innovative data collection strategy. The quantitative element appeared in the data analysis phase, whereby researchers noted the frequency of the thematic elements in children's drawings and interviews. There have been a few studies that were predominantly qualitative, such as Dalton and Devitt's (2016) study of the effectiveness of a learning intervention for primary school children. Researchers used questionnaires and language tests to measure the intervention's effectiveness, but also consulted with students in focus groups to deepen their understanding of the data. Simmons, Graham, and Thomas's (2015) four-phase study included fairly even qualitative and quantitative strands. Starting with an analysis of Commonwealth policy, they moved to interviewing teachers and principals (n = 89) and conducting focus groups with primary and secondary students. Then, they surveyed students and staff, and wrapped up the study with action based on the data—professional development.

Quantitative

Quantitative studies, though the rarest research approach in the field of student voice, do exist. Examples include Reichert, Chen, and Torney-Purta's (2018) international civic engagement study, which used several scales to determine whether distinct groups of students could be characterized by different patterns in their perceptions of school contexts and if adolescents' perceptions of the school climate correlated with indicators of emergent participatory citizenship. Another quantitative study (Krauss, Kornbluh, & Zeldin, 2017) serves as an example of what is possible for the field as it expands into its mature stage of research. Their study aimed to address the question: To what extent do youth–adult partnership and family functioning predict school engagement? Researchers used Zeldin et al.'s (2014) scale to measure the youth–adult partnership construct (i.e., Level 2 of Mitra and Gross's pyramid) and used several short (4–5 items) validated scales to measure the other constructs (cognitive engagement, emotional engagement, parental monitoring, and family cohesion).

It is not only integral to the growth of SVR to understand the questions and approaches to research design but also the "who" of the research conducted. Seeing as SVR is inherently about people and relationships, knowing whose perspectives are prioritized and researched is important if the purported goal is intersectional justice.

STUDY SAMPLE POPULATIONS IN STUDENT VOICE RESEARCH

The majority of the student voice research surveyed took place in English-speaking countries: primarily the United States, the United Kingdom, Australia, and New Zealand. Non-English-speaking countries represented were mostly in Europe, with the largest portion of research coming from Spain, and followed by Latin American and Scandinavian countries. When explicitly stated, the urbanicity of the studies often overlapped with other factors such as race and socioeconomic status (SES). Most of the research that considered urbanicity took place in urban contexts in a variety of school settings—public, private, religious, alternative, or independent. Approximately one quarter of the student voice research examined dealt with race as a factor, specifically students of color, indigenous students, and immigrants' experiences (e.g., Hajisoteriou, Karousiou, & Angelides, 2018; Johnson & Levitan, 2021; Krauss et al., 2017; Levitan, 2018; Levitan & Johnson, 2020; Mitchell et al., 2017; Pomar & Pinya, 2017; Zeldin et al., 2016). About a third of those studies that included race as a criterion for inclusion or examination specifically mentioned low SES as a further descriptor (e.g., Brasof & Peterson, 2018; Koomen, 2016; Mansfield, Fowler, & Rainbolt, 2018; Quinn & Owen, 2016; Rodgers, 2018). A small number of studies focused specifically on student ability, mostly students with dis/abilities, and a few dealt with "gifted" students (e.g., Barnard-Dadds & Conn, 2018; Honkasilta et al., 2016; Saggers et al., 2017). One case, Capewell (2016), examined youth experiences with inclusion criteria of teen motherhood, low SES, and dis/abilities. It is important to note, however, that these studies examined these students' individual experiences with learning and never as co-researchers, or included in school decision-making structures or within systems change. Similarly, a few studies note nondominant language immigrant and/or English as a second language (ESL) students' experiences (e.g., Hajisoteriou et al., 2018; Reyes, 2019). One study focuses on LGBTQ students' experiences (Wernick, Woodford, & Kulick, 2014). In examining SVR study populations, it is significant that many studies implicitly involve identity intersections (Crenshaw, 1991), and thus highlight the necessity for research designs to consider students' identities and their contexts.

Geographic and sample information about SVR is of particular importance because of its tendency to take place in Western societies and to "involve" marginalized student populations. Although these students' input (Level 1) is integral to designing better educational experiences, if we are to move toward "radical collegiality" and intersectional justice, then we argue students must be involved at higher levels of research design.

Role of Students in Student Voice Research

The vast majority of the student voice literature surveyed viewed the role of the student as being a source of data (Level 1 of Mitra and Gross's pyramid). In other words, researchers collected students' reflections, opinions, and input through interviews, focus groups, surveys, drawings, and poems. These data were then interpreted for meaning by researchers using various methods and to various ends, such as reports, actionable directives for school change, and academic papers. If we accept Fielding's (2001) understanding of student voice as an assortment of activities through which students can influence decisions that affect their lives, it is unclear as to whether or not the majority of the research surveyed creates opportunities for students to do so.

Indeed, the next largest category of student voice research did not directly ask for student input through the above-mentioned methods. Instead, data were collected through researcher observation of students, both in person and through audiovisual technology, and through examination of documents produced by or about students. Again, meaning was gleaned by researchers through various, mostly qualitative research methods. Without active involvement from or with students, this type of research, though seemingly helpful and innocuous, should perhaps be critiqued as it is often done in a way that objectifies youth rather than fostering partnerships (Seltzer-Kelly et al., 2012). In this way, this type of scholarly research may unknowingly preserve youth–adult inequities. Academics investigating student voice initiatives hold the power to collect and interpret data from students. Consequently, researchers may uphold the very hierarchical relations they aim to dismantle (Chadderton, 2011). Instead, to achieve quality youth–adult relationships (Level 2 of the Pyramid of Student Voice), adults must listen respectfully to a range of youth expressions (Cook-Sather, 2006b), and students must feel their voices are influential and lead to action (Bron & Veugelers, 2014).

As such, with perhaps an aim to rectify these inequities, some student voice research takes a different approach to student involvement. In an attempt to respond to the resounding call for students to co-construct curriculum, pedagogy, and assessment to increase ownership and content relevance (Bundick et al., 2014; Fielding, 2011; Robinson & Taylor, 2007; Saeed & Zyngier, 2012; Smyth, 2006, 2007, 2012), various methods have emerged in the research.

Member checking (Capewell, 2016; Conner, Brown, & Ober, 2016; Pazey & DeMatthews, 2019; Powell et al., 2018) asks students to review researchers' interpretation of collected data (Level 2). Youth participatory action research (Carrington, Allen, & Osmolowski, 2007) and students as co-researchers (Levels 2 and 3) (Bergmark & Kostenius, 2018; Biddulph, 2011; Davies, Popescu, & Gunter, 2011; Gunter & Thomson, 2007a; Johnson & Levitan, 2020; Kellett, 2010; Levitan & Johnson, 2020; Robinson, 2011; Rose & Shevlin, 2004; Yonezawa & Jones, 2007) actively involve students at various stages of research design, implementation, and interpretation (Level 3). In one such study, Mayes (2019) "deliberately sought to involve students in design, enactment and analysis, listening to and acting on the views and insights of the 'consequential stakeholders' of schooling" (p. 509). Another study had a student act as a cultural broker (Reyes, 2019) interpreting other students' responses, whereas Cook-Sather (2009b) had students act as pedagogical consultants. Finally, in a more mixed-methods approach, Dare, Nowicki, and Smith (2019) had students interpret and structure the data through sorting and rating activities. Students were asked to sort generated items into meaningful groups and then rate items according to their importance using a 5-point unipolar rating scale. The researchers then applied statistical analyses to the sorted data to produce charts showing how the group as a whole structured the data.

CONCLUSION

Much of the extant student voice research is focused on the lowest level of Mitra and Gross's (2009) Pyramid of Student Voice, or gathering youth input. Currently, qualitative research is by far the most common methodological approach to studying student voice. This fits with Edmondson and McManus's (2007) framework, as the field is relatively new in comparison to other fields of study. A robust qualitative base of research provides a conceptual foundation to be able to generate further mixed-methods and quantitative studies. Finally, many study participants live and attend school in urban communities where the language of instruction is English. Recognizing the reality that school systems in these communities are built on a long history of white supremacy and assimilationism and thus disadvantage students who are not white citizens, many researchers have specifically designed studies to learn about Black, Indigenous, and people of color (BIPOC) and immigrant students' experiences in schools.

Being student voice researchers, a field that is centered on the concept of "radical collegiality" (Fielding, 2001b), our work requires an activist stance. Our mere existence as a field challenges the traditional student-teacher dynamic. As scholars, we continue to challenge ideas of who leads research projects by partnering with students as co-researchers. We can also specifically design research that informs practice or even embed practical applications into our study design, like the data-based professional development in Phase 4 of Simmons, Graham, and Thomas's (2015) study. Quantitative approaches should not replace qualitative studies, but they can build on the findings of smaller case studies and make practices contextual and generalizable to other schools.

The challenge to all of us, as student voice researchers, is to move beyond the first level of student voice toward more studies of youth–adult partnership and building capacity for youth leadership (the latter of which includes studying the mechanisms and structures that amplify meaningful youth leadership). This can be done in what we study (e.g., examples of youth–adult partnerships and student leadership in educational contexts) as well as how we study those phenomena (e.g., collaborating with young people throughout the research study rather than just during the data collection phase). Specific suggestions for the latter include researchers focusing on reflexivity at the outset and inviting students to co-create the research questions, select the study methodologies, share their ideas in multiple formats during data collection, take on an interviewer role, make meaning of the data collected, and co-author the final manuscript.

As we do this, we can also utilize Crenshaw's (1991) notion of inter-sectionality to study the intersections of student identity and the ways in which the various identities that youth hold beyond the stakeholder role of "student" impact experiences of schooling. In addition to further studies of race and nationality, there is much to be learned from studying additional student identities, including, but not limited to, ability, linguistic culture, par-enthood, sexual orientation, and gender identity beyond the binary (i.e., transgender and nonbinary students). These intersections in research can ad-vance the aims of radical collegiality (Fielding, 2001b) and justice for all students.

CHAPTER 6

Reflection and Reflexion on Student Participation and System Change

Pat Thomson

This chapter takes the form of a montage rather than an argument. It does not present a conclusion. Rather, it is an incomplete researcher reflection/reflexion on two sticky questions that are connected. I wonder about the edges of student voice research: when does "voice" stop, and when does it move from "voice" to "voiced"? What are the connections between student "voice" and research that supports educationally just changes for children and young people? The answers to these musings are not straightforward. I use research projects I engaged in as a means to explore these questions. My reflexive montage relates specifically to the issues of researcher reflexivity, power dynamics, and intersubjectivity in the Student Voice Research Framework. I push the range and limits of what, how, and why voice and voiced practices are undertaken to push the field.

SETTING THE STAGE

Australia has a long history of "student participation." Beginning in the mid-1970s, student participation was embedded in educational politics that worked for democratic schools, social justice, and inclusion (Connell, 1993), active citizenship (Thomson, 2007), and a negotiated curriculum (Boomer et al., 1992). Student participation was variously endorsed by state governments with support for statewide student conferences, for student councils, and for students on school governing bodies. The Australian version of student participation[1] favored/favors activities where students are change agents (Holdsworth et al., 2001; Thomson & Holdsworth, 2003; Thomson, McQuade, & Rochford, 2005). Yet, because student voices could be hijacked for instrumental ends, and often were, the appropriation of students' energies and voices and their diversion into trivial activities was/is critiqued in the Australian context (Holdsworth, 2000).

Early on, Australian youth activists used Hart's "ladder" (adapted from Arnstein, 1969; published in Hart, 1997) as a rough evaluative tool for activities that claimed to be student participation. The ladder—which goes from manipulation, decoration, and tokenism, to child-initiated activities and child-initiated, shared decisions with adults—is not simply a list of different kinds of engagement, but also a moral hierarchy. Activities at the "bottom" are not only less agentic, but also less ethical and acceptable. Student participation was positioned, as was I, to prefer particular kinds of approaches to working with students. Students-as-partners-in-activities was deemed good, students-subject-to-adult-designed-projects-and-decision-making was bad.

THE POWER OF "VOICE"

In the mid-1980s I was appointed as principal to a K–12 school in Australia known for its previous leader's cavalier attitude toward social justice. The school had no sexual harassment policy, despite this being mandatory. The staff were deeply divided about questions of race, gender, and class and saw me either as villain or savior. I learned very quickly that the only way to approach change was to ask questions: "Do we need a sexual harassment policy? Have we got a problem? Why don't we find out?"

A volunteer committee, all women, organized a one-day conference for 200 girls, a group representing every class. In the morning, drama workshops generated stories of everyday experiences of name-calling; bra-strap, hair, and underwear pulling; and rankings of apparent attractiveness. There were other darker stories of groping and assault. It quickly became apparent, if we had ever had any doubt, that a policy was required. In the afternoon, the girls brainstormed ideas for action. Supported by teachers, the girls devised an innovative scheme where each class would have trained peer "buddies" who could support victims of harassment and bullying and help them to report the issues. "Buddies" would also monitor incidents and be involved in annual policy reviews. But how to persuade the hostile staff members that there was a problem in the school that required serious attention? A group of 8th- and 9th-grade girls had an answer. They would come to a staff meeting and tell their teachers what was going on. Four teachers volunteered to support the girls to make their presentation.

The memory is vivid. Seven small girls holding hands, some clearly trembling, telling stories of being in a hostile masculinist school culture. Staff, some of whom had previously dismissed the very idea of sexual harassment as a feminist plot, were clearly moved, some distressed by what they heard. The girls got more confident as they persuasively presented their ideas for trained class "buddies" and a monitored policy. There was no opposition to further development and implementation of their proposal.

The school culture did of course not change overnight. A few staff left the school at the end of my first year. Harassment and bullying did not disappear, but it was not denied and was dealt with. The policy was sustained through annual training and monitoring in which students always took a significant role. When an inspection team visited the school some 8 years later, they reported that every random student they spoke to was able to tell them about the harassment policy and how it worked.

If I had had any doubts, I learned that students could tell truth to power and make positive and lasting change.

LADDERS, QUESTIONS, AND FRAMEWORKS

The ladder metaphor has been critiqued by many, notably by Hart himself. Writing some years after his initial formulation, Hart (2008) said that the ladder had been intended as a dual-purpose intervention designed to (a) speak out against tokenistic and manipulative models of children participation, and (b) produce critical discussion. He had not intended the ladder to be universally applicable. Nor had he imagined that it would be used as a normative evaluative tool. He noted that

- the ladder only addressed formal interactions with adults, and that children also independently developed autonomy and agency through play and interactions with peers. Children did not always need to be "given" agency;
- the ladder metaphor suggested that children are the only agents that matter. However, children's participation often needs to be scaffolded, and thus the commitment by, and supporting practices of, adults also needs to be made explicit;
- the ladder can be misread as developmental stages, with children advancing through the various levels as they mature. All children, regardless of their age and stage, can have a say in what matters to them;
- it is not always possible for children to initiate projects and children may not always want to do so. They may, however, still meaningfully participate if they choose;
- the levels are not homogenous—there are, for instance, different ways in which children might be consulted with different effects;
- the ladder has been misread as meaning "children are in charge." In other words, children's rights trump all others. This is not desirable, ethical, or practical;
- the model is culturally specific and might look different in more collectivist contexts; and
- the model omits active resistance and passive hindrance, as well as tolerance and indulgence.

Hart suggested that the ladder had served its purpose and that it was time to develop other perspectives.

Among many other candidates for alternative conceptualizations are the philosophically based-questions developed by Michael Fielding. A critical educator, Fielding was concerned by the decoupling of ethical purposes from discussions of processes, including student participation. He worried that a focus solely on processes played into neoliberal policy hands. He saw the potential for the instrumentalization of students' voices and agency, and for the redirection of youthful energies to legitimate a rapidly narrowing English education system, where test and exam scores mattered over more wholistic and socially just, human-centered approaches to schooling (Fielding, 2001a, 2001b, 2006). Fielding proposed questions that might be asked of any student participation project—who is speaking and who is not? What is allowed to be spoken about and what is not? Who is listening and who is not? What happens as a result? And in whose interests are these results? (Fielding, 2004). These questions offer a normative frame against which proposals and programs can be designed and evaluated.

Cahill and Dadvand's (2018) 7Ps framework addressed the dangers of separating means and ends, and offered further iteration, a guide to project development, and design geared to collaboration, shared reflection, and dialogue. The 7Ps framework asks researchers to attend to purpose, positioning, perspective, power relations, protection, place, and youth participation in programs. The 7Ps drew on feminist poststructural and critical theory, youth studies, and citizenship research and was located in an Asia-Pacific development context, perhaps going some way to address Hart's concern about the Eurocentrism of his ladder. Other models included (a) Mitra's (2008b) being heard, collaborating with adults, and building capacity for leadership; (b) Lundy's (2007) children's rights-based model, where the combination of space, voice, audience, and influence mattered; and (c) Anderson, Graham, and Thomas's (2019) 52-item evaluative student participation scale.

But were/are these enough?

STANDPOINT, EPISTEMIC SUBJECTS, AND EPISTEMIC JUSTICE

I moved from Australia to the UK in 2003, having already shifted from schools into higher education. My colleague and I were tasked with evaluating a reforming school, Kingswood High School (a pseudonym). Heavily committed to student participation practices, my co-researcher, Helen Gunter, and I asked if it would be possible for the school to allow us to work collaboratively with students (Gunter & Thomson 2007a). A student reference group was set up to assist us with designing a survey (Hollins, Gunter, & Thomson, 2006).

Through students' analysis of the survey results, the initial evaluation morphed into student-initiated and designed research about bullying
(Gunter & Thomson, 2007b; Thomson & Gunter, 2006, 2008, 2011). With
our support, students designed creative visual prompts for conducting peer
interviews—ambiguous visual scenarios that their peers had to interpret—
and narrative scenarios for teachers to complete. The visual prompts and
scenarios were based on students' own "funds of knowledge" (Gonzales,
Moll, & Amanti, 2005), their expertise in being students, and their lived
understandings of how youth cultures, framed by class, location, gender,
and race, intersected with school practices of sorting and selection.

Because we wanted to account methodologically for the marginalized
student knowledges used as the basis for designing and carrying out the
research, we turned to standpoint theory. *Standpoint theory* argues that
knowledge is not neutral, that it is produced through language, and that it
is derived from one's social position. Yet standpoint theory is critiqued for
presupposing that marginalized groups share a universal position, homogenous experiences, and common interests (Harding, 2004). However, it is
also a political position for speaking back (Foley, 2002). Taking these critiques on board, we proposed a students-as-researchers standpoint methodology that would

- address issues that were important to students and thus in their
  interests;
- work with students' subjugated knowledges about the ways in
  which the school worked;
- allow marginalized perspectives and voices to come center stage;
- use students' subjectivities and experiences to develop approaches,
  tools, representations, and validities;
- interrupt power relations in schools, including, but not confined to,
  those which are age-related; and
- be geared to making a difference (Thomson & Gunter, 2007).

This formulation allowed for heterogeneity among students but pointed to
common patterning caused by the school and wider social structures/cultures.

Looking back more than a decade later, I see that I assumed an easy correspondence between student participation in school change and student
participation in research. I carried into research the implicit moral hierarchy
that had students-as-researchers as preferable to research in which students
were consulted/were "data." However, I also knew that it was not always
possible to work with students as co-researchers. Not all school leaders were
up for the challenge of student participation as the principal at Kingswood
was. I also realized that students-as-researchers projects were more likely to
be relatively small-scale and thus limited in their capacity to make a difference. Kingswood students, for example, could have benefited from changes

to national assessment practices, national policy on student grouping, and subject setting and national resource allocations (class size was an issue related to the bullying students were researching).

So began a line of thinking about how to do larger-scale research that was not designed by students but that recognized their experiences, valued their knowledges and perspectives, and made their understandings and experiences the basis of analysis and conclusions/recommendations. Research in which perhaps some participation was better than none at all (Lundy, 2018). Research where questions about epistemic justice could perhaps inform research processes.

I began to think about ladders and research again. Many advocacy organizations had continued to work with the ladder model. Sound Out, a U.S.-based organization dedicated to promoting student participation in school change, suggested a murky middle layer of student-centered activity, information, and consultation (Fletcher, 2021). Research that positioned students as subjects could potentially sit in this gray space. However, Hurlbert and Gupta's (2015) split ladder of participation offered a complex model that assessed the level of participation needed for particular kinds of activities that tackle policy and/or problems of practice. Minimum student participation is necessary for well-structured problems that are often characterized by "substantive agreement on norms, principles, ends and goals surrounding a policy problem and agreement on the knowledge inherent in solving the problems" (Hurlbert & Gupta, 2015, p. 101). But as each of these areas become less clear or agreed upon, Hurlbert and Gupta argue, wider democratic participation is necessary. In other words, this ladder appeared to offer a less binary and more strategic approach to student participation.

However, these did not address my comfortable conflation of student participation in reform with students-as-researchers projects. Sometimes students-as-researchers projects were directly designed to change an institution, but this was not always the case. I knew that colleagues had struggled with how to do research that was not led by students or undertaken collaboratively with them but that still worked in their interests and honored their perspectives. In the feminist tradition research, which creates a space for hitherto unheard perspectives to enter the public realm (Fine, 1992; Smith, 1987), such research activity is generally understood as "voiced." Smyth and Hattam (2001) argued that voiced research working with young people was different from tokenistic, decorative, or consultative research

> because of its epistemological commitment to a more democratized research agenda . . . (it) is a way of providing a genuine space within which young people are able to reveal what is real for them. . . . This means that research questions can only really emerge out of 'purposeful conversations' (Burgess, 1988; see also Burgess, 1982, 1984), rather than interviews (whether structured or unstructured). . . . When taken seriously, this represents a significant reversal of the

way power generally tends to operate in research settings; the researchers know and young people are expected to willingly comply in supplying and surrendering information. Voiced research seeks to reverse those dynamics of power. (pp. 407–408)

Smyth and Hattam's research was undertaken with young people labeled as "at risk," young people who were not interested in being involved in data analysis or determining project outcomes. These young people were prepared to tell their stories and negotiate about how they were told, but that was all. Reluctance to participate is not an unknown phenomenon. The literatures on student voice research with vulnerable populations (Faldet & Nes, 2021; Nind, 2011; Tangen, 2009) offer various views on the right to participate and the right to refuse; researchers suggest a need to recognize full participation as a complex ethical question. Researchers accordingly negotiate whether and how much young people want to be engaged in participatory research, rather than assume it as a given.

But of course, the notion of "voice" and "voiced" can be as problematic as that of standpoint (Thomson, 2011). Political voice is often multiple (voices), multimodal, and used in different forums with different effects. Focusing on the medium and process can shift the emphasis away from what is being spoken about, and what needs to happen after the "speaking." Aware of these issues, the shift that Smyth and Hattam proposed was more than simply "voice"—it included space created by the researcher, purpose, ethical conduct, and a normative Habermasian (1987) view of dialogic reciprocity. Smyth and Hattam recommended considerable researcher reflexivity throughout a research project, including postproject publications and presentations. Their view suggests that the consultation and information that sit in the middle of Hart's ladder may be of quite different orders and perhaps effects.

I began to consider research *with*, as opposed to *on*, students as an ontological and axiological question—a question of whether the researcher saw their participants as equally and differently possessed of valued knowledge and know-how. Some anthropologists now talk of research participants as epistemic counterparts rather than informants or collaborators. Working with epistemic counterparts may mean forms of collaborative action (Criado & Estalella, 2018; Estalella & Criado, 2019), but may also mean research conducted according to ethical principles grounded in epistemic justice. Fricker's (2007) formulation of epistemic justice and injustice holds that unjust practices are those used to silence and exclude the understandings, experiences, and interpretations of peoples marginalized by class, race, gender, able-ness and neurotypicality, sexuality, and age. Subordinate views are systematically rewritten, abstracted, and reinterpreted; misunderstood; distorted; misrepresented; distrusted; manipulated; excluded; and dismissed.[2]

The implications for researchers here are clear. Research that works against the practices of epistemic violence and injustice means taking participants' words, narratives, meanings, and truths very seriously, taking them as legitimate and significant knowledges.

A focus on research "ologies" opened a different line of thinking about research with and not on students—a line of thinking I have not yet fully traversed. But I can see that this line of travel does suggest that there might sometimes be good reason to do large-scale work that students have not designed, but where their knowledges and the principles of "doing" epistemic justice might produce challenges to repressive and inequitable educational practices—and thus work in their interests.

STUDENT-LED SYSTEMIC CHANGE

After many years as a school principal but before moving into higher education, I had a brief stint as a senior education bureaucrat in Australia. It was just long enough for me to organize two statewide student conferences. This was an annual event I had hoped might last after I left, but it did not, demonstrating once again that much institutional student participation—as opposed to self-organized student political action—is fragile and dependent on the commitment and sponsorship of powerful adults.

The second student conference in 1997 was focused on environmental questions. At the time there were a number of government-sponsored citizen science and conservation projects running in schools. There was also a strong curriculum push for sustainability education to be taken more seriously. As my brief included the development of a new futures-oriented policy document, I decided that students might helpfully bring their understandings and concerns about the environment to the then Conservative government.

The student conference, called the Youth Environmental Council (YEC), produced two recommendations—that there be regular state consultation with students and that the South Australian waters in Great Australian Bight be declared a whale sanctuary. The whale sanctuary proposal was unexpected and arose from the floor of the student conference. The students' whale sanctuary proposal dovetailed with government debates about the legal status of the ocean and the very possibility of ocean-based sanctuaries. A great deal of behind-the-scenes work by adults would be necessary to make students' recommendations a reality.

The recommendations were presented by students to the Minister for Education and the Minister for the Environment. The students on the conference day and in the newly formed YEC added weight to their proposals and considerations; through their "selves" they were serious, persuasive, well evidenced, clearly capable, rational, highly concerned, and keen to be constructively engaged. As I watched children and young people give their views to these two very powerful adults, I could see again the ghost of that school-based sexual harassment conference from when I was principal where the "bottom-up" power of students was significant in producing change. The Youth Environmental Council was formed on that conference day and still exists. The legal classification of the waters was changed from marine park to aquatic reserve, thus creating a whale sanctuary.

But it is not always possible for students to speak directly to adults who have the position and power to produce systemic change, particularly via research.

DIGITAL POSTCARDS ABOUT ART EDUCATION

In 2016, and in partnership with the Royal Shakespeare Company (RSC) and Tate (a prestigious national art museum in London, Liverpool, and St. Ives), my colleague Chris Hall and I began a new research project called TALE (Tracking Arts Learning and Engagement).[3] TALE investigated the benefits of arts education for high school students and was designed and conducted in the context of a serious decline in enrollments in senior secondary arts subjects. The drop in arts learning was the direct result of a new school audit measure (the English Baccalaureate), which prioritized core subjects—English language and literatures, math, the sciences, geography or history, and a language. Our research furthered an interest in seeing how arts teachers made their professional learning into pedagogical practices and what students gained.

The TALE project worked in 30 schools and was designed around two teachers in every school (with staff turnover, n = 64) and their senior secondary classes. In each school and each year, we interviewed the teachers and teaching assistants (n = 180), and at least one focus group of students across 3 year levels (n = 323 groups, 1,447 students). We observed lessons, interviewed a senior school leader, and made extensive photographic records of arts activities. We also administered a survey to all senior secondary students regardless of whether they had chosen to continue with the arts or not (n = 4,477).[4]

The research was not designed as a student voice project. While we could have formed a student reference group, we did not know how we might really do this, given funding and time limitations. So, rather than establish a tokenistic committee, we chose to conduct the project conventionally, hoping it would work in the long-term interests of students. We knew that perhaps the best we might do was to be "voiced" and epistemologically ethical (see the earlier discussion of voiced research). But at the end of the project, we were struck by the huge corpus of student data. With 6,000 responses from young people, we had the largest data set in the UK of young people's view on the arts. We knew that this data was our greatest research "asset" and an important aspect of our "contribution." We started to think about how we might get young people involved in some analysis and in disseminating the results.

The TALE results launch, a high-profile event at the House of Lords, was titled "Time to Listen," to make the point that the discussion about the importance of arts education had largely been conducted by adults in the sector. Because young people had rarely been asked what they thought, let alone been given center stage, we decided we might address their silencing.

Using some 40 pages of student quotations that we supplied, the RSC worked with drama students from one of the case study schools. Students chose the words that meant most to them, devised a short verbatim theater script, and performed their interpretation of research results on the launch day. Later, the RSC used the same student-selected quotations as starters for conversations in teacher professional development sessions. Tate also worked with its Youth Collective, a few of whom had been involved in the research, to choose quotations to be made into signs for the first day of school across the nation. These one-off events showed (again) that using students' words was a powerful way of presenting "evidence" to various publics. It also demonstrated that involving students in the latter stages of research was possible.

Inevitably, selected students' words also ended up in paywalled academic journals, expensive books,[5] and university repositories. Some of these papers take students' understandings as significant subjugated knowledges and seek to present and explain their perspectives. One paper (Thomson et al., 2019b) explains how many TALE students saw choosing an arts subject as an act of resistance to dominant pedagogies and to family advice to conform to the English baccalaureate performance requirements (EBacc), and to the EBacc policy itself. Another paper (Thomson & Hall, 2021) begins with students' reports that the art room was "relaxing" and asks how the organization of space, time, relationships, curriculum, and assessment construct this "atmosphere." We see these papers as a form of academic "epistemic justice," taking students' knowledges seriously.

But building on our launch day experiences, we decided that, despite having no funding, we would work with the RSC and Tate youth collectives to design a more public communication strategy. We did not, however, get as far as setting dates for meeting with young people before the pandemic hit. Our plan for postproject student participation vanished.

Time moved slowly on, and so did Chris and I—to the primary school equivalent of TALE, the RAPS project: Researching Arts in Primary Schools.[6] But in semi-lockdown and when working from home, I was still occasionally bothered by how little we had made public of students' words, and how little they/we had answered back.

On a whim, and unable to contact the RSC or Tate where staff were on furlough and youth collectives no longer met, I decided to make postcards to be posted online to support the 2021 UNESCO Arts Education Week, an international effort held each year in May to recognize art education as a necessary part of a comprehensive education. I had no idea at the start how many postcards I could or would make. I went back to the original TALE thematic analysis and several hundred pages of snippets of youthful talk. I selected 20 quotations that matched key themes we had identified and chose an image for each quotation; some images came from TALE and other research projects, and some from the public Flickr albums of one of the TALE schools, Thomas Tallis. Each quotation and image was accompanied by a short interpretative statement. I released four postcards a day on my social media accounts on Facebook, Instagram, and Twitter using the event hashtag (see Figure 6.1).

The response to the postcards surprised me. Twitter Analytics reports that the first postcard in the series was seen 18,777 times. These figures increased steadily throughout the week, but there is no way of knowing how many were repeat engagements. In social media terms, these are not particularly startling figures, not enough for any of the postcards to "trend." As a point of comparison, a tweet I made in the same month advertising a survey on headteachers' workload earned a far greater number of impressions. But I got a number of emails in response to the postcards asking where they could be bought in hard copy. There were also numerous requests for a downloadable digital postcard set. I have obliged with a PDF, which is freely available on the RAPS website.

Figure 6.1. Sample Postcard

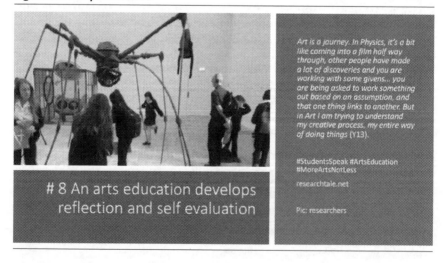

MUDDLING WITH VOICE AND VOICED RESEARCH

I am still pondering the murky middle of participation ladders, the points where children and young people have neither designed nor carried out any aspect of the research but where researchers inform and consult students with the aim of (a) representing their marginalized views in order to (b) make a difference that (c) works in their interests. I wonder, can researchers really get beyond adult ventriloquism of heavily mediated research materials? But what about those times when this is the only way for students' views to be heard?

I can think of multiple reasons why the TALE postcards and voiced research might be dismissed. One set of problems are related to the words themselves. The words on the postcards are neither "authentic" nor "true." The TALE focus groups were not representative but selected—students who were nominated by their teacher and who agreed to talk with us. We steered the conversations; we had questions we wanted to ask. Students may have told us what they thought we wanted to hear or been influenced by their peers in the group to say some things and not others. Students' ideas are not fixed; they may think one thing one day and something else the next. The conversations were transcribed by someone outside the research team, and the transcripts have been deconstructed into themes. Of course, some quotations were chosen by young people for use in public events. But I also chose some quotations for papers and postcards and put them into a multimodal form where an image and a researcher interpretation might further steer the ways in which the words can be read—a myriad of manipulations and mediations.

Or I might take a more theoretical perspective on the truth of quotations, telling myself that young people are not unified rational subjects (Loewenstein, 1994) but socially and culturally shaped. Students cannot be taken as a singular homogenous self. Furthermore, intersections of class, race and ethnicity, gender, able-ness, neurotypicality, sexuality (Crenshaw, 2015) mean significant diversity among the 1,447 young people we spoke with. How can this multiplicity be represented on postcards? But as a group, these young people were also positioned as students, framed by dominant educational discursive formations (Arnot et al., 2003) and their responses may thus bear family resemblances. Were these then what researchers call "themes"? If we cannot claim that these student quotations and postcards are "pure," what is their status in/as research?

And if I make a claim for voiced research, I also know that it's easy for researchers to get things wrong when they aim to "let research subjects speak," in the manner of earlier feminist standpoint research. The case of English poet Kate Clanchy's book, *Some Kids I Taught and What They Taught Me,* is salutary. Clanchy, her publisher, and the Orwell Foundation who lauded the book were heavily critiqued for failing to recognize ableist and racist tropes in the text, and their genealogical connections with eugenics and phrenology. Public scrutiny of Clanchy's book has raised the level of debate, and perhaps understanding, of the dangers of speaking about and for others from positions of privilege.

Among the many constructive suggestions for writers—and scholars—wishing to work with the words and lives of oppressed and marginalized peoples are these questions from Professor Sunny Singh:[7]

1. Why do you want to write this? What is your motivation?
2. What is your personal, emotional, psychological, ethical investment in writing it?
3. Can someone else tell this story better? Is it someone else's story to tell?
4. What does YOUR telling of the story do? Does it replicate prior violence, oppression/injustice? Does it provide new understanding or insight?
5. What is your power balance/imbalance as a writer to the subject matter?
6. Should you write/publish this at all? As with most ethical questions the key is not can one but should one.

These questions seem particularly pertinent to researchers who, like me, want to foreground the perspectives of young people and are wrestling with work at the kind of scale that might influence the thinking of policymakers. While I do not want to tell stories of individual young people, as Clanchy did, Singh's questions are still highly pertinent.

I could easily convince myself that the use of students' research-generated narratives and statements are nothing but a form of manipulation, fabrication, and distortion—nothing but more adult researcher ventriloquism through a simulacrum of student voices. Even if the young people's words on postcards have "verisimilitude" (Garman, 1994), I fret whether they are worthy of the idea of voice, as in conceptions of student voice, and voiced research.

More worries arise when I think about the alternative—*not* using the words we have in hand. I ask myself, is focusing on whether the young people are modernist subjects, shaped and framed by dominant discourses, just another form of epistemic injustice? How much does it matter that young people were not involved beyond agreeing to take part in conversations with researchers who promised to make their view public? I worry that we/I might not honor our ethical obligations to make students' views known outside of their classroom and school. I wonder if it is possible that when we focus only on these very research-ish perspectives, we implicitly diminish these young people's gift of words and lived experiences.

I am still considering these moral imperatives, holding them in tension. Are the postcards, and other artifacts like them, ways of supporting submerged perspectives to enter troubled public conversations a better, if not ideal, option than students' views not heard at all? What good have we done as researchers if youthful points of view are sequestered away for academic eyes only? If words accomplish work in the world, then what do we gain from thinking about what is lost from the ways in which the words were generated? What realpolitik might make these words produce some difference and support more just social and educational change?

Hard questions. I am considering, weighing, engaging with moral hierarchies and tangled knots. Scale, participation, epistemic justice . . . voice, voiced, inform, consult. . . . I have no ready answers. This is not a conclusion. This is an incomplete reflection/reflexion on two sticky questions that still bother me.

NOTES

1. Student participation was stimulated and documented, most notably through the work of Roger Holdsworth and the crowdfunded Connect magazine. See https:// www.asprinworld.com/Connect1.

2. Bourdieu (1977, 1989) also makes this argument when he talks about the symbolic violence of dominant truths, and Smith (1987, 1990) graphically shows how the production of spoken and written texts are integral to the relations of ruling.

3. The TALE project can be found at https://researchtale.net.

4. The TALE survey had items in common with a regular national arts participation survey, and we were able to compare the arts participation and activities of students across the schools with the national average.

5. TALE publications (Hall & Thomson, 2021; Thomson & Hall, 2020, 2021; Thomson, Hall, Earl, & Geppert, 2018, 2019a, 2019b, 2019c, 2020) are also available on the TALE website together with two research reports.

6. The RAPS project is available at https://artsprimary.com and https://www .youtube.com/channel/UC4jOwF3V9VFIVaqEldPMiCA.

7. See https://www.twitter.com/ProfSunnySingh/status/1423334775260127232.

Part III

STUDENT VOICE METHODS IN ACTION

CHAPTER 7

Making Meaning and Planning Change with Students Using Photo-Cued Interviewing

Kayla M. Johnson

As an educator and education researcher invested in improving practice and policy, I think a lot about how students perceive and experience education. The growing field of student voice research encompasses many philosophies, approaches, and goals that generally converge around the belief that involving students in research about their education can effectively contribute to student learning and development and school improvement (Mitra, 2005, 2006). As I reflexively describe below, my foray into student voice research began with uncovering my own voice as a student and reflecting on how my own perceptions and experiences could be leveraged to improve education.

A few years after my teaching fellowship in France, I was asked to share what I had learned with international educators hoping to improve the design and implementation of study abroad programming. It had been my first time traveling outside of the United States, but as transformative as the experience had seemed to me, I struggled to articulate anything meaningful about my experience aside from the photos that now adorned my living room walls. I opened Facebook and furiously clicked through the many photo albums I had curated from my adventures abroad: "Paris," "Rome," "Berlin."

"Amsterdam." The first photo in this album featured a train departure board in Paris with nearly every train marked "RETARDÉ," or delayed (see Figure 7.1). I immediately remembered panicking, running from platform to platform trying to find my train to Amsterdam, where I had planned a weekend getaway. When I realized that none of the trains were moving, I paused and looked around at the hundreds of people calmly sitting on benches and suitcases, reading newspapers and sipping espressos. I frantically approached a man and asked what was going on. He said:

"A train conductor was attacked last night. Every conductor in France is on strike to protest for safer working conditions."

"So, there are no trains today? I'm supposed to go to Amsterdam!"

"We will all get where we need to go eventually."

I had not thought about this experience in several years. That day, I learned the importance of collective action and the virtue of patience, and recognized my own self-centeredness. And as I thought about how I might leverage this moment for my presentation, I recognized the power that photos, and reflection on those photos, can play in understanding how students perceive and experience study-abroad programs.

Photos are powerful tools for eliciting stories and facilitating reflection (Margolis & Zunjarwad, 2018). Many types of photo-elicitation research methods exist (see Hurworth, 2004 for a comprehensive overview), and many researchers have used them to explore students' perceptions and experiences in educational settings. To achieve my goals of understanding students' experiences and improving education, I combined student voice philosophies with photo-elicitation-type approaches to develop photo-cued interviewing (PCI; Johnson, 2020)—a unique contribution to qualitative methods and to student voice research. With PCI, like my train board photo, students take

Figure 7.1. Train Departure Board in Paris, En Route to Amsterdam

and select photos that are meaningful or significant to them in some way and engage in reflective dialogue with the researcher to collaboratively make meaning from their experiences.

The ubiquity of photo-taking, smartphones with cameras, and digital interaction that uses images makes PCI a contextually responsive data-generation strategy for many students. PCI provides students with more agency in the research process than other, what might be considered traditional, qualitative approaches. By using their photos to prompt intersubjective conversations about their experiences, students start the meaning-making process, affording researchers opportunities to reflexively consider phenomena from the students' perspectives. Through this collaborative meaning-making, educators can understand students' perceptions and experiences and use these understandings to inform and improve practice and policy. In these ways, PCI uniquely connects photo-elicitation research to all four principles of the Student Voice Research Framework (SVRF).

In this chapter, I explain and demonstrate the utility of PCI as a student voice research strategy. I first identify the purpose and value of PCI as it relates to the SVRF. Then, I illustrate and discuss the PCI method in practice. I ground this discussion in data from a student voice study of migration and Indigenous student identity formation in Peruvian higher education. I walk readers through our research process, highlighting key points for student voice researchers to consider in their own projects. I end with logistical considerations and practical recommendations for others who want to use PCI to understand students' educational experiences and to improve their practices.

PURPOSE AND VALUE

Exploring how students perceive and experience educational phenomena can help educators develop more comprehensive approaches to improving teaching practices, learning and development outcomes, educational policies, and school environments (Brasof & Mansfield, 2018; Fielding, 1999b; Mitra, 2006). With their SVRF, Brasof and Levitan (Introduction, this volume) underscore the utility of student voice for educational improvement and provide valuable guidance for educators and researchers looking to effectively involve students in change-oriented educational investigations. By centering the voices, experiences, and realities of students, and with the intention to use these realities to improve education, PCI is, foundationally, a student voice-oriented method (Johnson, 2017). In ways I describe below (and illustrate later), the PCI method can attend to all four principles of SVRF—intersubjectivity, reflexivity, power dynamics, and context. Like Brasof and Levitan, I believe that the success of student voice research methods like PCI relies on the researcher enacting all four principles.

Below, I align PCI with the four SVRF principles by illustrating how I use it in my research. For more specific guidance on these strategies, see Appendix A in the online materials for this title (accessible from the product page for this volume on www.tcpress.com).

Intersubjectivity

Being intersubjective means to build productive, mutual understandings of experiences between researchers and participants (Borer & Fontana, 2012). Brasof and Levitan say that building intersubjectivity in student voice research requires researchers to make meaning *with* students through dialogue. Dialoguing with students strengthens the relationship between the researcher and student and lowers chances for miscommunication or misinterpretation.

With PCI, students discuss photos they have taken. This is done in an interview setting—with a researcher, their teacher, etc.—to collaboratively make meaning of their experiences. PCI uses postmodern reflexive interviewing techniques (Denzin, 2001) to enable the researcher and participant to share in an experience, effectively blurring the lines between researcher and participant to create a collaborative interview space (Borer & Fontana, 2012). Through conversation about and around students' photos, students and teachers have space to illuminate perceptions and experiences, to interrogate assumptions and biases, and to develop more comprehensive understandings.

When leveraged as a research tool, photos can help elicit and tell stories that may otherwise go untold in traditional interview formats (Margolis & Zunjarwad, 2018). The photos students take and share in PCI enhance the potential for intersubjectivity because they enable the researcher to visualize and reflect upon—and the student to vocalize and reflect upon—an experience that may otherwise be obscured, ignored, forgotten, or taken for granted by either the researcher or the student. Being able to see and subsequently discuss a student's experience helps researchers more comprehensively understand how students experience educational phenomena. Using photos as the interview prompt also helps researchers acknowledge and overcome previously held assumptions by grounding the conversation *in situ*, through the students' eyes. Finally, the learning that happens through PCI can be mutually beneficial—in some studies I have found that PCI facilitates important learning for students as well (e.g., Johnson, 2020).

Reflexivity

Reflexivity is the critical, active interrogation of personal biases and privileges and how these things come to bear on the research process (Lahman, 2008). Brasof and Levitan argue that reflexive student voice researchers interrogate their assumptions about students as well as how their own experiences with and perspectives on the phenomena they are researching might bias their approaches to and interpretations of data. Engaging in reflexivity in student voice research is particularly critical as adults tend to hold certain biases against youths' knowledge(s) and abilities and tend to hold positions of power above them (Costello et al., 1997).

Reflexive researchers also understand and interrogate the underlying assumptions or biases of the methods they use and the theories that frame their investigations. I developed PCI after interrogating the assumptions and biases that underpin other photo-elicitation methods. For example, photovoice (Wang, 1999) is commonly used to conduct needs assessments with marginalized communities. However, in my research, and especially in the research with Indigenous students that I discuss in this chapter, I did not want to assume that they *needed* anything. Most photo-elicitation methods also consider photos as a primary data source (Hurworth, 2004), but I did not want to assume that students' photos conveyed the significance of their experiences. For example, my photo of the train departure board in Paris in no way conveyed the lessons I learned that day—it only prompted my reflection of the event. While photos can help students, researchers, and audiences make sense of the conversation, the primary data source in PCI is *what students say* about their photos.

Selecting PCI as an appropriate data-generation strategy with students carries many other assumptions and biases that need to be interrogated. First, relying on photos to elicit data requires having trust in students. We need to trust that students will take and select photos that are appropriate and useful, and that their photos will help to illuminate (not obscure) important aspects of their experiences (e.g., Johnson, 2018b). Second, using PCI assumes that photos are culturally appropriate in the research context. Researchers need to consider the beliefs that students (and their various communities) have about photos and whether taking photos is (un)welcome in each setting.

Finally, in studies where I have used PCI (e.g., Johnson, 2017; Johnson & Levitan, 2020), I carefully select multiple, contextually appropriate theories to broaden my understanding of the meaning(s) of the data and expand the possibilities for decisions that I might make from the data (see Levitan, 2018). PCI can be combined with any theory(ies), but I would encourage student voice researchers to select theories that can best illuminate and make sense of students' lived experiences and that are oriented toward transforming education.

Power Dynamics

Just as PCI enables intersubjectivity and reflexivity, it also can productively attend to problematic power dynamics that hinder research processes between adults and youth. Educators and educational researchers tend to hold power, privilege, and/or authority over their students and study participants. Brasof and Levitan argue that building intersubjectivity and practicing reflexivity help make the uneven power dynamics between educators/researchers and students/participants more equitable. Effectively addressing power dynamics in student voice research requires researchers to enable students to claim their power within research projects and the decisions made from them.

PCI is a participant-driven approach that puts the student in the driver's seat to start the conversation. When I ask students about their photos, I pose open-ended questions or make inviting statements (e.g., "Tell me about this photo") that make space for students to shape the conversation around interests, experiences, and goals for the conversation. Although I may prompt students to consider certain concepts or phenomena when taking and selecting photos to share with me, I emphasize that students may share anything they wish to share. Doing so allows the students to claim and exercise their power, which can address and productively complicate traditional perceptions about the role of the "researcher" and the role of the "researched."

Fielding's (2001b) four-level typology of student voice participation provides helpful guidance on how researchers might address power dynamics by inviting students to participate in the research process. While not inherent to the use of PCI, I often invite students to be co-researchers (Level 3) in research studies. In this capacity, students play an active, collaborative role in the development and implementation of research processes. However, I also believe, and have found, that not all students will want to be active collaborators (which takes time and energy) and often choose to be active respondents (Level 2) instead. PCI could also feasibly be used in a study where students are the source of data (Level 1) or students are the researchers (Level 4). Of course, the researcher would need to carefully consider the ethical and logistical implications of each approach.

One important point about power dynamics in educational research is that not all power held by the researcher needs to be mitigated. Student voice researchers need to recognize when their power can enhance the research process. For example, when it comes to enacting change, researchers must be ready and willing to wield their power to help meet students' needs and accomplish their goals. With PCI, researchers may exercise their power by gaining access to spaces for displaying students' photos or telling their stories, by communicating the utility of photos (and dispelling myths about them), and by ensuring that students' photos and stories are not co-opted or exploited.

Context

Finally, as Brasof and Levitan conclude, student voice researchers select research strategies that—in addition to building intersubjectivity, enabling reflexivity, and attending to power dynamics—align with students' contexts, cultures, experiences, and perspectives, and that will effectively access the knowledge researchers seek. One key way to attend to students' contexts is to use inquiry strategies that can be implemented in a noninvasive, enjoyable way. Today's young people are prolific photo-takers. Like my reflection on my photo of the train departure board, young people use these photos to recall memories, reminisce, tell others of their experiences, and make meaning from their experiences through reflection. PCI leverages the ubiquitous photo-taking habits of today's young people into a pseudo-naturalistic inquiry tool to help both researchers and themselves better understand their experiences.

Photo-based research like PCI brings up several ethical dilemmas, such as who can or should be depicted in photos. Engaging in photo-based research with "protected" communities (such as Indigenous communities) or with minors (under the age of majority) often requires additional ethical considerations and consent/assent procedures. I encourage researchers to begin conversations with their institutional review boards early in the research planning process.

METHOD IN PRACTICE

In the following sections, I detail my use of PCI in a study about the impacts of rural-to-urban migration on first-generation Indigenous students. Our research team traveled to Cusco, Peru to learn from 28 postsecondary students about how migrating to urban Cusco from their rural communities in the Andean highlands and the Amazonian rainforest affected their identities, their ability to accomplish their goals, and their sense of self and well-being. We also invited them to share recommendations for how to improve access, experiences, and outcomes for other rural Indigenous students who wish to pursue higher education. This study arose from the research team's years-long research and work with Indigenous Andean communities, which has illuminated the opportunities and challenges facing students who seek formal education opportunities (e.g., Johnson & Levitan, 2020; Levitan, 2015; Levitan & Johnson, 2020). The ultimate goal of this research was to impact educational change that would make higher education more responsive to the identities, needs, values, and goals of rural Indigenous students like our participants (see Johnson & Levitan, 2021 for more details on this study).

Below, I describe the most important facets of our PCI research process as they relate to the four SVRF principles—intersubjectivity, reflexivity, power dynamics, and context.

The Positioning

With any research study, but especially with student voice, researchers must make evident, reflect upon, and ethically and responsibly act on their positionalities, privileges, and powers (Mansfield et al., 2012). Engaging in research with students requires educators to reflexively consider how students may perceive them as authority figures, evaluators, gatekeepers, or other power brokers and how these perceptions may influence what students are willing to share with them (Bower, 2003; Delamont, 1976). In our study, the student participants were not our students (they were not enrolled in our courses nor our institutions). A few of them had benefited or knew others who had benefited from nongovernmental organizations that we are involved with in rural communities.

While we were not the students' teachers, the research team and I were all educational researchers who embodied identities that complemented and complicated our abilities to be relational with them. As I describe our positionalities and how we reflected and acted upon them, I encourage readers to think about how who they are might come to bear in their research with students. Starting with the most senior member of the research team, Joe is a white man from the urban United States and an assistant professor of education. He has worked with Indigenous communities in Peru since 2009 and speaks fluent Spanish. Natalia is a Peruvian woman and first-language Spanish speaker from Lima (the capital city of Peru, located on the Pacific Coast) who previously worked for Peru's Ministry of Education and was earning her masters in educational leadership. I am a White woman and emerging Spanish speaker from the rural United States and was a postdoctoral researcher in higher education at the time of the study. I have worked in Peru since 2015, and like our participants, I was also a first-generation college student. We all developed our Spanish language skills within the Peruvian context, meaning that we had shared local vocabulary with participants that allowed us to build intersubjectivity and understand nuance and contextual meaning a little more quickly than if we had learned Spanish elsewhere. All three researchers were in their late 20s to early 30s at the time of the study, like many of our participants (who were 18 to 36). All the participants were fluent Spanish speakers, but Spanish was not their first language. No one on the research team is Indigenous.

Throughout the project, we used contextually appropriate strategies to connect and engage with potential participants. For example, we used word-of-mouth networking with our existing partners and collaborators to recruit participants. This allowed us to connect with participants from a place of preexisting trust—if their friends or family trusted us, then they felt they could, too. We met with each participant individually to explain the study and invite them to participate. In these informal meetings, usually in a public location over tea and snacks, we shared a bit about our own identities and experiences and allowed them to ask questions about our backgrounds and expertise. As we would be asking them to share intimate details about their own identities and experiences, reciprocating that intimacy was important.

As students shared their own experiences with us in individual interviews, we reflexively considered how our own educational experiences, our experiences in Peru, our racial and socioeconomic identities, and our knowledge and expertise as educational scholars may influence how we hear our participants. To mitigate our assumptions and biases, we often discussed our initial interpretations with the participants directly during the interviews.

The Prompt

PCI data collection begins with a prompt, a guiding question or statement that primes students to consider and illuminate something specific about their perceptions or experiences. The prompt is given to students at the outset of the study (e.g., before engaging in a specific activity) to guide them in the kinds of photos they may take but could be used *ex post facto* as a lens through which to examine photos they have already taken.

In this study, we wanted to know how students' identities developed or changed as a result of migrating from their rural communities to urban Cusco for their higher education, which is the common migration pattern for rural Indigenous students in this region. We gave the students a simple prompt: "*Who am I?*" Secondarily, we asked students to consider: "*Who was I before coming to Cusco? Who was/am I in Cusco? And* (for those who had already graduated), *Who am I now?*" Open-ended prompts like these allow students to select and reflect upon their experiences without "priming" students in ways that might bias their photo-taking. While we were ultimately interested in identity development, migration, and educational experiences, we purposefully did not include these academic terms. Doing so might have influenced students to share less authentic accounts of their perceptions and experiences (Cleary, 1996; Johnson, 2018a; Roberts & Nason, 2011). So, a broad, open-ended prompt helps to alleviate the influence of the researcher on the research process and enhances the intersubjectivity of what "identity" in relation to "educational experiences" and "migration" could mean.

The appropriate or necessary amount of orientation or priming will vary depending on the study and the students. Depending on the students' ages or skill sets, their relationships with the researcher, or their comfort with photography, the researcher may need to provide additional guidance for students to understand what kinds of photos they should take. In a few instances, students asked for clarification on what their photos might look like or represent, so we offered neutral examples that illustrated how the method works without featuring a topic they were likely to use. For example, Joe shared a simple photo of a soccer ball and talked about how his identity as an intercollegiate soccer player shifted after he graduated. This example was neutral (intercollegiate sports do not exist in Cusco) but also contextually understandable (soccer is popular in Latin America), and illustrated how simple the photos could be and how students might think about their identities in relation to different times and places. We also emphasized that students' photos could be metaphorical or symbolic, such as a tree to represent life or a cemetery to represent death.

We gave students 2–3 weeks to take photos. During this time, we anticipated that students might spend time at school, in their home communities, at work, and in other places that might be meaningful to them. We believed that allowing time for students to visit many places that are meaningful to them would yield more diverse photos and deeper reflections on their identities and experiences over space and time.

The Selection

We asked each student to select five to eight of their photos that most meaningfully represented their response to the "Who am I?" prompts. These photos mostly depicted mountain landscapes, busy streets and markets, foods, clothing, cultural events, and family and friends. We had explicitly instructed participants not to photograph anyone without their verbal consent, and not to photograph children under the age of 18, but some participants did not follow these instructions. As a result, we are unable to publish many of their photos. Nonetheless, we can use the discussions concerning those photos in publications, and we can include descriptions of the photos in publications. It will not influence the validity or value of the discussion and analysis. This is a suitable alternative that aligns with the PCI principle that photos are not the primary data source. However, not publishing the photos could lessen the impact of the research (a picture is worth a thousand words, after all). To mitigate this issue in other projects, we have provided written and verbal instructions to students that more clearly explain the ethics of photo research and what kinds of pictures are not ethical.

The Interview

We met with each student individually (or, on a few occasions, with two students who were close friends or a couple) to discuss their selected photos in a semi-structured interview format. (See Appendix A in the online materials at www.tcpress.com for our interview protocol.) To illustrate the PCI method in action, I use small excerpts from an interview with Román. Román was 33 years old and grew up in an Asháninka community in the rural Amazonian rainforest. He had studied nursing at an *instituto* (trade school) and then religion at a seminary and is now pursuing a degree in education. Román is interviewed by Joe, who was the same age and who shared Román's interests in religion, philosophy, and education. In these excerpts, Román and Joe discuss some of Román's photos. As you will see, their conversation arose from Román's photos and commentary on them but also diverted to other topics—some more obviously about his educational experiences than others. Nevertheless, our conversation helped us to understand (a) how Román thought about his identities at different points in his life, and (b) how postsecondary institutions in Cusco can better respond to Román's identities.

The following excerpts represent only portions of Joe's interview with Román but illustrate how we enacted the four SVRF principles through our use of PCI. I provide commentary that highlights important components of the conversation and reflections on how we made sense of the conversation to inform our research goals.

> Joe: *Did you choose any photos that represent your life before coming to Cusco?*
> Román: *Yes. The school* [see Figure 7.2].

Joe situates the conversation in a specific time—Román's life before coming to Cusco—but allows Román to choose which photo to begin with. Joe then displays the school photo on a large screen TV.

Figure 7.2. The Primary School in Román's Community

Román: I'll describe it. The school is small, very rustic and is for people who live in the community. The school had a custom that the parents, when we went to school, were always there, from time to time as a form of support.

Román notes a few characteristics of his primary school that set it apart from what we already know about postsecondary institutions in Cusco: it is small, it is rustic, and it serves the local community. We also learned that his parents' involvement in his early education was important to Román. In thinking about how to make higher education responsive to rural Indigenous students' identities, these are useful action points.

Joe: So do you identify with this school?
Román: Yes, a lot. When we are children nobody wants to go to school [. . .] but I found familiarity there. I found spaces for dialogues with the children and with the teachers more than anything—an extreme trust with the teacher. And the teacher was also from the campo *[rural communities] and understood our needs. She did not make you feel less, or more—equitable. We had a river and she would say, "Do you want to go fishing?" And we would go fishing.*

Here, we learn more important characteristics of his school and the people in it. Román's primary school was a space where he could "dialogue" (which seems distinct from "talking") with kids like him and with his teacher. Román's teacher emerged as an important figure from his life before Cusco— someone who came from a similar context and who understood how to support him (like engaging in culturally relevant activities, such as fishing).

Joe: Is this experience one reason you want to be a teacher?
Román: Umm . . . Subconsciously it may be because I haven't questioned it that much. [. . .] Something subconscious that reminds me of the teachers who treated me well or who gave me that space, that warmth. It may be that I carry it subconsciously.

The conversation has moved away from the school in the photo and to what the school might represent. Joe starts to intersubjectively interrogate Román's experience by offering an initial interpretation for why Román has decided to study education. Román acknowledges that, while he hadn't yet thought deeply about his motivations, his positive experiences with his primary school teacher might be one reason. This type of in-interview reflection and realization has been common in my research using PCI, which I also believe to be one of its greatest strengths (Johnson, 2017).

Joe: How was her pedagogy?

Román was studying education, so Joe used this technical term to acknowledge and honor his expertise, building intersubjectivity and leveling power dynamics.

> *Román: Ah very good. She gave us a lot of free rein, right? We're in the campo, so, the teacher, she was so intelligent [. . .] there were resources such as plants, or stones, or the garden itself* [see Figure 7.3]—*so she took us there.*

After talking at length about his life in his rural community, Joe transitioned the conversation toward Román's life in Cusco. This explicit temporal and spatial shift allowed us all to make sense of how Román experienced his education in different places and at different times in his life, which helped us understand any identity shifts that he might have experienced.

> *Joe: Alright. Now, let's talk about your life in Cusco. [. . .] Did you pick some photos about your time in Cusco?*
> *Román: Yes, the one of the entrance to my* instituto [see Figure 7.4].
> *Joe: Do you identify with the* instituto?
> *Román: Identify? No, not that deeply. But I have memories, right?*

Rather than assuming Román selected the photo of his *instituto* because it represented something about his identity, Joe asked Román if it did, which he denied. Through this denial, we see a clear difference in how Román

Figure 7.3. Trees Bearing Fruit in Román's Community

Figure 7.4. The *Instituto* Román Attended in Cusco

identifies (or rather, does not identify) with his postsecondary institution—a modern-looking trade school in Cusco—compared to the "small, rustic" school in his community, which he did identify with.

> Joe: *Do you have more photos from your time at* instituto?
> Román: *I have more from the area where I grew up. There, we used mules for transportation* [see Figure 7.5].
> Román (continues): *I chose this because I had a lot of experience with them. When I was little, I had to walk 12 hours, or could use a mule for 9. I began to appreciate the true sacrifice. Of sweat, of the heat, of hunger, thirst. It marked me. [. . .] It is obviously my identity.*
> Joe: *And what does this photo of mules represent about your identity?*
> Román: *It shaped me. As an identity, it would be to be courageous, to value the sacrifice that I made at that time. Because now every-thing is easier.*

This claim—that life in his community was more challenging than his current life in Cusco—stood in stark contrast to the narratives of nearly every

Figure 7.5. Román and His Father With Two Mules

other student, who felt Cusco was more challenging. It also surprised us because Román had just painted a happy picture of his primary school years against the mere mention of his *instituto*. So, Joe probed a little further:

> Joe: *Let's talk a little more about your time [after leaving your community]. So you went to the seminary, and then you worked?*
> Román: *Yes, as a nurse with an Italian NGO [nongovernmental organization] that provided social assistance to people who needed it most: health, basic sanitation, water, electricity. I took the opportunity because (1) it was a challenge, and (2) the people spoke Quechua, which was easier for me to understand.*

Because Román grew up in the Amazon, we had assumed that he spoke Asháninka, not Quechua.

> Joe: *Is Quechua your first language?*
> Román: *Yes, in fact, my parents speak both Quechua and Asháninka. They are bilingual. There is this taboo, though, of "No, my son has to speak Spanish," right? But I learned Quechua because at school everyone spoke it.*

We find it significant that Román's parents are bilingual in two Indigenous languages and that his primary school taught in Quechua, yet they expected him to learn Spanish. This revelation underscores the pressures and challenges that Indigenous students can face.

At this point, our conversation begins to move away from what Román's photos depicted. This is one reason why photos are not considered as the primary data source with PCI, because I have found that (a) what students want to share about an experience is not always easily represented in a photo, and (b) dialoguing about photos opens the conversation to tangential, yet critically important points that might be missed if too much attention is given to the photos themselves. Sticking only to the photos can stifle student voice.

> Román: *The very fact that they spoke Quechua made you feel close, right? [. . .] If you speak Quechua, they trust you.*
> Joe: *Interesting. So [community members] have a distrust, fear of people who speak Spanish?*
> Román: *Yeah. [. . .]*

Here, our preexisting knowledge about school settings in Peru kicked in again. Given that most educators beyond primary school in Peru teach in Spanish (Hornberger & De Korne, 2018), Román's perception about the distrust of Spanish speakers is troubling. Trust with teachers is critically important to student success (Cook-Sather, 2015; Mansfield et al., 2012).

> Joe: *So what was the relationship like between the community, the NGO, and you as an intermediary?*
> Román: *The NGO always comes up with the proposals, right? "We are going to make these changes." Then I, as the intermediary, consider if this change is really fair or not. Because they say "Yes! Now!" Among themselves they will say "It suits them." But it is more sincere to say: "Look, these are the cons and these are the benefits. Does this work for [them], or not?"*

Román continues to reflect upon the troubling dynamics that can arise between Indigenous community members and non-Indigenous peoples. Román perceived that the NGO, whose purpose was to address community needs, defined those needs themselves without considering whether their ideas matched local realities. This paternalistic development approach goes against the numerous sets of ethics of engaging with Indigenous community members, which converge around the idea that Indigenous community members must define the scope of the work to be done, and to what end (e.g., Ball & Janyst, 2008; Snow et al., 2016; Sumida Huaman, 2020). As an Indigenous man, his experience with the NGO seems to have contributed to his distrust of "outsiders."

Joe: Did this experience affect your identity?
Román: My identity, no. In part, it has strengthened me.

This brief exchange was important. Román's description of his role as an intermediary fits with our conception of identity (e.g., it is a role that he plays; Levitan et al., 2018), but Román does not consider it part of his identity. This is another reason we typically did not use the word "identity" in our prompts or interviewing (Román was one of our first interviews, so we adjusted our wording shortly after). It is also why centering the students' voice—rather than our own assumptions—helps to uncover more accurate understandings of their experiences.

Joe returned attention to Román's *instituto* photo.

Joe: What was the university like?
Román: The professors come, they give their lecture, and that's it.
Joe: Did you like this teaching?
Román: Partly yes, because they told me new things.

Unlike Román, most other students did not like the way that professors lectured. We are still grappling with the implications of this disagreement for improving practice.

Joe: How did you feel studying and living in Cusco?
Román: I missed the customs, the food, the air itself, the people.
Because at least they tell you: "Hello." That trust, that respect
that they give you, right? But there is not that here. Everything
is empty. It's cold. It makes you feel very far away. It is difficult,
very difficult.

This is Román's first detailed description of life in Cusco. It isn't clear whether he means the people in the university or people in the city more generally. Given our focus on the impacts of migration for education, it really doesn't matter. Still, Joe probed for that information.

Joe: What about the education?
Román: I don't like the system. The curriculum is not adequate. It
doesn't really reflect the needs, human needs. The knowledge
they give to us is very globalized. Our knowledge is no longer
valid.

This aligns with our previous research about curriculum in primary and secondary education in Peru, so we now have evidence of it at all levels of formal education. This finding highlights the systemic lack of culturally grounded curriculum and the importance of systemic changes.

Joe: *The last thing—We have talked about some of your experiences and how they impacted you. Do you have any recommendations for how to improve the transition from rural communities to urban institutions for students like you?*

Román: *When I aspired to continue studying, I encountered many problems, right? One was economic—there is no food, there is no space to live. It would be much better if the State cared. If [they helped you with] a room [to live in], you wouldn't be worrying about how am I going to do it? How am I going to pay? You would be concentrating on studying.*

That Román's initial recommendations are to meet students' most basic needs—shelter and food—is significant. As he aptly states, without a place to live and food to eat, it is difficult for students to concentrate on studying. The economic concerns that face students from rural communities clearly inhibit their abilities to focus on their education even when they can access it. This was an apt reminder to our team that culturally grounded curriculum will do no good if students' most basic needs are not met.

The interview goes on for another 30 minutes or so, with Joe returning to some of the specific challenges and opportunities that Román mentioned and probing for recommendations to improve education based on those reflections. Román recommends, among other things, (a) helping students to identify career paths that align with their strengths, (b) implementing more dialogic instructional strategies, and (c) developing curriculum that better reflects Indigenous values, realities, needs, and ways of knowing.

The Analysis

As evidenced in my commentary above, we performed some analysis in the interview itself. We tested our hunches, gained clarity, and formed preliminary, intersubjective understandings about Román's experiences and how they influenced his identities. More formally, after data collection we reflexively considered Román's and others' experiences and reflections through multiple theories and frameworks. This multi-theory approach allowed us to better interrogate how we understood the students and helped us to interpret their experiences from multiple angles. For this study, we used coloniality of power (how top-down power structures influence and colonizes people's choices and options in life; Quijano, 2014) and *Mink'a* epistemologies (mutuality and relationality with others and the natural world in work and community life, Sumida Huaman, 2020)—two contrasting yet complementary and contextual theories about relations of power and life options (e.g., Johnson & Levitan, 2022)—to understand how colonialism oppressed students and/or how Indigenous community values empowered them.

To illustrate, let's examine Román's mule story through these two theories. From the viewpoint on coloniality, we might see the use of mules as transportation as a symbol of enduring colonialism. Román has to transport crops via mule for 9 hours—presumably to a nearby urban center to sell them to make money. As Román says, this is a sacrifice, which from coloniality could be viewed as an oppressive force that keeps Indigenous communities subservient to market forces. From *Mink'a* epistemologies, however, we can see the mule as a symbol of roots, of hard work, and of Román's persistence that enables his community to sustain itself. Román seems proud of the mule—he is smiling in the picture and speaks fondly of it—and claims that this experience "strengthened" him. Still, considering the mule from the two opposing, yet interrelated perspectives helped us to form a more comprehensive understanding of Román's childhood experiences and how they shaped who he is and how he views the world today.

Then, to more clearly understand how these forces interacted in students' lives, we mapped their oppressive/empowering experiences onto an ecological systems framework (Bronfenbrenner, 1994), which considers how different levels within a system—with the student at the center of it—interact and influence the student. This secondary analysis affords student voice researchers the ability to make connections between students' experiences and to identify "leverage points" (Abson et al., 2017; Olson & Raffanti, 2006), or facets of a system that can be manipulated to create sustainable and systemic change.

The PCI method can be combined with a plethora of theories and frameworks, but researchers should be careful to select theories that are contextually appropriate, that reflect how students see their world, and, ideally, that enable change.

The (Re)Presentation

Student voice researchers must make principled decisions about how they (re)present data. That is, how researchers represent students' voices through their interpretations and analyses, and how they present those interpretations and analyses to others, should align with the basic principles of student voice work.

First, students should be invited to participate in the interpretation, analysis, and representation of their words. In-interview meaning-making is one way of doing this through PCI. We also invited all our participants to take part in data analysis, though only one student chose to assume this role in a formal sense. The same student also helped us to select poignant photos and quotes that most accurately and comprehensively represented students' perceptions and experiences. In addition to our contextually appropriate, change-oriented multi-theory approach described above, we checked our analyses against other research and our own experiences in Peru to enhance the validity of our interpretations.

Second, students should have a say in how their perceptions, experiences, and ideas should be presented to others, and to what end. At the outset of our study, we shared with our participants that one of our anticipated outputs was a public gallery exhibition that would feature their photos and stories. We selected this output among others after reflexively considering the goals of our research study and how those could be most effectively communicated and achieved. Like some other photo-elicitation methods (e.g., Wang, 1999), the potential for public persuasion is foundational to PCI. Through students' photos and representative quotes, we aimed to communicate their perceptions, experiences, needs, values, and goals in a way that garnered attention, prompted action, and resulted in change. However, we did not assume that this approach best suited the students' visions for the research, so we did invite them to provide feedback and suggest alternatives (they all agreed, and also suggested smaller presentations to institutional leadership). By identifying this as an intended output at the outset of the study, and by inviting their feedback, we helped to ensure that students understood and could shape how their voices would be portrayed.

In the end, we held a public gallery exhibition in a heavily trafficked corridor of the Municipal Palace of Cusco, a publicly accessible building containing the administrative offices of the regional elected officials. We thematically arranged students' photos and accompanying quotes to illustrate important facets of their identities and how their experiences migrating to Cusco to attend postsecondary education affected them. At the end of the exhibit was a wall of their recommendations for improving higher education, along with a blank poster board and pen that invited visitors to consider the students' experiences and provide their own recommendations (which built further intersubjectivity). At the inauguration of the exhibit, we invited the students to speak about their experiences, share poems and other artwork, and talk with local government officials about the importance of supporting rural Indigenous students.

Not all PCI projects will use these strategies. However, student voice researchers should carefully consider what they will do with the photos and stories that students share and should prioritize students' ideas and opinions.

CONCLUSION

There are many possibilities and challenges to leveraging PCI as a student voice research method. Using PCI in this study helped us and our participants to achieve our learning goals and will be instrumental as we continue to work toward institutional change. PCI helps to (a) build intersubjectivity within the interview space, (b) reflexively examine our biases and assumptions,

(c) level researcher–participant, settler–Indigenous, and other power dynamics, and (d) respond to the unique contexts and lived experiences of our participants. The resulting photos and narratives compellingly illustrate the complex identities that rural Indigenous students embody and how migrating to Cusco impacted—for better or worse—who they are and their abilities to achieve their goals.

Designing and implementing a study that uses PCI can be challenging. Navigating the ethics review process—in which the ethics of institutional review boards and the ethics of students, communities, and schools can contradict (Levitan, 2019a)—can cause tensions and disagreements around how to ethically engage in such research and to what ends. Logistically, using PCI can be time-consuming and requires both defined time parameters to keep the process moving as well as flexibility. Researchers may need to train students on how to take good photos, and they should discuss the ethics of photography and provide sufficient time for photo-taking. Conducting PCI interviews can be mentally arduous as researchers must balance flexibility and structure to ensure that the interview is participant-driven but also achieves the goals of the research while also engaging in in-interview interpretation and analysis.

But even against these challenges, PCI can be an invaluable and rewarding research tool for educational researchers hoping to improve education practice and policy. PCI has enabled me to gain deeper understandings of students' experiences. It has revealed and prompted student reflection, learning, and development. It has raised awareness of and prompted advocacy for the issues facing marginalized students and communities. I have found that students enjoy participating in studies that use PCI, which invariably adds to its value as a student voice strategy. For educational researchers seeking a method of collaboratively exploring and making meaning with students, I recommend PCI as an intersubjective, reflexive, power-relational, and contextually responsive strategy.

I offer a special thank-you to Mr. Claudio Bonatto Gamio and Ms. Allison Peoples for their help with transcribing, translating, and making sense of the data represented in this chapter.

CHAPTER 8

Participatory Visual Data Analysis
Tools for Empowering Students Toward Social Change

Lisa J. Starr

I have worked in the field of education for almost 30 years, yet I continue to be struck by how much research takes place in schools that excludes the voice of students. A certain logic or common sense suggests that student voices should be heard loudly and often. As Cook-Sather (2006a) so aptly suggests, there is something fundamentally wrong with examining, researching, and remodeling a system without consulting those the system is designed to serve. Perhaps this is the reason that action research has such wide appeal in education. The cyclical nature of inquiry, design, action, and reflection that underpins action research resonates with that common-sense approach to engaging young people in research. Though the voices of students have become more prominent in educational research, more can be done to ensure students' experiences inform policy and practice in schools. In this chapter I will discuss two participatory visual methodologies (PVMs), photovoice and cellphilms, as youth participatory action research methods to promote student voice. PVM is aligned with what Charteris and Smardon (2019) characterized as *learner-oriented discourses*, where students are active participators or co-researchers engaging in partnerships that focus on a co-construction of knowledge and meaning.

Photovoice and cellphilms as youth participatory action research also align directly with the principles of the Student Voice Research Framework (SVRF). These projects develop *intersubjectivity* through multiple communication modalities (video, audio, discussion). Photovoice and cellphilm projects engage students and adults in *reflexive* dialogue throughout the research process, and the projects require participants to think through the *power dynamics* between the student creators and the adults working with them. Finally, photovoice and cellphilms are inherently *contextualized,* as they are projects meant to illuminate students' realities.

Both photovoice and cellphilming are methods that rely on images as a social medium to record reality, communicate events and attitudes, and then prompt critical discussion often on topics that may be known but perhaps misunderstood. In the original use of photovoice by Wang (1999), women in Chinese villages were tasked with photographing their everyday work and health realities to both enact greater understanding and create a pathway to change. Cellphilming is the act of taking a short video often between 1 and 5 minutes using either a cellphone or a tablet. The goal of cellphilming is for the students to represent their perspective on an issue in their everyday lives. Dockney and Tomaselli (2009) originated the term "cellphilming" by combining *cellphone* and *film* to describe the merging of two technological mediums in one device. Mitchell, De Lange, and Moletsane (2018) confirmed that photovoice and participatory video like cellphilming are effective in "engaging community participants, and especially in altering some of the typical power dynamics related to the researched/researcher, and to ensuring spaces for marginalized populations to both speak about and then speak back" (p. 4).

Essential in the use of both photovoice and cellphilming is that the experiences portrayed and then critiqued remain in the voice of those who experienced it firsthand. This key feature is directly reflected in the SVRF, particularly with regard to intersubjectivity, power dynamics, and context. A good participative researcher can facilitate photovoice and cellphilming to highlight the distinct experiences, perspectives, and insights of youth in ways that don't require them to be led by the researcher down a performative path where youth simply reaffirm what the researcher expects of them. By adopting a more intersubjective stance, youth engaged in photovoice and cellphilming can more freely offer authentic critical perspectives. By preserving the images, analysis, and discussion in the voice of those young people who have created them and having the researcher play a facilitative role more than an interpretive one, the power dynamic between youth and researcher justifiably favors the youth. This participative approach reduces the likelihood of meaning being filtered or co-opted by others with more power, namely the researcher(s). The photographs or cellphilms are not the focus of the meaning that is being constructed but rather the catalyst. Finally, photovoice and cellphilming are methods that engage youth in cultural representations using a medium that they are arguably experts in: cellphones. The use of a cellphone as a tool for research often serves to elevate youths' perception of themselves as experts, which in turn strengthens their position as researchers.

In less participatory methodologies used to work with students, particularly in the field of education, understanding or the meaning associated with the situation or phenomena being studied is often described as being co-constructed through social interaction with teachers. The implication in that co-construction is that a balance of power and agency is maintained in the process. In reality, students do not always have or are not always allowed to have the agency necessary to truly co-construct knowledge with teachers. In my experience as an educator, I have consistently found that young people are incredibly insightful and often quite honest when sharing their thoughts and beliefs, particularly about topics of importance to them. In my work in schools both locally and internationally, I have used photovoice and cellphilming to delve into difficult topics like gender-based violence. When students show their understanding through PVM, the ideas shared and exchanged by students have a profound and lasting impact on themselves as participants but also on those responsible for policy and change.

Mitchell and Moletsane's (2018) transnational research project, Networks for Change and Well-Being: Girl-Led "From the Ground Up" Policy Making to Address Sexual Violence in Canada and South Africa, is an excellent example of research that powerfully uncovers the impact of sexual violence on girls and young women, especially Indigenous girls and young women in Canada and South Africa. Through the use of participatory visual methodologies, girls and young women were positioned as both knowers and actors. Through cellphilm production and in working with photographs, participatory visual research creates ways to disrupt what might otherwise be regarded as normative structures by "revisiting their own visual productions, reflecting on their work, often changing their minds, and productively challenging and contradicting themselves" (Mitchell & Moletsane, 2018, p. 6). Through the use of participatory visual methodologies, the process was led by girls and young women, to engage in what Choudry and Kapoor (2010) refer to as *learning from the ground up*. We regard this use of the arts not only as speaking (or speaking up and voicing) but also as speaking back or seeking to disrupt dominant narratives.

This is a particularly powerful way to disrupt narratives because the viewer cannot escape the image, so they form deeper understandings of the issues through the critical engagement with the imagery, whereas in conversation or dialogue, the words once spoken become filtered through the listener's experiences and memories or possibly even forgotten. This is particularly problematic for students faced with the power structures embedded in schools where they are often seen as the least influential.

Photovoice and cellphilming also allow students to forge authentic connections through shared experience and the critical analysis that comes with creating an exhibition around a common theme. Photographs and cellphilms act as a prompt and open access to knowledge and awareness about sensitive social issues. In photovoice and cellphilming, students capture and represent issues from their own point of view and the world around them to bring to the fore issues that are rarely talked about. Once the photographs are developed, there's an opportunity to reflect and share this perspective or point of view with peers and community members, and also with people who can assist toward disrupting inequities in society and bringing about positive social change.

YOUTH ENGAGEMENT IN CELLPHILMING AND PHOTOVOICE

In the two examples I refer to throughout this chapter, one focuses on a cellphilming workshop facilitated with 16- to 18-year-olds from Mozambique who were beginning their teacher training. In Mozambique, young people can begin their elementary teacher training at colleges throughout the country as early as 16. Teacher training programs for the elementary level are 2-year programs that prepare them to enter classrooms throughout the country in rural areas. In Mozambique, young people are particularly engaged in social media and bring enthusiasm to the cellphilming workshops, as well as much insight and a desire to make change. The students shared with us their understanding and experiences of gender-based violence that had been heard of and sometimes witnessed within their own colleges. It is important to note here the ethical implications of this type of work. In cases where students may have experienced gender-based violence and are asked to represent those experiences in the images or the photographs that they share, the researcher runs the risk of re-traumatizing young people. This is always a point of concern that researchers must attend to.

The second example focuses on the use of photovoice with students ages 14–17 enrolled at a small English-speaking high school in Quebec, Canada. The topic of the photovoice activity was to simply have young people share their experiences at that particular high school. They were prompted to communicate their thoughts and ideas of what the school meant to them but also what they wanted adults to know. The commonly held belief among staff was that they were providing a very positive familial learning experience to students. As researchers, our team wanted to hear firsthand from students about their perception of their experiences and then to help students create an exhibition that represented those experiences. The exhibition was shared with their teachers, parents, and other key stakeholders in the school community.

Both of these examples, and other research I have participated in, continue to have a profound impact on me as a researcher. The honesty and authenticity of students is inescapable. The reaction of the adults is often predictably defensive—illustrating the challenge for fostering intersubjective understandings between adults and youth about the schooling experience. Students show a willingness to not only share their beliefs and ideas, but have those beliefs and ideas make a positive impact. It is this latter desire that is perhaps the most profound when using PVM to promote student voice. Perhaps the most significant challenge is in engaging the adults with whom the decision-making authority resides.

PULLING BACK THE CURTAIN ON WHAT IS KNOWN
AND UNKNOWN

In working with students in Mozambique, our research team sought to understand how students see gender-based violence and what should be done about it in their teacher training colleges. In Mozambique, the political and social climate has yielded seemingly clear messaging to the wider society that gender-based violence is unacceptable. The Ministry of Education recognized and condemned all acts of gender-based violence and developed policy to reduce these acts of violence. The Teachers' Law/Act appeals to teachers not to start relationships with students inside or outside of the teacher training colleges. Educators cannot use their position to gain advantages that are illegal or immoral. Yet gender-based violence persists. Despite the government's political will to respond to sexual harassment, there is no clear mechanism or credible way to report and refer cases of violence. There is a lack of information about teacher training colleges reporting mechanisms, which deals with older youth who are not necessarily children but who remain vulnerable.

Women, particularly young women, continue to be manipulated to provide sex for grades; improved stature in the community; and at times, simply access to education. We sought the most honest representation that we could obtain from them in our investigations. As a white female from a western Canada prairie town, in situations like this one of the biggest obstacles that I and other researchers face is that we remain outsiders. Thus, we must recognize that traditional modes of research will inhibit our ability to obtain a more intersubjective understanding of this problem. When addressing a topic like gender-based violence, we acknowledge that at times we can only get just under the surface because we don't live in their communities and we do not walk their paths.

PHOTOVOICE IN PRACTICE

Embedded in the art of photovoice is an iterative analytical process. In the example at the local Quebec high school, the research team posed a very broad question: What is your experience of school? One of the sub-questions was, what do you want people to know? At the time we posed these questions to the students, we had been observing teachers and administrators contemplate a significant change to their model of curriculum delivery. This new model, NEXTschool, was intended to have schools refocus their efforts and delivery around five educational drivers: space, time, andragogy, relationality, and communities. Discussions took place among teachers on how to disrupt traditional class scheduling and how to reimagine classrooms as purpose-driven learning spaces as opposed to a standard, traditional class.

Inquiry and project-based learning were also considered. One common thread woven throughout was teachers' belief that the students loved the school and that their efforts were all for the betterment of the students. Yet in our observations, we had not heard directly from a single student about how they felt about school or what, in their minds, was needed to improve their learning experience. With the approval of the school administration, we gathered together a group of diverse students and sent students in pairs to take 8–10 photographs throughout the school that in their view was a response to the guiding question, *what does your school mean to you?* The research team emphasized that the students were the experts of their own experience and encouraged them to tell their stories as openly and honestly as they felt able.

In facilitating photovoice, I prepare students by stressing the following:

- I explain the background of photovoice as a research tool, the nature of photovoice, and the impact it can make. This explanation helps students to see themselves as researchers and that the photovoice activity and subsequent message is in their hands. Often, I include examples of previous work to help them visualize the process and outcome.
- I encourage students to work together to discuss questions, concerns, and hopes. This helps students to create a depth of meaning that is key to both finding their voice and communicating their message
- I emphasize that discussion of the photographs and their meaning should clearly reflect the guiding question. At times, ideas emerge that diverge from the main focus of the photovoice theme or topic. I do not ignore these ideas but rather discuss them with students to find out how they are interpreting the main theme in relation to them. The goal is to guide students in choosing their message and what is important to them.
- I stress that photographs are more than a way to tell a visual story. A visual image can profoundly influence people's thinking and even their well-being, "With their messages—both explicit and hidden—[images] help[ed] to shape our concepts of what is real and what is normal" (Spence, 2003, p. 2). Essentially, photos and the subsequent discourse they foster become evidence.

Because cameras are ubiquitous in the lives of young people and even adults, it is easy to understand how a cellphone camera can be used to creatively capture and share life experiences. Students often do not realize how influential pictures can be in shaping policy. The image itself does not shape policy, but rather the images influence how to focus on one's worldview. Photographs can capture attention and influence awareness and understanding of a reality that can be quite different from one's own. However, students taking photographs is not the key to photovoice. The critical engagement with the photographs as well as the resulting discussions that are prompted by them is where real learning takes place. To revisit Cook-Sather's (2006a) earlier words, it stands to reason that when talking about schooling, the voice of those directly impacted by it should be much more pronounced. By increasing awareness and knowledge about experiences including, as well as differing from, their own, students can help to develop a broader and more inclusive understanding of a range of important issues. As a tool, photovoice emphasizes individual and community action because information and evidence are not created simply for the sake of creating knowledge; they are created for the purpose of social action and change. Simply examining community problems and struggles is not enough. Energy must be put toward identifying community solutions and doing what is needed to implement those solutions. The photographs and images produced by students can be a powerful means to an even more powerful end. In the Quebec school example, the photovoice exhibition, which was the culmination of the research, set off a series of deeply reflective conversations among teachers about their identities as teachers and as a school. It further led them to engage students directly in their beliefs about what was needed in the school community.

In the first stage in which I provide background information about the impact of photovoice, I also discuss the basic principles of photo ethics. At the university level, ethics can be both complicated and complex. I intentionally explain photo ethics around five key points:

1. Students should not engage in trespassing or going in areas that are considered out of bounds in order to obtain a photograph. This is not to suggest that there are areas that they should not depict but rather no trespassing is to ensure their physical safety.
2. Students should respect privacy. I explain to students that they should not take pictures that would invade an individual's privacy or put that individual at risk.
3. Students should obtain permission in the form of verbal consent to take pictures of a person or a small group of people. Taking pictures of large groups of people without permission is allowed provided they are taken within a public domain like a park or a coffee shop.
4. Students should not take pictures of any illegal activities since this could put them and others in danger.
5. Neither students nor the camera should be hidden while taking pictures. The student should make themselves visible and whenever possible explain what they're doing if anyone asks.

We have intentionally kept these ethical points simple and easy to follow so that students can engage in the greatest amount of depth possible for the activity without putting themselves or anyone else's safety at risk.

In the second stage, in which I ask students to engage in discussion, I also challenge students to take photographs that represent their response to the guiding questions posed. In this stage, students can work individually or in pairs but should be provided with guidance on how many photographs are required. In the Quebec example, the research team worked with 18 students. We organized them in pairs and tasked them with taking 8–10 photographs within the immediate school area. Before going out into the school area, we showed them examples of photographs that other groups of students had taken. We spent a brief period of time discussing what students noticed in the pictures and what they thought the photographers were hoping to achieve. We intentionally kept our instructions simple and focused so as not to be overly prescriptive about what images students should be depicting.

Figure 8.1 is an example of one of the display panels curated by the students. The introductory paragraph was guided by the instructions provided by students. The images were taken by students. The accompanying hand-written text was generated by students following an exercise that asked them to caption the images to further convey their intended message.

Once students generate their set of pictures, we enter step 3, a critical discussion and reflection of the photos and the experiences depicted in them. At times, the result of this reflective exercise means that students go out to take additional photos because an idea or prompt emerges that students agree is an important additional consideration. This step is more common among students who are engaging in photovoice for the first time, and though it is not required, leaving space for news and important ideas that students identify is important. Depending on what equipment is available, we use small wireless photo printers that students can send their pictures to and print onsite. Once the photos are printed, we hang them throughout the room that we are in so that students can wander and look at each other's pictures. After a general discussion, students enter a more critical analysis stage known as the SHOWeD model (Wang, 1999, p. 188). The SHOWeD model prompts students to consider these questions:

What do you *see* here?
What is really *happening* in this photo?
How does this relate to *our lives*?
Why does the strength or problem exist?
What can we *do* about this?

These prompts provide a structure for engaging in reflexive dialogue and ground the voices of the students. The SHOWeD model also requires adaptation of methods (such as video, arts-based, or other data collection

Figure 8.1. Example of a Photovoice Exhibition Panel

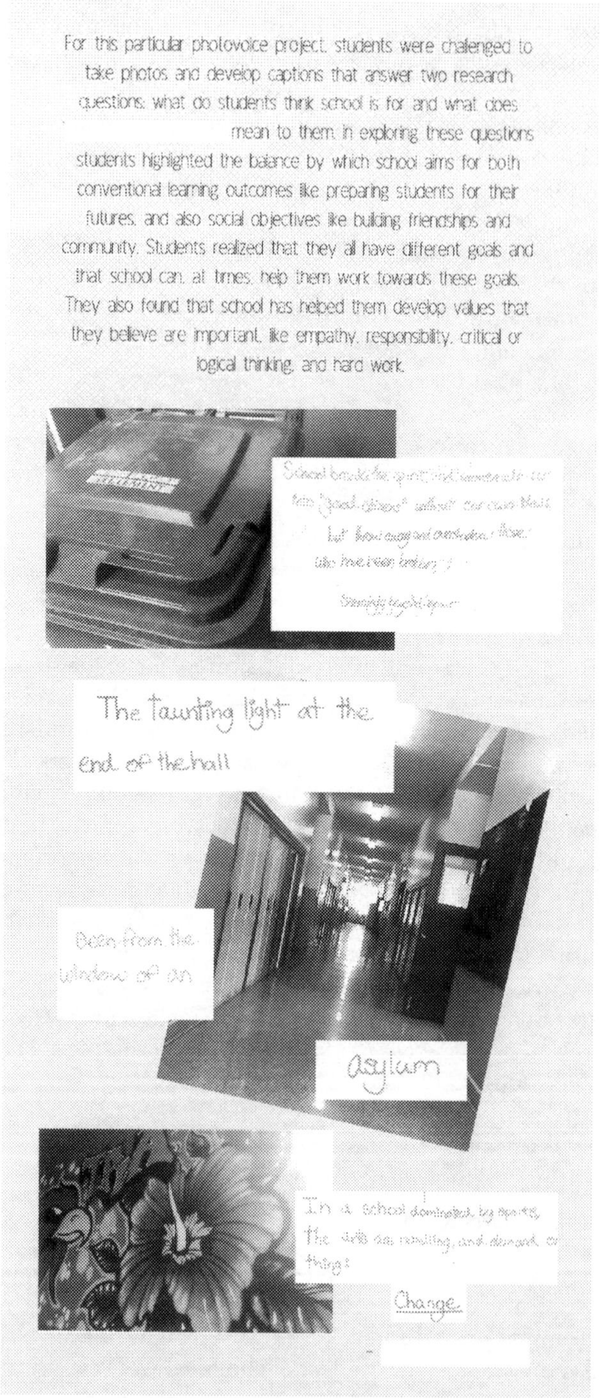

For this particular photovoice project, students were challenged to take photos and develop captions that answer two research questions: what do students think school is for and what does _____ mean to them. In exploring these questions students highlighted the balance by which school aims for both conventional learning outcomes like preparing students for their futures, and also social objectives like building friendships and community. Students realized that they all have different goals and that school can, at times, help them work towards these goals. They also found that school has helped them develop values that they believe are important, like empathy, responsibility, critical or logical thinking, and hard work.

methods), as well as adaptation of analytical technique, to create a strategy congruent with students' contexts, cultures, experiences, perspectives, and knowledge. Students analyze their own photographs to better understand not only their intention but also the meaning they hope to represent.

In stage 4, students begin by choosing two photos to be part of a wider exhibition. The theme of the exhibition is the original guiding question, *what does school mean to you?*. After engaging in the analysis and choosing two photos, students write captions or narratives to accompany each photo. These narratives are intended to support the meaning depicted in the photograph, focusing more on intent than interpretation. Students are then tasked with replacing the photos and the captions that were originally hanging and again engage in a gallery walk. The intention of the gallery walk is to become familiar with the other messages and to consider how these messages and images might be either categorized or organized around important themes. After the gallery walk, students brainstorm different categories or themes. Students then reorganize the order of the photographs and accompanying captions in accordance with those themes. The themes become large-scale panels as part of the exhibition.

In step 5, students begin to plan their exhibition, considering the what, where, when, and how. Students are challenged to consider who they would ideally like to view the exhibition and what, if any, is the main message.

The final step engages students in writing a curatorial statement. This statement is a short paragraph that gives context to the exhibit, which can be developed as a group after the photos and place have been chosen. The curatorial statement includes (a) a title, (b) the context and aim of the photovoice project, (c) the names of photographers (with their consent), (d) the prompt guiding the photos, (e) the theme or main message, (f) a question or two to prompt or challenge the audience, and (g) acknowledgments of any funding support or special permissions.

CELLPHILMING IN PRACTICE

When engaging students in cellphilming, a typical approach includes nine stages (Thompson, Mitchell, & Starr, 2019):

1. Students choose the topic. Choosing to identify the topic beforehand or collaboratively depends on the students' interests and availability. It is also in this stage, like in the photovoice example, that students consider the importance of visual ethics. In the Mozambique example, the research team posed five guiding questions to prompt students thinking:
   - Is this photograph or cellphilm okay to show in a public setting?

- Do you think this person knows they are being photographed or filmed?
- Is this photograph or cellphilm revealing of someone? Why or why not?
- What could you do to make a picture or a cellphilm less revealing?
- How do visual ethics link to human rights?

2. Students choose a genre for their cellphilm. They can choose from several different genres, including melodramatic story, media messages or public service announcements, talk shows, interviews, or documentaries. Questions that influence the choice of genre include asking: *What is the purpose of the cellphilm workshop?*

Figure 8.2. Student Engaging in Cellphilming in Mozambique

Who is the audience for your cellphilm? How long will your cellphilm be?

3. Students engage in a critical analysis of select images to gain a better understanding of the ethical implications of cellphilming. Not all photographs or cellphilms without people or people's faces in them are necessarily anonymous. An item of clothing, a bruise on an arm, or a landmark may serve as identifiers. To increase anonymity in cellphilming, a no-faces-approach can promote creativity and abstract thinking. Examples include filming objects, filming scenes or buildings without people in them, filming people shadows, or filming handwritten signs or making a notecard video.

4. Students typically work in small groups of four to six people. They brainstorm story ideas as a response to the guiding question or prompt. Usually these ideas are written on chart paper or poster paper so that they can be shared with the wider group. Once a number of ideas have been generated, students narrow down the possibilities for what they may want to film. Ideally, students reach consensus over one idea to focus on.

5. Students create a storyboard. Storyboarding is a planning activity where students work in small groups to plan and sketch out their ideas and stories sequentially and in detail before they begin filming. Here are some helpful questions to guide student planning:
   - Who is your audience?
   - What evidence will best illustrate your story/theme?
   - How can you tell this story via different mediums (images, text, other audio visuals)?

This stage helps students organize their ideas and begin to consider the technical aspects of filming. Students then share their storyboard ideas with their peers for feedback. Doing so gives groups the opportunity to revise or fine-tune their storyboard before filming.

6. Students begin filming. Four important details are important for students to consider:
   - What location will be used?
   - Will there be any interference with sound?
   - Are other groups filming close by, and will you be able to hear them?
   - Does the student filming have their finger over a microphone?

Because the films are very short, groups are encouraged to film them several times to improve them.

7. After students have completed their cellphilm, the wider group comes together to screen it. If possible, cellphilms should be screened using a projector. Before screening each cellphilm, a student from each group introduces the cellphilm, including the title and a short summary. After the screening of each cellphilming, students engage in a question-and-answer session. Each group responsible for a cellphilm sits at the front of the room as a panel and invites the audience to offer comments and ask questions. The facilitator can encourage questions and comments about the themes and issues found in the cellphilm by posing such questions as the following:

   - What do you like best about the cellphilm?
   - What is the main message and why is it important?
   - Who is the audience and why did you choose this audience?
   - What would you do differently next time?

8. Students engage in a critical reflection about the issues presented in the cellphilms. For facilitators and or instructors, getting groups to engage in discussion about the ideas and themes in the cellphilm is a very important part of the process. Students are often very self-critical about the technical aspects of their productions, including length, sound quality, and lighting. These are important components of cellphilming that should be taken up at some point, but in the discussion about the issues presented in the cellphilms, students should focus on the topic and the content regardless of the video quality. There can be several different layers of reflection about the cellphilming process. Students should reflect on their involvement in the cellphilming activity and reflect on each other's cellphilms as a response to the following questions:

   - What are the explicit issues being represented in the cellphilm?
   - How does the cellphilm help to address these issues?
   - What do you think about the issues presented?
   - In the cellphilms, is anyone portrayed negatively? Positively?
   - Who is a change agent?
   - What do the issues have to do with those roles?
   - How do these scenarios reflect and reproduce real life?
   - What stereotypes are being enacted?
   - Does the cell film challenge norms or stereotypes? If yes, how? If not, how can and should they be challenged?

9. In the final stage, students consider possible audiences for the cellphilms: Who should see this film, and why?

THE VALUE OF PVM AS A TOOL FOR EMPOWERING STUDENT VOICE

The more I engage in participatory visual methodologies like photovoice and cellphilming with students, the greater the confirmation of how knowledgeable and socially engaged young people are. A key facet, and perhaps the most empowering, particularly in the examples shared, is that the words and images of students are original and unfiltered. The issues and topics depicted are not chosen by a researcher or a teacher or an administrator, making them distinctly personal. As researchers or facilitators, we do not edit or change the photos or the accompanying narrative. It is the originality of the photos and films that prompt the most depth of thinking among the students and those who view their work.

Perhaps the most valuable lesson that I have learned in facilitating PVM with students is how accurate and powerful their words and images are. In the Quebec example, the facilitators helped the students organize the exhibit and provided them with nine printed panels that were 2.5 by 4 feet each. Those panels were displayed in the main hallway in the school. The most surprising outcome was the reaction of the teachers. As mentioned earlier, this was a small school and one that prided itself on the sense of community it provided to students. And though the majority of the photos and captions depicted a very positive experience of schooling, not all of it was as positive as teachers assumed. In keeping with the creative analytical process implicit to photovoice and cellphilming that I have discussed throughout this chapter, I have included the following poem as an example of the common struggle that students experience in being heard by their teachers. The words captured in the poem are a composite of the words from students' photograph captions and the reactions that teachers had to those images and captions. The boldness of the font is intentional.

My Voice Isn't Loud Enough to Be Heard

Our students love it here . . .
    . . . *The staff works hard to help us*
This is home to them . . .
    . . . *I like time with my friends*
Our small school is more like a family . . .
    . . . *I struggle in school but teachers want to help me improve*
    . . . *school breaks the spirit*
That's not true!
    . . . *Being in class is like a weight in my hands*
We are there for our students!
    . . . *the amount of work is overwhelming*
We work hard!
    . . . *the anxiety builds up and you feel stupid*

The students didn't say these things.
What will parents think?
Take these pictures down!

Students did in fact like many aspects of their school experience and appreciated the efforts made by their teachers, but they did not do so blindly. Students wanted teachers to better understand the challenges they experienced daily. When students showcase their experiences through imagery and subsequent critical discussion to delve into the deeper meanings shown in photographs and cellphilms, teachers are sometimes confronted with realities that, as in the poem, are difficult to accept, yet capture the reality of students' lives. As a result of the photovoice activity, teachers were deeply uncomfortable with the reality that students were not as happy as the teachers believed them to be and perhaps the efforts of teachers to create that familial environment were not landing as firmly as they thought. The exhibit was also viewed by prospective parents, much to the chagrin of the teachers who worried that the honesty of the students painted the school in a negative light. Some teachers did not believe the exhibition should have been public. In fact, some teachers wanted to know which students said what (we did not tell them), so that they could talk to them directly about why they felt negatively.

What was most interesting was that the teachers were forced to question their own beliefs about the education and the learning they were providing for students. The honesty of the students disrupted their teacher identity and caused a degree of discomfort. Some teachers found this to be a good thing. It was an opportunity to reflect and critique some of their own assumptions about their teaching in the school itself. For other teachers, their identity was shaken. These reactions are a testament to how powerful PVM can be at representing students' ideas and beliefs.

CHAPTER 9

Listening to Relations of Power and Potential with Material Methods

Eve Mayes

The student voice encounter is not a neutral zone. It is a zone where neither young people and adults, nor young people themselves, can ever be unproblematically "equal." Relations of power between young people and adults in student voice work, as well as relations of power between young people themselves, have been thoroughly explored in previous research. This chapter extends these previous discussions of power in student voice work to pose one research method for exploring power dynamics: using a ball of yarn in reflective conversations—though the methodological argument that I make is not exclusive to yarn. I draw on two studies where this method was used—an ethnography of a secondary school students-as-co-researchers group (Mayes, 2016a), and an evaluation study of student voice in primary schooling (Mayes, Finneran, & Black, 2018). Primary school in Australia is for younger school-aged students—from Foundation (from 5 years old) to Year 6 (generally, 11 or 12 years old). Thinking with this method, which materialized different insights in these two studies, I explore how material objects are intertwined in the re/production of power relations in student voice, as well as in schooling more broadly. I consider the ways in which the materials that researchers use in our methods can evidence the workings of power and potential in student voice encounters, and how they can support collaborative reflection on these power relations. Working with these examples of the work of a ball of yarn, I argue for the productive potential of turning attention to matter for cultivating collective response-ability—that is, the capacity to respond, in the moment—for what happens in student voice research and practice.

POWER DYNAMICS IN STUDENT VOICE

Student voice efforts frequently aim to shift macro-political structures and governance processes. For example, shifting power relations is attempted through the representation of young people in school and system-level decision-making forums (Brasof, 2015), as well as through young people conducting their own research with the broader student body and sharing their research with their teachers and school leaders (Groundwater-Smith, Mayes, & Arya-Pinatyh, 2014). Yet, the invitation for students to "have a voice" is usually initiated by adults, highlighting the "powerful authoritarian role of teachers to that of students" (Robinson, 2011, p. 444). When adults and students speak, there are always already macro-political institutional asymmetries of power, as well as immanent micro-political workings of power—before students open their mouths to speak, during the voice encounter, and influencing what will happen as a result of their voice work. Students may hesitate at the invitation to "have a voice," and self-censor and "tone police" their voices and research findings to say what they think is expected of them, and to avoid causing tension or offending adults (Biddle & Hufnagel, 2019; Mayes, Finneran, & Black, 2019). In turn, the questions asked, the methods offered, and the material conditions of the voice encounter shape what is said and what is not said or unsayable. For example, students who meet with their school principal in the principal's office to "have a voice" may say something quite different to what they might say in a focus group run by other students in the school playground. After students "have a voice," adults may question the credibility of students' perspectives and research findings to justify not acting on them (Edwards & Brown, 2020), reshaping or co-opting students' ideas and research findings to fit adults' preestablished concepts (Bourke & Loveridge, 2016; Fielding, 2004), not following up on students' recommendations (Parr & Hawe, 2020), and/or using student voice initiatives to compel students to accept school reforms on the basis that students have been consulted about them (Bragg, 2007; Mayes, 2020). But there is no full domination—even when institutional power is exercised, there are more visible and less perceptible forms of resistance, including students' solidarity, subversions, and laughter (Mayes, 2020; Nelson, 2017).

At the same time, students are also enmeshed in their own intrapersonal relations of power and everyday felt tensions when they engage in voice work. It is not the case that, just because a focus group is facilitated by a student, it is necessarily more empowering or experienced as an equal space by students. In school life, there is a tendency for young people who are confident, high-achieving, popular, and articulate (which often align with white and middle-class markers of privilege) to be selected or to volunteer to speak, to represent and to lead other young people (e.g., Silva, 2001; Whitty & Wisby, 2007). Teachers (and researchers) may have their own ideas about which students will be "most appropriate" to lead and/or participate in student voice work "(mostly referring to the best or calmer [students] in class)" (Schäfer & Yarwood, 2008, p. 124). In Cox and Robinson-Pant's (2006) study of primary-school student representative councils in the United Kingdom, trust between student representatives and the broader student cohort was affected by representative students "deliberately imposing their own views" rather than listening to their peers (p. 519). In a multi-sited case study of the enactment of student voice practices in three primary school contexts, Rosalyn Black, Rachel Finneran, and I found, in the study introduced further below, that there was a tendency for student representatives to act as mediators for other students—particularly those deemed to be too young to "understand what it [having a voice] means," or those deemed to have just "silly" ideas for change (student quotations, in Mayes et al., 2019, pp. 164, 165). When student representatives "adjudicat[e] the voices of other students, they may inadvertently speak for others (Alcoff, 1991) and underestimate the capacities of other students, even in attempts to broaden student voice across a school community" (Mayes et al., 2019, p. 167). Even when students engage in their own research, student-led research (that is, without adults) does not create less hierarchical power relations; young people "resist, challenge, acknowledge or negotiate power amongst themselves" (Schäfer & Yarwood, 2008, p. 132). Within any voice encounter, there are multidirectional glances, imperceptible affective flows, subtle silencing, tensions, resistances, and evolving relations between bodies that dynamically shape what occurs (Mayes, 2016b).

The problem with power, methodologically, is its tacit quality. Power can be vaguely sensed, enacted and reproduced by habit, felt in its subtle effects but elusive to explain. It is hard to explain what you know about pedagogical and research power relations to an educator or researcher who embodies particular forms of institutional power. It is hard for students to articulate the fraught relations of power that shape how students relate to one another, and the capricious instability of these power relations, even within the ostensibly equal zone of student voice work. As Christopher Kelty puts it, there is always already a "soft part of the social fossil" of what is experienced across bodies in space and time that has "decayed or disappeared" (2019, p. 9)—and that may not even be consciously articulable. Researchers, teachers, and students seeking to represent other students need to learn how to attune, even if imperfectly, partially, and open-endedly, to how power and potential shift and move in student voice encounters. Below, I do not claim to solve these issues but hesitantly offer one method to support collective reflection on the complexity and intractability of power in student voice.

THEORIES OF POWER AND THE MATERIALITY OF METHOD

This chapter contributes to the third principle of the Student Voice Research Framework (SVRF): consideration of power dynamics. I am interested in the methodological potential of attending to and learning from the material residue of voice encounters for collective reflection on power relations in student voice and students-as-researchers work. There are a range of theories of power that are explicit and implicit in student voice research and practice. These theories of power broadly range from critical theoretical views of power as a possession or structure that can suggest that power can be balanced, democratized, or transcended (e.g., Taylor & Robinson, 2009), to feminist poststructuralist conceptions of power, inspired by Michel Foucault, that conceptualize power as relational, dynamic, and productive (Luke & Gore, 1992; see Mayes et al. [2017] for a discussion, written by students, teachers, and researchers, of various conceptions of power). I think about power with the conceptual insights of 17th-century Dutch-Jewish philosopher Baruch Spinoza, the French philosopher Gilles Deleuze's reading of Spinoza, and the work of contemporary feminist activist materialist researchers. For Spinoza, power manifests in two modes: as *potestas* and *potentia*. The Latin word *potestas* is associated with power in its fixed, forceful, formal, institutionalized mode, concerned with the formation of subjects—students and teachers, for example (Deleuze, 1988, pp. 128–129). *Potestas* can also be thought of as power *over*—institutional asymmetries of power like student/teacher. Power as *potentia* is fluid and dynamic—formed in immanent (here-and-now) relations, becoming perceptible in flashes, where a body's capacity to act increases (Deleuze, 1988). *Potentia* can also be described as power *to*. To think about power is to question a body's capacity—what *power to* affect and to be affected that the body *feels* in a particular moment in time, in particular historical, material, textual, and affective conditions that are continually changing. The important point, for the discussion below, is that bodies are not only human—the word *body* encompasses human and nonhuman entities: living beings, matter, objects, affective intensities, and thought (Deleuze, 1992, p. 256). Thinking about power in this way sharpens my analytic focus not only to official institutional manifestations of power (such as the structures and roles that determine who makes decisions in schools), but also to the immanent conditions of, for example, a student voice meeting or a participatory research event.

This chapter tells two stories about a ball of yarn in two student voice research encounters, to consider the materiality of methods and power. The uses of yarn that this chapter discusses are to be distinguished from Australian First Nations yarning research methodologies: a "method of knowledge exchange that embodies the oral traditions of Indigenous cultures" (Shay, 2019). It is important to note that yarn was the material that happened to be used in these two student voice research encounters, but the argument that this chapter makes is not exclusive to yarn as a material object. Thinking with Spinoza, material objects (for example, a ball of yarn) are not separate from the voice of the student or teacher or researcher. In student voice research, material objects are frequently considered to be methodological tools—separate from the humans involved in the research—inert and to be used to *elicit* the inner voice of the student subject. However, it is not so much that a ball of yarn is a tool to elicit voices; rather, a ball of yarn is *entangled* with the production of a spoken statement (a voice). In other words, when a ball of yarn is part of a research encounter, it affects the utterances that can and cannot be spoken. Any spoken utterance is constituted in and through the dynamic interplay of ideas, matter, materials, and human and non-bodies that intra-weave and transform each other in encounter. A ball of yarn may be a "vibrant theoretical-conceptual-affective-material" body, as Niccolini, Zarabadi, and Ringrose have described the work of yarn in an arts-based workshop in a tertiary gender studies classroom (2018, p. 325). They draw out how yarn itself is an "enfleshed word"—"etymologically tied to guts and innards through the Sanskrit *hira* "veil, entrails," and Greek *khorde* "intestine, gut-string" (p. 330). Like Niccolini et al., I also draw upon feminist philosopher of science Donna Haraway's (2016) discussion of the game of Cat's Cradle:

> Cat's cradle invites a sense of collective work, of one person not being able to make all the patterns alone. One does not "win" at Cat's cradle; the goal is more interesting and more open-ended than that. It is not always possible to repeat certain patterns, and figuring out what happened to result in intriguing patterns is an embodied analytical skill. (p. 70)

A ball of yarn, and its movements in and through student voice encounters, carries and creates potent affects (cf. Renold, 2018); yarn can become an "affective conductor" (Niccolini et al., 2018, p. 329).

For readers who are interested in other examples of research that foregrounds the material for intervening "into the live political ecology of education" (Renold & Ringrose, 2019, para. 5), I recommend reading the work of Renold & Ringrose (2019) with jars; Renold (2018) with sharpie pens and rulers; Ivinson and Renold (2020) with embodied movement; Zarabadi and Ringrose (2018) with veils; and Hickey-Moody et al. (2019) with paint and collage. In such work, attending to the material is argued to (a) "increase attention to complexity, feeling, and new ways of seeing" (Cahnmann-Taylor & Siegesmund, 2018, p. 1); (b) create unexpected insights and responses to everyday experiences and emerging research problematics (Page, 2018); (c) give "form to speculative possibilities" and "speculative new futures" (Hickey-Moody et al., 2019, p. 201); and (d) unsettle, materialize, and validate knowledge creation beyond familiar and numerical, verbal and linguistic modes of knowing and communicating (Leavy, 2017).

In the following section, I include photographs of these balls of yarn during and at the end of particular research encounters. These photographs are blocks of sensation that memorialize affects from particular research conjunctions of bodies and materials (Grosz, 2008). I consider the possibilities of working with the material insights of these strings and balls of yarn. I argue that the materials that teachers and researchers (and students working with other students) use in our student voice work *matter*. These materials are part of the knowledge, voice, and action that are generated in the research encounter; they variously shape, extend and/or block, enable and constrain, what can be said and done (Lee, 2001; Mayes & Kelly, forthcoming).

WHAT CAN A BALL OF YARN DO?

I will tell two stories of what a ball of yarn can do. I do not have a prescription for how to use a ball of yarn—in many ways, what a ball of yarn can do depends on the lived histories, current relationalities, and anticipated futures of the gathered group of human bodies who play with the yarn. These two stories, below, are suggestive of the different insights about power and potential that materialized, with a ball of yarn, in different settings, and at different times. In what follows, I contextualize two research studies and describe the work of a ball of yarn, before discussing the methodological implications of reflecting on and with a ball of yarn.

Yarn Webs Can Connect

The first story comes from an ethnography of a students-as-researchers group at one government secondary (years 7–12) school in southwest Sydney in 2013. This school had, over a period of 4 years, spent significant time and resources on student voice, but this concept had been controversial (e.g., Groundwater-Smith et al., 2014). The student voice group (called the Steering Committee) had not been like the typical polite "representative" student group. Each year, a different group of students conducted their own research about what their peers were feeling. Few of the members were the typical student representative type (that is, high-achieving, white, middle-class students) and, at times, were quite outspoken about what was not working at the school. I had previously been an English and English as an Additional Language teacher at this school; in 2013, I was undertaking my doctoral fieldwork. Over the course of the year, I visited the school between 2 and 5 days a week. I spent time (in formal focus groups and interviews, and in informal ethnographic conversations) with students previously and currently involved as co-researchers in the student voice group, as well as with school staff, generating accounts of student voice and the 4-year school reform process. A total number of 100 students, staff members, and parents were involved in 68 formal interviews and focus groups. I also observed and participated in Steering Committee meetings.

The ball of yarn was used at the final meeting of the Steering Committee in December 2013. The meeting was intended to wrap up the students' work for the year, and to be a time when the students and adults who had worked together could reflect on what they had done together over the year. In 2013, this particular group of students had researched how teachers were feeling and preparing for a new Australian Curriculum for History (e.g., Mayes et al., 2013). This group of 20 students ranged in age, from students in year 7 to year 11. At the same time, the meeting was bittersweet, since the students and adults there were aware that the school leadership had decided that the Steering Committee was not going to be resourced by the school in the following year (e.g., Groundwater-Smith et al., 2014; Mayes, 2020).

The meeting began with students sitting in a circle on the front lawn on a warm early summer's morning. Most of the Steering Committee students were there (though a few had class activities that they could not miss), as well as Miss Frazzle (pseudonym), the facilitating teacher of the Steering Committee; Susan Groundwater-Smith (who had been an academic mentor to the school over the 4 years); and Helen Beattie, a visiting North American advocate for student voice who joined the group for this day. I invited the students, in turn, to respond to the following prompt: *What experience/event associated with the Steering Committee "glowed" for you this year? Try to describe what you saw, heard, felt, touched, tasted in that experience/event.* I was thinking about MacLure's (2013) discussion of data that "glows" as a form of data analysis. I introduced the following protocols: the person holding the ball of yellow yarn could speak for as long or as short a time as they'd like, without interruption, indicating when they had finished speaking. The next person who wanted to speak would then raise their hand, and the ball of yarn was thrown to them, with the first person keeping hold of their part of the yarn. After each person had spoken, another ball of green yarn was introduced; students then shared what "glowed" for them from what someone said—that is, what connections they could make between what someone else had said and their own experiences. These protocols could be described as "enabling constraints"—that is, "sets of designed constraints that are meant to create specific conditions for creative interaction where something is set to happen, but there is no preconceived notion of exactly what the outcome will be or should be. No deliverable. All process" (Massumi & McKim, 2009, p. 15)

By the end of the discussion, two entangled yarn webs formed across the circle—one yellow and one green (see Figure 9.1).

I wrote in my fieldnotes about what happened next (all students' names are replaced with pseudonyms chosen by the students):

As the students pass around the yarn and hold it taut, a web begins to emerge. The first web is yellow—highlighted against the green grass in the photos I take. Tyson wears his cap backwards, and loops the thread through the hole in the back of the [non-uniform colored] cap, so that it is as if two threads erupted from the front of his brain. His clothing is entwined with the thread. This frees his hands up to bend his knees upwards and wrap his forearms around his knees. Shaza, sitting next to Tyson, wraps the thread around the back of his neck, so that any pull

Figure 9.1. Two Yarn Webs

Photograph by author

of the thread by the group might draw him closer into the group. With the collective tension of the thread of the group, xPeke leans backwards, holding two threads as if they are the ends of a surf ski handle.

When the second ball of yarn comes around, this time in green, it is harder to see against the green grass when photographed. It is almost camouflaged. As the students add to each other's words from the first round of the thread, we are quiet, attentive, except for the whirr of a cicada perhaps and the occasional whirring of a plane overhead. The only person who speaks is the person who has the ball of yarn. Eyes fix on this person. I am aware of who is not there though: Christian, and his wise words, and James, who if he were here, might finally feel a sense of belonging, that he is listened to and not laughed at. In this moment, it feels like we are connected. But this is a fleeting moment, and not everyone is there.

When I get up to take a photo of the web, MiaRose and Isaac offer to take hold of my corners of threads, to keep the web intact.

The bell rings, and we need to move to an inside room to continue our meeting. I ask what they want to do with the yarn—do they want to leave it on the ground where it is and take a picture of it? No, some of them say, let's walk with it. Let's see how long we can hold onto it. I wonder aloud, won't that be embarrassing, for others to see you walk through the hallways linked to others via this yarn? No, they say, it's not embarrassing. I agree then, and we begin to move together, each grasping at our corner of the yarn.

We walk through the foyer, walking past a teacher as we clasp hold of our corners of thread, walking together, in proximity to each other, through the narrow doorways, then towards the door of the common room. I ask if someone can hold my end while I unlock the door. MiaRose says she will and takes hold of the two corners. I unlock the door.

As the entangled students and adults come in, Dale puts his foot through the web somehow, and laughs. Someone says, you're breaking it! Dale laughs and says, I'm sorry. I ask what should we do. They try to regain the web, but it is gone. I suggest they drop their thread on the spot and move to a seat. The students do this and move to their seats. There is a tangle of yarn on the floor near the door *(see Figure 9.2)*. The yarn is no longer spread taut in straight lines, but has grouped together in curves and folds on the ground. When I try to wind it back up again, it gets knotted, it cannot become one straight line of thread again, but it also cannot regain the straight and jagged lines of the web that weaved over and under the other lines *(see Figure 9.3)*.

Later in the meeting, I invite those who were part of the yarn web to write, on a sticky note, something about the experience. Responses include:

> "Web outside was AH-MAZING!" (Student)
> "The web symbolized the deconstruction of existing dynamics in schools (messy), leading to a stronger more equal structure of teaching and learning." (Teacher)
> "THREAD = AWESOME." (Student)
> "I believe it is a visual representation of equity." (Student)

It seemed to me that the yarn webs materialized a felt sense of connection between human bodies in this particular group, in this particular place and time.

Yarn Webs Can Be Material Evidence of Flows of Power

The second story comes from a 3-year research evaluation study conducted by myself, Rosalyn Black, and Rachel Finneran, commissioned by the Victorian Student Representative Council (VicSRC) (e.g., Finneran, Mayes, & Black, 2021; Mayes et al., 2019). The VicSRC describe themselves as "the peak body representing school-aged students in Victoria," working "to empower all student voices to be valued in every aspect of education" (VicSRC, 2021, para. 1). In 2018, the Primary School Engagement (PSE) program was a newer initiative of the VicSRC that had previously worked predominantly

Figure 9.2. Tangled Yarn on the Ground

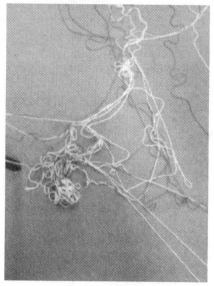

Photograph by author

Figure 9.3. The Ball of Yarn Afterward

Photograph by author

with secondary school settings. The PSE program sought to support student voice practices in primary school settings through facilitating student voice workshops for schools and offering support resources to teachers and students. In 2018, during the first year of the study, the evaluation investigated the situated accounts of students, teachers, and school leaders of their student voice initiatives and their participation in the VicSRC's Primary School Engagement project through a close study of the experiences of three case study schools. These three schools (two metropolitan and one regional) were nominated and approached by the VicSRC to be part of this evaluation study; they were chosen because they were considered to have developed strong student voice practices. Evaluation methods included an interview with the school principal, an interview with the facilitating/support teacher, and two focus groups, with representative students from these three schools. One of these student focus groups was conducted in the first half of the year and the other focus group in the second half of the year.

In the second student focus group, students reflected on their student voice work that year. Topics discussed included describing their student voice activities at their school, and the impacts and challenges of their student voice work. The students who were part of these focus groups were selected and invited to participate in these evaluation focus groups by the facilitating teacher at their school. Of the 23 participating students, 13 of these students were in year 6 (the final year of primary school) and 21 were in their school's SRC (or equivalent). Of the 23 participating students, there were 16 females and 7 males. The research instruments included the prompt question and description of the use of a ball of yarn:

> Can you tell me what has been happening with the Primary School Engagement program at the school since we last spoke? What has been a highlight? Have there been any challenges?
> [Example yarn activity: a student describes a highlight or challenge while holding onto an end of yarn, and then passes the ball of yarn to another student to add their highlight or challenge, and so on, to form a web.]

This activity was initially designed as a strategy to ameliorate the awkwardness of focus groups (where there is nothing to do with one's body but sit still). It is important to note that, unlike in the first story, the researchers (Finneran, Black, and I) had not known these students for very long before we facilitated this research method, though the students knew one another. Different patterns of the web may have emerged if a student had facilitated the activity with their peers or if their teacher had facilitated it. Unlike the meeting in the first story, where I offered enabling constraints for how to speak, listen, and throw the ball of yarn, in this study we did not advise students in advance on how they might take turns. With these caveats, the first time that Finneran and I facilitated this activity, we noticed the unevenness of the web; some students seemed to take a lot of turns to speak, whereas others sat back in the focus group discussion. By the end of the focus group, the yarn became material evidence of who had spoken and how often. Loops of yarn clustered around particular people's fingers, and webs laced between particular sections of the focus group circle. In Figure 9.4, for example, the loops around one student's finger and how the number of strings pulled taut in three directions suggest the directionality of the flow of conversation. It became possible to count the number of turns that were taken between particular human bodies in a focus group circle.

By the end of the discussion, the yarn web materialized the turn-taking pattern of the focus group (see Figure 9.5 as an example). Certain directional lines were thick, evidencing back-and-forth movements of the ball of yarn between two bodies, whereas other lines were solitary. In some of the groups, other students intervened at times, telling each other to try to make the yarn's movements more dynamic and not so bidirectional ("*We're losing the web! Pass it to someone else!*")—that is, to stop the interactional pattern of only two people dominating the conversation.

Toward the end of the discussion, I drew attention to the web and encouraged students to write on a sticky note how they made sense of the webbed configurations of yarn. Here are samples of what students wrote:

> *The yarn shows who talked and contributed a lot and who didn't.*
> *I think the yarn thing means who is speaking up and talking a lot. It's showing who is answering the questions.*

Figure 9.4. Yarn Loops Around a Student's Fingers

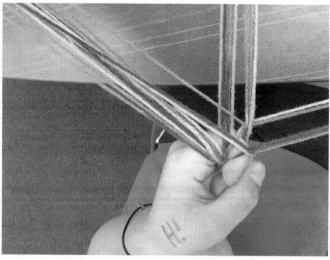

Photograph by Rachel Finneran

Figure 9.5. An Uneven Yarn Web

Photograph by Rachel Finneran

In a number of the focus groups, students said that they'd like to use the yarn in their representative student voice meetings, though they didn't always say why. At the time, I didn't ask for elaboration—perhaps they wanted to bring the yarn to their own meetings to support collective reflection on their embodied habits of turn-taking in the group. It seemed to me that the yarn web had become a useful material method for reflecting on interactional power dynamics between bodies.

CONCLUSION

Yarn has helped me, as a teacher and researcher, to think about and play with questions of power in student voice research and practice. As Niccolini and colleagues have written, the literal material tensions of yarn are an "an agentic and material co-presence" that threads experience together (2018, p. 325). When yarn is threaded to and with human bodies, it can afford "a material capacity to play and think with and through tensions of identity, self, and other privileging relationality" (p. 335).

To be clear, I do not view the work of yarn as a metaphor for power relations; the yarn is *part of* dynamic movements of power. As suggested in the second story, there might be literal tussles over whose turn it is to hold the ball next and power relations at work in throwing the ball between bodies. In the first story, students wanted to keep the tension of the yarn between human bodies tight and connected, walking with the web to keep it taut. The yarn, in this moment, was coextensive with a felt sense of connection to each other and *potentia* (the power to act). Their embodied histories of collaborative work were entangled, perhaps, with concern about the precarious future of these connections. This web was fragile and was dropped to the ground, yet it continued to tremble affectively (for me, at least) beyond the immediate research encounter. Most of the adult and student bodies in the first story had worked together over the year, building relations of care and connection. Playing with yarn, there was a call and response, "the answer to the trust of the held out hand" (Stengers, 2011, in Haraway, 2016, p. 34). The yarn became "an entanglement of our differences"—though only temporarily and precariously (Niccolini et al., 2018, p. 330). The patterning of power fell in the hands that grasped the yarn, pulled it taut, hung it loosely, snaked it in curves (cf. Haraway, 2016).

The tension needed to keep a yarn web taut materializes insights about power. In the first story, I directed the group, offering enabling constraints about how to work with the ball of yarn and how to listen to each other. Although it is entirely possible that this use of power was experienced as oppressive, to exercise power is not necessarily nefarious. Nelson (2017) has eloquently demonstrated, in her analysis of turn-taking in student voice work, the "ambiguous and complex realities of dealing/playing power" (p. 192). Institutional power—*potestas*—such as an adult directing students in a classroom or research activity, does not foreclose student agency and capacity to act—for example, in the first story, for the students to improvise and call for an embodied continuation of the web. Encouraging students to slow down and listen carefully, too, may be a generative use of power (*potentia*)—productively inhabiting a role (here, teacher-researcher) to enable all to speak (if desired).

There are ethical obligations for how this method is used. As these material yarn webs form, and participants listen to each other, those holding the web are drawn into entanglement, caught up together. Great care is to be taken in how we (researchers, teachers, students) respond to how the web forms—how to speak to each other, how to embody a response—not to shame the other or compel silence or speech. Donna Haraway (and many others) calls this disposition *response-ability*: the capacity to respond and attune carefully to the relational ontologies that encompass but exceed human bodies. Collective response-ability entails considering the re-patternings of tension and power that are possible: for example, asking, *what other ways of speaking-listening-attuning might modify existing habits and create new patterns?* In the game of Cat's Cradle, like the yarn webs described above, the challenge is to keep the ball of yarn in motion—to trust, attune, and listen. With yarn, avoiding friction is impossible; yet, it is these knots and tangles that hold the web together. The challenge may be, as Niccolini and colleagues put it, "finding give within tense relations" (2018, p. 335).

Yarn can do many things, in different configurations, with different bodies, histories, present experiences, and imagined futures. I have not provided a "how to" guide or protocols for the use of a ball of yarn, because this method is utterly contingent on the histories and present embodiments of the bodies who might use it. Yarn materializes how generative it is to work with power, felt as tension that connects and works across bodies. Rather than trying to resolve this tension, or to flatten out any sense of power, I have argued that it is productive to think *with* these tensions. Like Niccolini and colleagues (2018), I am cautious to avoid suggesting that yarn, or any material method, is necessarily emancipatory—it entirely depends, and the method may be differentially experienced across a group. Thinking with long-standing feminist critiques of critical pedagogy (including student voice), methods may not always feel empowering (Ellsworth, 1989), but they may still be productive—that is, they *do* something, even if the researcher cannot prescribe or know in advance what they will do.

Reflective Questions (for Adults Working with Student Voice Groups, as Teacher and/or Researcher)

- What materials do you tend to use in your work with students?
- What physical materials are left behind after you have been working with students? What could this material teach you?
- (If using the ball of yarn) How much did you, as an adult, speak? Who steered the conversation, and how did this steering happen?
- What might happen if turn-taking was done differently?

Reflective Questions (for Students Engaged in Student Voice Work, After Tracking Turn-Taking in a Focus Group with a Ball of Yarn)

- How did it feel to bring a ball of yarn into the conversation today?
- What did the ball of yarn show you about the dynamics of the group? For example, what does it make you think/feel about the knots and tangles of the group's work together?
- How do you think other people, in the conversation, experienced these group dynamics? Do you think everyone felt the same way? Why or why not?
- Who tends to speak the most in student voice meetings? Who is quieter? Why?
- How could we [the students and adults who you are working with] be more attentive and attuned to each other?

CHAPTER 10

Balancing Breadth and Depth

Using Mixed Methods in Scale Development Research

Lindsay Lyons

Up to now, student voice research has been predominantly qualitative. This makes sense. Not only is the field in a relatively nascent stage (Edmondson & McManus, 2007), the field is inherently qualitative. A qualitative approach is necessary to better understand diverse student experiences and the impacts of the unique programs that exist to foster student voice. However, the strength of this approach and its depth of understanding is also its primary limitation. A school leader interested in amplifying student leadership throughout the school would need to interview hundreds or thousands of students to get a full picture of students' experiences. Although it would be deeply informative to undertake a project such as this, it is likely too time- and resource-intensive to be practical. Additionally, the call for equity in education is urgent. While a study that focuses on one school can be incredibly beneficial to that educational community, there is a systemwide need for more equitable structures and practices. Quantitative studies enable researchers and practitioners to advance educational justice for far more students across many contexts. Furthermore, educational institutions value quantitative data. The inclusion of quantitative evidence in educational research may contribute to its perceived value by adult stakeholders (Creswell & Plano Clark, 2011), and thus may increase the likelihood school leaders will be moved to act when they see the research findings.

In considering both the practical needs of school leaders and the interest in understanding student leadership experiences at scale, I sought to design a study that could capture varied student experiences while also retaining the depth of understanding made possible through a qualitative approach. Conducting a study to collect longitudinal data or evaluate the impact of student voice programs would require the ability to measure the student leadership experience. As there were very few instruments that measured these experiences, particularly in K–12 settings, I chose to develop such an instrument—a reliable set of scales—using a mixed-methods approach.

In this chapter, I describe how a mixed-methods approach enables researchers to strike an optimal balance between deep understanding of student experiences in specific contexts and a broad understanding of student experiences across contexts, such as identities and school environments. I begin with an introduction to mixed methods and its alignment to the Student Voice Research Framework (SVRF). Then, I provide a step-by-step look at the study design and implementation of a scale development study. Lastly, I use the reflexivity and context tenets from the SVRF to present the lessons I learned from designing, implementing, and reflecting on the study. Such reflections include (a) questioning my true purpose in conducting the study, (b) navigating performative responses from students and staff, (c) discussing the limitations and language considerations of a survey used across contexts, and (d) the implications of the timing of the study, which prevented students from participating in all parts of the study.

MIXED METHODS, SCALE DEVELOPMENT, AND THE STUDENT VOICE RESEARCH FRAMEWORK

Scale development research, a primarily quantitative endeavor, can utilize a two-phase mixed-methods study design. The mixed-methods approach to research is relatively new, forming around the late 1980s, and possesses transformative potential in taking research beyond the QUAN-QUAL (quantitative-qualitative) binary to better understand the depth of student experiences across a wide breadth of identities and contexts. When designing a mixed-methods study, the researcher must consider whether the qualitative and quantitative strands will be independent or interactive, whether one strand will be more dominant, whether the strands will be used sequentially or concurrently, and at which point the strands are mixed (e.g., during data analysis, data collection, at the design stage). A mixed-methods scale development study is well suited to address the various tenets of the SVRF, as youth—power dynamics may be less likely to silence students in an anonymous predominantly quantitative survey and qualitative elements of the study are necessary to facilitate intersubjectivity and understanding of student contexts.

Creswell and Plano Clark (2011) suggest mixed methods when a researcher wants to explain initial findings and more deeply understand a problem through multiple phases. In a scale development study, a qualitative phase could precede the quantitative scale development phase to ensure scale items reflect the word choice students use to talk about the constructs being studied. Alternatively, or in addition to, an initial qualitative phase, a qualitative phase could follow scale development, whereby students are asked to reflect on the data collected and share their interpretation of scale responses and trends in the data. While the two prior examples reflect a sequential mixed-methods design with a pure qualitative phase following or preceding a clear quantitative phase, a scale development study can also take the form of an embedded mixed-methods design. In this case, the researcher might embed open-ended questions (QUAL) into a survey (QUAN) or include a Q-sort, a procedure in which participants organize or rank constructs (QUAN), within interviews (QUAL) (e.g., Gehlbach & Brinkworth, 2011).

Quantitative data helps determine how phenomena are experienced among a wider variety of participants and enables the development of validated instruments (i.e., a scale). To ensure the scale is valid and reliable for respondents in various contexts and for various populations, participants should include students from different schools and school types. A mixed-methods approach makes this possible, because digital survey distribution relieves the researchers from traveling to each school, and if students are part of the research design, digital survey distribution can create a network of student leaders at various schools. The collection of qualitative data also helps determine how phenomena are experienced across different school contexts, improving the quality of data interpretation and analysis.

The mixed-methods approach to scale development aligns to the SVRF, particularly to the tenets of reflexivity and context. Researcher reflexivity is an important part of scale development. In particular, ensuring respondents represent a range of youth voices is critical to a scale's success, as it should be validated for students with diverse backgrounds and experiences seeing as these characteristics may influence a student's level of agreement to scale items (Worthington & Whittaker, 2006). This helps to address issues that can emerge when researchers view students monolithically. Additionally, a study with various opportunities for students to contribute qualitatively to a predominantly quantitative study (i.e., at multiple times in the study and in multiple formats) will strike an ideal balance between deeply understanding students' experiences in context and broadly understanding systemwide educational trends, needs, and ideas for improvement.

Selecting context-appropriate strategies for students can be challenging in scale development research. The scale developer walks a fine line between having a large number of items to ensure variability of responses and keeping the survey short enough to hold students' attention until the final question (DeVellis, 2017). Along the continuum of student involvement in research, students could help develop and refine the language of scale items, provide data by responding to surveys, and help interpret the data through participation in Phase 2 focus groups. In the following sections, I share how I embedded opportunities for these types of student voice in a scale development study as well as critical reflection on how I could have better integrated the SVRF tenets during the study.

DEVELOPMENT AND VALIDATION OF STUDENT LEADERSHIP
CAPACITY BUILDING SCALES[1]

The purpose of my study was to develop and validate three scales that measure the degree to which a school builds student leadership capacity. To expand the research on student voice and student leadership to a school level, I aimed to develop a set of scales that measured Mitchell and Sackney's (2011) three levels of capacity building in schools: personal, interpersonal, and organizational. This framework had been previously used by Brasof (2014) to research student voice at the school level. In addition to determining what factors emerged around these three capacity-building constructs and possible correlations between them, I wanted to get a deeper understanding of students' perceptions of student leadership competencies and the structural mechanisms that enabled students to access leadership opportunities in their schools. I also wanted to determine whether differences emerged across subgroups of students (e.g., year in school, socioeconomic status, first language, race, dis/abilities, academic performance, prior leadership experience). Finally, I wanted to employ qualitative data collection to triangulate the findings, namely, to determine how the scale results aligned with both student and teacher perceptions of student leadership opportunities and experiences. I also sought to understand how school leaders planned to use the findings to further develop student leadership capacity.

Study Design

I used a mixed-methods explanatory sequential design of QUAN(qual) → qual for the study. The purpose of an explanatory sequential design is to explain the quantitative findings. I wanted to center students' voices in an attempt to ground the study in the pursuit of justice with the understanding that the educational system typically excludes students' voices from important conversations about schooling and (at least in the United States) is intimately tied to the aims, policies, and practices of white supremacy. Thus, I employed a transformative perspective, the purpose of which is to identify historical and present-day injustices and challenge them, in part, by elevating the voices of marginalized participants (Mertens, 2003). This study's design aimed to center students' voices in both the quantitative and qualitative phases, using adult voices as points of additional triangulation, but not as the main source of data. This approach seeks to invert the typical power dynamic of adults and students in school settings. Students are often expected to be quiet and compliant and are rarely included in school leadership and decision-making roles, aside from nominal positions in student government organizations whose purview is usually limited to planning social events (e.g., Ozer & Wright, 2012; Pautsch, 2010).

In line with the transformative perspective, I used emancipatory theory in the design and interpretation of research data. Specifically, I examined the degree of inclusion of diverse student voices through an intersectional justice lens, paying particular attention to gender, race, socioeconomic status, first language, and dis/ability. In addition to centering historically marginalized voices, I included space for school stakeholders to discuss and develop a plan of action to transform the structures that have promoted hierarchy and silenced students. This design choice, grounded in justice, was intentional. To disrupt oppressive systems and prompt transformation, the study needed to do more than simply collect data. This aspect of the study design also speaks to the research paradigm of pragmatism, as schools are less likely to take steps toward amplifying equitable, inclusive democracy if the research remains theoretical and does not lead to practical next steps. The paradigm of pragmatism also pairs well with mixed methods as it rejects the traditional quantitative–qualitative binary in favor of a pluralistic use of theories and methods to answer research questions (Johnson & Onwuegbuzie, 2004), which deepens understanding of students' perspectives within and across many school settings and supports the praxis of reflexivity.

Phase 1: Scale Development (QUAN)

The first phase of the study began with the development of three scales designed to measure student leadership capacity building across Mitchell and Sackney's (2011) three dimensions: personal, interpersonal, and organizational. Following the development, review, and pilot of scale items, I used exploratory and confirmatory factor analyses (EFA and CFA) to determine a model fit for each of the proposed scales. The goal of EFA is to find how many constructs underlie the set of items, define these constructs, and reduce the original set of items to only the most relevant items to the constructs. The purpose of CFA is to confirm the initial model is a good fit by analyzing how well the model proposed during the exploratory factor analysis fits and how well individual items fit within the model (Hinkin, 1998). Then, I wanted to know if the items from all three scales would fit into one overarching scale, so I ran the EFA and CFA again for a single-scale model. I also conducted tests to determine if student responses significantly differed by demographic group.

Construct Definition. Prior to generating scale items, a theoretical model along with clear definitions of constructs should be developed (DeVellis, 2017). Clear construct definition is critical for scale reliability and validity scores later in the process (Spector, 1992). A researcher can use existing construct definitions or create original definitions, but it is important to explain the rationale for each decision (Abell, Springer, & Kamata, 2009). A guiding principle in the selection or creation of construct definitions, particularly for scale development, is to ensure a specific construct is being used rather than an overly inclusive category (DeVellis, 2017).

As this study was grounded in the existing student voice literature while also aiming to expand the scope of student voice to the school leadership level, I chose to create my own definition of the central construct the study aimed to measure, which I called student leadership. I defined student leadership as *students working collaboratively to affect positive change in their educational environments with support from adults and mechanisms in the school.* I supported this definition with existing literature such as Redmond's (2013) theory of youth leadership, which highlights the need for students to have both individual leadership skill development and support from adults and school systems and structures. Whereas the construct of student voice speaks to the individual, I chose to develop and use this definition of student leadership because it supports the transformative and emancipatory aims of the study by speaking to the larger structures in place that can systematically exclude or include students from leadership opportunities rather than locating responsibility for voice or leadership activity solely on individual students. Mitchell and Sackney's (2011) three dimensions of capacity building were also used as key constructs around which, I hypothesized, the three sets of scale items would cluster. These dimensions also speak to Redmond's (2013) call for both individual skill development (personal capacity), adult support (interpersonal capacity, known in the student voice literature as youth–adult partnerships), and structural support from the school (organizational capacity).

Other constructs used in this study included three leadership competencies: critical awareness, inclusivity, and positivity. These constructs were specifically chosen to more concretely define student leadership, as youth leadership is far less defined than the field of adult leadership, and also to center justice through the selection of critical awareness and inclusivity as two of the three constructs. Finally, eight student voice mechanisms were used as constructs: radical collegiality (Fielding, 1999a), governance structure, recognition, pedagogy, research, relationship, consistency, and group makeup. These constructs were named and defined as part of a literature review of student voice studies (Lyons, 2018). Identifying these mechanisms helped bring to life the pragmatic aspect of this study. I developed scale items that measured a mechanism construct to enable students and educators to see how specific structures and practices contributed to or limited students' opportunities to exercise leadership in school. The goal was for school stakeholders to be able to pull practical next steps from reading the scale items and student responses. For example, if the scale item "Students and teachers at my school attend workshops or trainings together" received a low score, school leaders would know that an action step could be to design a workshop that served both students and teachers and to ensure that both stakeholder groups were given an opportunity to participate.

My inclusion of these specific constructs and their definitions was based on existing scholarly literature viewed through both transformative and emancipatory lenses. However, the voices of students were critically absent at this point in the study. Looking back, I realize I was hesitant to include students at this point because I assumed students might not identify with the critical aspects of some of the constructs, preferring to focus on the less provocative definitions of leadership that traditional education espouses. The rush to complete the study and frankly, as a graduate student, to stop racking up student debt, also contributed to my decision to exclude students from construct development.

Item Development. The second step was to develop a long list of all possible items. Bernstein and Nunnally (1994) suggest the domain-sampling model of item development in which items are created to represent each domain or subscale within the construct. I used a crosswalk-style table (with the three capacity-building dimensions as columns and the three leadership competencies as rows) to ensure I created at least two items that would measure each construct. I also color-coded the eight mechanism constructs as I drafted items in the table to ensure all mechanism constructs were represented by at least two items.

The initial list of items is supposed to be long. While there are different suggestions for how many items should be drafted, DeVellis's (2017) recommendation of three to four times the number of items anticipated in the final scale represents a middle ground. Considering the study's transformative and emancipatory aims, it was also important to consider the accessibility of the scales to students who struggle academically or for whom English is a second or additional (3rd, 4th, etc.) language. For this reason, the number of items needed to be manageable for students who, because of these learning struggles, have likely been disproportionately excluded from leadership opportunities. Similarly, I chose to avoid using negative items as the additional mental strain of processing negative items can confuse the respondent and ultimately decrease the reliability of a scale (Gehlbach & Brinkworth, 2011).

I developed the items as statements with a six-point agreement response scale: 1 (strongly disagree), 2 (disagree), 3 (somewhat disagree), 4 (somewhat agree), 5 (agree), and 6 (strongly agree). The initial item pool contained 77 items, which I analyzed to ensure the lowest reading level possible using the website Rewordify.com. Across each of the three proposed scales, the Flesch-Kincaid reading score ranged from 5th to 8th grade with 12 low-frequency words, one of which was defined in the context above the item. I asked several researchers, educators, and students to review the items for clarity and construct alignment. Students also had the opportunity to ask questions or provide verbal feedback in lieu of or in addition to written feedback so as not to preclude students who have difficulty writing from providing feedback.

Pilot. I delivered the scale items to participants in the context of a survey. Surveys should be organized like a conversation, paying particular attention to the order of questions (Baron, 2018). Immediately following a small number of questions that determine eligibility for inclusion in the study, Baron advises beginning with interesting questions that draw in the respondent and help them reflect on the topic. The first page of my first scale read began with a definition of leadership skills: "Here you will be asked to think about the opportunities you have to develop leadership skills in school. Examples of leadership skills are critically reflecting on your actions, considering different points of view, or identifying your strengths." Following this contextual statement, the overarching question read, "Thinking about learning leadership skills in school, how strongly do you agree or disagree with the following statements?" From there, students responded to items that presented a specific example of what this might look like in their school. The goal of conversational-survey design is to maximize the value and minimize the frustration of the participants. Questions should be broken into sections by topic, and an open-ended question should follow each topic area to provide space for additional comments or reflection. Demographic questions are best placed at the end of the survey, as they are not engaging, nor does it follow a natural conversational flow to ask a list of demographic questions at the start. An optimal survey length is 10 to 15 minutes.

To support alignment between research strategies and students' contexts, I conducted the pilot test with 38 students to ensure that student respondents understood the items and directions and that they could smoothly complete the survey. Pilot test participants included students in one of my multilingual high school classes who were learning English as a second or additional language. No significant changes were made to the personal or interpersonal scales. A few items in the organizational scale were changed after the pilot.

Data Collection. The prescribed sample size for factor analysis varies, but a common suggestion is 300 respondents in order to achieve statistical significance and reliable internal consistency (Nunnally, 1978). In addition to ensuring an appropriate size, the sample must be representative. Worthington and Whittaker (2006) noted that it is "not necessary to closely represent any clearly identified population as long as those who would score high and those who would score low are well represented" (p. 816). However, it is wise to include a diverse set of people in case certain characteristics influence the construct being measured. If a sample is not representative, the relationship between items and constructs may vary from the relationship in the larger population (DeVellis, 2017).

In this study, student participants attended either an urban or a rural public high school. All students had an opportunity to take the survey within the school day as long as they had been in the high school for a minimum of 3 months. Seven urban schools located in New York City, one rural school in New York state, and one rural school in Vermont allowed me to invite their students to complete the survey. All urban schools in the study were portfolio schools, which meant students completed portfolios in lieu of standardized tests for graduation. Three of these seven schools were designed specifically to serve students who were new to the United States and new to the English language.

At each school, I distributed paper fliers with a QR code or emailed the survey link for students to access the survey. I chose this approach because students at my school regularly used their school-provided iPads to scan QR codes in academic settings. Three of the schools in the study shared one lunchroom in which students had to stand in a long line for typically 10–15 minutes to get food, so this was an opportunity for students to use their phones to complete the survey while waiting in line (demonstrating the SVRF principle of being responsive to students' contexts, which helped with response rates). Students were given time to complete the survey in study halls, advisories, town hall meetings, lunch time, or (in one school) as a bellringer activity in students' Social Studies class. The first page of the survey informed students participating in Phase 1 of their rights to remain anonymous and to refuse participation. In addition, I verbally informed students of their right to refuse in person (or in the case of the two schools I could not travel to, via video). Despite this precaution, comments from respondents in one school indicated that the way the survey was presented to them and the time it was presented (during their Social Studies class period) may have made some students feel pressured to complete the survey, which was a clear outcome of my inability to present the study face to face. After completing the survey, the last page invited students to email me if they were interested in participating in a focus group to discuss student leadership further.

Data Analysis. Following data collection, I cleaned the data prior to analysis because one group of students (students from one of the rural schools) was heavily overrepresented. To do this, I used a randomly selected subsample from the overrepresented group in the final sample ($n = 280$). I analyzed the survey results using exploratory factor analysis in IBM SPSS and CFA in Amos. In addition to the factor analyses, both SPSS and Amos were used for descriptive and comparative statistics related to the leadership competencies and mechanisms for building student leadership capacity.

Factor analysis is a data reduction process that seeks to determine the fewest number of items that can fully describe and measure the constructs. I conducted an exploratory factor analysis using principal component analysis (PCA). PCA uses the term "components" instead of factors and measures the total variance of items. Components are defined by how participants respond to scale items (DeVellis, 2017). I retained factor structures accounting for approximately 60% or more of the variance, and I deleted items that did not load on a component at .40 or higher or that loaded on more than one component at .40 or higher. Cronbach's alpha is "one of the most important indicators of a scale's quality" and, specifically, its reliability (Nunnally, 1978, p. 94). He goes on to say that "reliability is a necessary condition for validity" (p. 131). Cronbach's alpha ranges from zero to one and serves as a measure of reliability that indicates how well items in a scale vary together. For good reliability, Cronbach's alpha should be higher than .70 but less than .90 (p. 248).

Following PCA, I conducted CFA to confirm the initial model fit. During this procedure, I tested the scale for convergent validity (strong correlations with existing scales measuring similar concepts), discriminant validity (low correlations with scales measuring different concepts), and predictive validity (ability to predict outcomes). I considered modification indices over 15 and standardized residual covariances over 1 for deletion. I tested the resulting models for goodness of fit. In making decisions about the final models, it is important to make sure the factor models have practical relevance. Pragmatism is a relevant lens here. As DeVellis (2017) warns, sometimes too many factors are included and "there is no guarantee that a more complex model that statistically outperforms a simpler alternative is a more accurate reflection of reality" (p. 198). In line with the study's transformative, emancipatory grounding, I reviewed all the final scale models for optimal length (to reduce student fatigue or excessive cognitive strain) while also ensuring model quality.

Following CFA, I conducted comparative analysis to determine differences between demographic groups. Demographic questions in the survey included grade, length of time in the school, race, home language, and dis/ability (whether a student has an Individualized Education Program [IEP]). I ran metric invariance in Amos to determine if participants' responses to scale items significantly differed by demographic group. For example, this analysis helps determine whether students with IEPs reported feeling less support from the school in developing leadership than students without dis/abilities. I computed mean scores for each construct and analyzed these data to determine if significant differences existed between schools on mean scores for student leadership competencies or mechanisms.

Phase 2: Focus Groups, Interview, Open-Ended Survey Questions (QUAL)

The purpose of the qualitative phase was to deepen understanding about students' opportunities to build leadership capacity. In addition to the open-ended survey prompts (e.g., if you have any specific examples or comments about "x" you would like to share, please type them here), I conducted post-survey focus groups and interviews to determine the degree to which school stakeholders found the scale results to be reflective of their experience at their schools and useful for practice. In this phase, participants also suggested improvements to how survey data was collected from students and how results were reported to schools.

I offered all survey respondents the option of giving narrative responses to the open-ended survey questions. Student participants were eligible for the interviews or focus groups if they completed the Phase 1 survey and indicated their interest in participating in a follow-up discussion. After completing the survey, students were invited to email the researcher if they were interested in participating in Phase 2. This preserved anonymity, as participant names were separated from survey responses. Adult participants were eligible to participate in the focus groups or interviews if they worked with students who took the survey (e.g., teachers, paraprofessionals, instructional coaches, administrators). Students needed to obtain a guardian's signature on the consent form in addition to their own signature on an assent form prior to the start of the focus group. Focus groups were scheduled for times in which interested participants were available.

Data Collection. I received a total of 107 narrative responses from students in all of the schools in the study via the open-ended questions on the survey. One focus group consisted of three students from one school, and one focus group consisted of 10 staff members from the same school. One teacher from another school participated in an interview. First, I showed participants all of the schools' mean scores for the items measuring the eight mechanisms, with their school's scores highlighted. Then, using a semi-structured interview protocol, I asked participants to answer several questions. Predetermined questions for focus group participants were as follows:

- What are your thoughts about these results?
- How useful is this information to your work?
- How do you plan to use this information?
- How could the survey or report of results be improved?
- What are your thoughts about the underlying leadership competencies of critical awareness, inclusivity, and positivity?

Data Analysis. I used the process of inductive coding suggested by Boyatzis (1998) to analyze my qualitative data. Once focus group and interview data were transcribed, I used memoing to create categories and indexed the raw focus group and interview data into categories. Next, I produced an outline by reducing the raw information, identifying themes in the subsamples, and comparing themes across subsamples. I applied the codes to the narrative responses to the open-ended survey questions and identified differences in subsamples in relation to the identified themes. I synthesized qualitative findings from the different schools into overarching themes that may be transferable and useful in a variety of school contexts.

While no students expressed interest in helping to code the data, there were several opportunities to include participant voices at this point in the study. I could have returned to the Phase 2 participants to ask if they would add anything given the additional narrative from other respondents. To better triangulate the analysis, I could have also invited students who had not yet participated in the study to help make sense of the data and push back on my interpretation.

LESSONS LEARNED

Up until this point in the chapter, I have shared the considerations and reflections on the research design and process of this mixed-methods study. I have alluded to the principles of the SVRF, but now I will reflectively and specifically name the strengths and limitations of this study using the tenets of the framework, in particular reflexivity and context.

Researcher Reflexivity

In the study design phase, there was intentional consideration of the question "Who (which youth) are asked to respond, and does this represent a range of voices?" Seeking respondents from both urban and rural settings and excluding suburban settings sought to disrupt the place-based power dynamics that often result in suburban students having more voice than students in rural or urban school districts.

I addressed my positionality as a researcher when this study was initially published as a dissertation. I acknowledged the contexts of my teaching experience (what, where, and who I taught) as well as my research interests and my presumption that student leadership is both possible and beneficial. However, I do not name my white skin, native language, or able-bodied advantages as part of the teacher–student power dynamic, and I do not interrogate the white liberalist idea of white saviorism, which I can now see that I brought with me when I first decided to teach in schools serving predominantly Black and Brown students. Had I answered Brasof and Levitan's suggested question, "Why do I do research with children?" when I began this study, I would have answered: to help students. By the end of the study, I was fortunate enough to have learned that student voice research is not intended solely to help marginalized students, but to improve all school stakeholders' experiences of the system of schooling. Had I named this intention up-front, it may have enabled students to see not just the value of their leadership but the need for it. Perhaps this would have yielded more honest data.

This also ties into the SVRF concept of intersubjectivity. I was a teacher at one of the schools that participated in this study. The student and educator focus groups consisted of participants from that school, certainly a limitation of the study on its own. While my existing relationship with study participants may have had a positive effect, as I had been able to create a foundation of trust with my students and colleagues (power dynamics) and I had demonstrated my support for student-led action research and activism, that familiarity may have also resulted in student performativity, particularly in the focus group. For example, one student seemed to justify a lack of leadership opportunities for students, citing the likelihood they would be irresponsible and sharing, "Now there are no more iPads in the hallways I guess because students were given too many opportunities and they took advantage of it." That performativity may have also shown up in students' responses to the survey, not just in the school where I taught, but in all of the schools that served students new to the United States. Many of the students in this network of schools migrated from countries experiencing instability, which interrupted students' learning. As a result, many of my students have told me (in other contexts) that they felt hesitant to critique their school, explaining they were grateful for the presence of a stable schooling experience and preferring to focus on the things the school did well. The power dynamics inherent in the school environment likely also contributed to students' tendency to engage in victim-blaming behavior rather than critique oppressive systems. Assuming this was the case for all students would be an inaccurate generalization, but it may have influenced some students' responses. Finally, the presence of a collegial dynamic between me as a researcher and the adult focus group participants may have brought school culture norms of what can and cannot be discussed into the conversation. Similar to Marc's story in Chapter 1, if I had raised questions that enabled student and adult participants to broaden the focus of our conversation to critically examine assumptions and patterns of behavior at the school and facilitate critical voice, we may have been able to break out of our old relationship patterns and form new relationships that better illuminated participants' experiences.

Strategy–Context Congruence

This tenet was a major consideration as I thought through my research approach. Initially, I wanted to design a study that created opportunities for students to be co-researchers. However, in talking to students about their desire and—perhaps more importantly—their capacity to take on the work of a co-researcher, I decided to rethink my study design. Returning to the importance of researcher reflexivity, I had to ask whether I wanted to engage students as co-researchers because it would actually advance student leadership or if it would just make me look like a better student voice researcher if a wide range of students actively participated. The study was conducted in the final 2 months of school, and students were spending all of their time and mental energy on studying for final exams or finishing their cumulative portfolio projects. I asked nearly 100 students if they were interested in being co-researchers on this project, and none of them expressed interest. A cynical read of that situation would have been that students are not willing to put in the work or do not want to be leaders. The reality of the situation was that this strategy was at odds with what I was aiming to achieve with the study. I hoped my study would enhance students' experience of school, but in pushing for students to join me as co-researchers, I may have had a few say "Yes" because they felt obliged to make me happy, and in doing so, I would have made matters much worse for those students.

The language of the survey was another critical piece for strategy–purpose congruence. My aim was to center historically marginalized students, which included students who may have struggled to understand challenging English vocabulary or complex sentence structures. To address this concern, I invited and received student feedback on each draft item, and I checked each item for readability. However, a more student-centered approach to item construction would have been to add a qualitative phase to the start of the study and invite students to talk through some of the concepts in an interview or focus group to generate items from the language students used. Of course, a challenge with this approach is ensuring the language used is representative and accessible for all prospective respondents, because student language may vary from school to school and from student to student.

Another challenge was how to hold the focus groups. On one hand, holding mixed stakeholder focus groups would have enabled students and educators to practice youth–adult partnership in analyzing and action planning around data. On the other hand, because my study did not lay the groundwork for that degree of collaboration, it may have further limited students' perception that they could speak honestly if they were speaking in front of teachers. Either way, triangulating the perspectives of three groups—students, educators, and myself as a researcher—provided opportunities to deepen everyone's understanding of how student leadership was perceived at a school and highlighted points of disagreement or mismatched perceptions.

Finally, the quantitative nature of scale development studies limited students' opportunity to fully share their perspectives on the topic of student leadership, whereas in a predominantly qualitative study, more detail would have emerged. Once more, this is a careful balancing act of demands on student energy and investment and centering students in all aspects of the research. If funding was available, paying students (one of the student voice mechanisms used in the study) to engage more deeply in this research project may have provided a solution that took into account the financial need of many students and conveyed a sense that their time was of value.

NOTE

1. For reference, the Building Student Leadership Capacity Scale is available at bit.ly/SLCBsurvey and is free for use.

CHAPTER 11

Intersecting Voices

An Integrative Approach to Applying the Student Voice Research Framework in Teacher Education

Alison Cook-Sather, Heather Curl, and Chanelle Wilson

In the Bryn Mawr/Haverford Education Program, in which we all have served as faculty, a student wrote the following about research:

> Research is not neutral or objective. It's historically founded on whiteness being the authority of knowledge and extracting that knowledge from Black, Indigenous, disabled, and/or LGBTQIA+ beings/bodies. People are not oil reserves to extract information from and generate wealth. Transforming social science research, I believe, means academics and "professionals" relinquishing their power and co-creating knowledge while prioritizing human connection, trust, care, and continued support in the after. (L. Lattimore)

This student's vision of research—as co-creation of knowledge that honors the humanity and capacity of all involved, particularly those who have been underrepresented in but often exploited by higher education—is the vision that informs our work as well. We see such research as a way of life in our profession and a mode of being in our program. The co-research in which we engage through a project called Teaching and Learning Together (TLT) constitutes the culminating phase of an approach to teacher education that enacts and advocates for an "intersecting voices" approach. This approach prepares college students to be future educators who embrace the fundamental understanding that teacher–student collaboration is the only way that learning meaningfully happens. Every participant in TLT—college students, university-based educators, secondary students, and school-based educators—is at once a learner, a teacher, and a researcher, and our practices strive for an integrative approach to applying the Student Voice Research Framework (SVRF) in teacher education.

In this chapter we begin by providing some contextual information about our program and describing the structure for the integrative approach that TLT enacts. We follow this programmatic description with a discussion of the theoretical framework that guides this work. We then explore our approach using the principles of the SVRF: intersubjectivity, reflexivity, power dynamics, and the use of research strategies grounded in student context and perspectives. We conclude with takeaways that may be helpful to others who aim to create approaches to undergraduate teacher preparation that integrates multiple voices and that positions all participants as simultaneous learners, teachers, and researchers.

TEACHING AND LEARNING TOGETHER IN TEACHER PREPARATION

Just over 25 years ago, Alison and a school-based educator created TLT in the context of the secondary teacher education program at Bryn Mawr and Haverford Colleges. The first iteration of an approach that has since come to define the Bryn Mawr/Haverford Education Program's mode of teacher education as partnership (Cook-Sather, 2021), TLT aimed to "re(in)form" the conversations (Cook-Sather, 2002a) through which secondary teachers are prepared for classroom practice. It did so by disrupting the normalized hierarchy that positions university-based theorists and researchers alone to generate pedagogical knowledge. This hierarchy is passed down to/imposed on teachers, with students as recipients of this knowledge and practice. The form of "radical collegiality" (Fielding, 1999a) that TLT enacts repositions secondary students, their voices, and their perspectives as central to teacher education (Cook-Sather, 2021; Cook-Sather & Curl, 2016; Cook-Sather & Youens, 2007) and positions all involved in that education as co-researchers of teaching and learning. If the cultivation of high-quality, person-centered, and socially just learning communities (Fielding, 1999a) begins during the pre-professional development stage of teacher education, prospective teachers are more likely to carry these convictions and capacities into their practice (Cook-Sather 2006a, 2009b; Wilson, under review).

Each of us has facilitated and further developed TLT—Alison from 1995 to 2008, Heather from 2008 to 2018, and Chanelle from 2018 through the present. Our approach enacts a research methodology that is premised on student voice principles and that uses qualitative methods to produce knowledge for each and all of the participant-researchers involved, both in the moment and over time. These participant-researchers include

- college students: undergraduate, preservice teachers who are seeking secondary teaching certification through the Bryn Mawr/ Haverford Education Program;

- university-based educators: instructors who teach the secondary methods course for undergraduate, preservice teachers in which TLT is situated;
- secondary students: high school students who are paired with each preservice teacher seeking certification through the Bryn Mawr/ Haverford Education Program; and
- school-based educators: teachers who serve as facilitators of the secondary students' participation.

TLT has five components, each of which constitutes and contributes to the project as a form of student voice research (see Appendix B online, accessible from the product page for this volume on www.tcpress.com):

1. One-on-One Electronic Exchanges
2. Weekly School-Based Conversations among Secondary Students
3. Weekly College-Based Class Discussions among College Students
4. Two, One-time, Reciprocal, Site Visits
5. Final Reflective Analysis

The interaction of these components is visually depicted in Figure 11.1, and expanded discussions of them, including prompts and examples, are included in Appendix B.

Figure 11.1. Interaction of TLT's Five Components

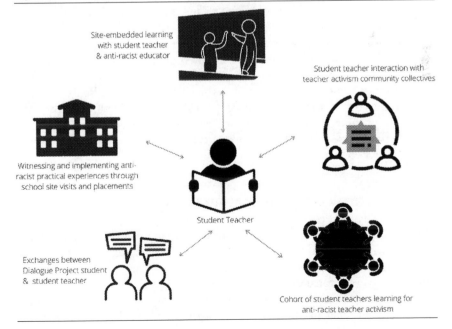

Site-embedded learning with student teacher & anti-racist educator

Student teacher interaction with teacher activism community collectives

Witnessing and implementing anti-racist practical experiences through school site visits and placements

Student Teacher

Exchanges between Dialogue Project student & student teacher

Cohort of student teachers learning for anti-racist teacher activism

Other assignments frame this multifaceted project for the college students, including reading theoretical and practical texts. The school-based educator invites a diverse group of students to participate in TLT each year, including students of various genders who are assigned to different tracks and who claim different racial, ethnic, and class backgrounds. Therefore, the data sources noted in relation to the five components of TLT are triangulated with theoretical (published) explorations of students' schooling experiences and field notes from (lived) school visits. The insights generated through the lived exchanges, and analyses of them, contribute to the knowledge the secondary and college students, as well as we (the college instructors), produce, thereby striving to enact co-creation of knowledge and prioritization of "human connection, trust, care, and continued support" that the education student, Lauren Lattimore, calls for in research in the quote with which we opened this chapter. When we seek ethics-board approval for research beyond the confines of the course, these data sources inform the scholarship we share with the wider community of teacher educators (e.g., Cook-Sather, 2006a, 2007a, 2007b; Cook-Sather & Curl, 2014, 2016; Curl & Cook-Sather, 2021).

TLT is designed to provide both one-on-one dialogue between a single secondary student and a single college student and exposure to the range of experiences and perspectives of all the secondary students and college students involved, thereby accessing depth and breadth of perspective. Because all undergraduates seeking certification to teach at the secondary level through the Bryn Mawr/Haverford Education Program are required to participate in the multipart, multiparticipant design we describe here, all participants engage in the co-investigation, co-analysis, and co-creation of knowledge about and practices of teaching. For the college- and secondary-student partners, the initial and most intensive phase of this co-creation unfolds over the course of a single semester, and then both groups carry their learnings into subsequent contexts. For the university- and school-based educators, the co-creation is an iterative process, enacted anew each year with each new group of student co-researchers, but also sustained over many years as part of an ongoing research project. For these reasons, we describe this project as one of intersecting voices.

THEORETICAL FRAMEWORK

The theoretical underpinning of our approach is that student perspectives and voices are essential to analyses and development of teacher and learner identities, teaching and learning approaches, and teacher–student relationships. These are informed by research methods grounded in humanization, arguments for young people's rights within their education, and student voice and student–teacher partnership as forms of equity work. We first ground our work in research focused on relationship building and humanization of both researcher and participant. We then review rights-centered, equity-focused arguments for student voice. Finally, we discuss how those emphases and arguments inform our approach to situating student perspectives and voices as central to analyses and development of teacher and learner identities, teaching and learning approaches, and teacher–student relationships.

Research for Relationship Building and Humanization

Though research is often framed as an objective and neutral process void of power and bias, it has been shown time and again that, as Lauren's words at the opening of our chapter articulate, research that does not intentionally disrupt power dynamics ultimately serves to perpetuate oppression, reifies societal power dynamics, and can lead to harm (Tuck, 2009). As the framework for student voice research explored in this book makes clear, engaging in research with young people from a *neutral* paradigm can lead to, at best, misinformed data and, at worst, the perpetuation of oppression of young people by researchers. As a challenge to research that perpetuates power dynamics and oppression, Paris (2011) argues instead for "humanizing research," which he defines as "a methodological stance which requires that our inquiries involve dialogic consciousness-raising and the building of relationships of care and dignity for both researchers and participants" (pp. 139–140). One can also conceptualize this work as starting with methods premised on mutual respect, acknowledgment, and feeling for shared humanity, and that refuse and resist anything that erodes or threatens these premises (A. Lesnick, personal communication, June 14, 2020). Similarly, as part of a project to "decolonize and humanize educational research," San Pedro and Kinloch (2017, p. 374) articulate a research methodology grounded in dialogic relationship building through storytelling. This framework of education research, named Projects in Humanization, is "enacted through the development of relationships, the process of listening and storying, and the dialogic engagements that occur during the telling and receiving of stories that have the potential to effect change" (p. 374).

The work of *humanizing* through dialogic *consciousness-raising*, *relationship building*, and *storytelling* serves as a foundation for the various forms of research TLT invites, including (a) the learning that both secondary and college students achieve through dialogue with one another, (b) the telling and receiving of stories accomplished in weekly seminars that serve as a source of learning, and (c) the listening, sharing, and learning engaged by both university- and school-based educators. Educators also have the potential to become more humanized, from student perspectives, as they model reflexivity and active learning as facilitators. And finally, students are humanized as their experiences and perspectives are taken up as texts and through relationships to learn from by college students studying to become teachers. The impact of teachers and their decisions—to foster or limit learning and growth—is revealed in the lives and stories of real students with whom relationships have been built. TLT is grounded in the belief that listening, sharing, and relationship building are foundational components of effective and equitable teaching. In this way, the research engaged through all parties in TLT offers an experiential pathway through which both students and educators can learn and practice these foundational components of education.

Rights-Centered, Equity-Focused Arguments for Student Voice

Although the United States is the only country in the world not to have ratified the United Nations Convention on the Rights of the Child (UNCRC), many teacher educators—and we count ourselves among them—feel that it is a matter of ethical imperative to create "rights-respecting" curricula and pedagogy that include the perspectives, voices, and participation of students (Curl & Cook-Sather, 2021; Lundy & Cook-Sather, 2016). As Lundy and Cook-Sather (2016) have argued, given that curriculum and pedagogy are the medium and mode of student and teacher participation in learning processes, "if student voices are absent from these, or only allowed in response to adult decisions and directions, then students' right to express their views freely in all matters affecting them and their right to have those views be given due weight, as specified in Article 12 of the CRC, are denied" (p. 267). As Alison has argued elsewhere, the assertion of students' rights through voice and participation is a call for a shift away "from an adult-centric, infantilizing and disempowering set of attitudes and practices" toward conceptualizing students as "among those with the right to take their place 'in whatever discourse is essential to action' and the right to have their part matter (Heilbrun, 1988, p. 18)" (Cook-Sather, 2006b, p. 370). To have a voice, as Solnit (2020) argues, is to experience three things: "audibility, credibility, and consequence" (p. 229)—to be heard, to be believed, and to matter. As Solnit (2020) explains, "if you matter, you have rights, and your words serve those rights and give you the power to bear witness," and if you are a person of consequence, "your words possess the authority to determine what does and does not happen to you" (p. 230).

Narrow conceptions of success and white supremacist, anti-immigrant rhetoric and policy limit education's enactment of rights-based education as articulated in Article 29 of the UNCRC. Stained with a founding that included displacement, murder, and enslavement of non-white peoples, the United States has developed an educational system that mirrors the inequity of its beginning (Curl & Cook-Sather, 2021). While this system once overtly enacted these inequities through banning education for some groups of people and, subsequently, racially segregating schools, it now "egregiously" invests unevenly in public schooling, both within and across states (Baker,

Farrie, & Sciarra, 2018, p. 23). Teacher education runs the risk of perpetu-
ating these inequities if it does not respond to the mandates of Article 29,
including that "children's education should develop a child's personality, tal-
ents and abilities to the fullest" and that educators "encourage children to
respect others, human rights and their own and other cultures," with a particular focus on education's role in "develop[ing] respect for the values and
culture of [students'] parents" (UNCRC, 1989). Though certainly not pur-
porting to "fix" the injustices (both historical and ongoing) just described,
individual projects such as TLT strive to enact tenets of Article 29 in two
distinct ways: (a) informing the mindset and beliefs of the college student,
and (b) understanding and practicing education in equity-focused, ecological, and sustainable terms (Curl & Cook-Sather, 2021). As Heather and
Alison have argued elsewhere, "Because TLT is itself premised on respect
for and attention to students' experiences and perspectives, it in turn fosters
the development of teachers who value and insist on encouraging children
to respect others, human rights, and their own and other cultures" (Curl &
Cook-Sather, 2021).

The equity focus and "ecological perspective" (Cook-Sather & Curl,
2014) embraced and enacted by TLT contribute to college students' learning—
and supporting their students in learning—to consider and combat inequities, live peacefully, protect the environment, and respect other people
(Curl & Cook-Sather, 2021). It structures student voice and pedagogical
partnership into teacher education to reveal and challenge inequity (Cook-
Sather, 2020). In human rights terms, it strives to enact a form of respect
"centered on notions of dignity and equality" that underpins "all rights-
based approaches" (Lundy & Cook-Sather, 2016, p. 273).

Centering Student Perspectives and Voices

A relationship-building, humanizing, rights-based, and equity-focused approach to teacher education ensures that student perspectives and voices
are essential to analyses and development of teacher and learner identities.
The experiences college students have in their teacher education influence
their conceptions of themselves as teachers (Beauchamp & Thomas, 2009;
Darling-Hammond & Oakes, 2021; Graham & Phelps, 2003; Hahl &
Mikulec, 2018). Whether they see themselves as authorities who deposit information into the empty heads of learners (Freire, 1998) or as partners in
caring relationships that focus on social and emotional as well as intellectual
development (Darling-Hammond & Oakes, 2021) will make a difference in
how they conceptualize and enact their teaching practice. Furthermore, if
future teachers develop an understanding of their own ethnic and racial
identities, prejudices, and implicit biases, they can more clearly see their students, view classroom interactions, and understand students' families from
positive racial perspectives (Wilson, under review).

Student perspectives and voices are essential to analyses and development of teaching and learning approaches. Students are often represented as receptors of knowledge transferred to them through educators; we challenge this notion, recognizing that considering socio-constructivist principles (Brau, 2021), all people in a classroom are contributing to the knowledge construction occurring during teaching and learning. Positioning secondary students as sources of knowledge for college students necessitates the understanding that education is constantly evolving, faster than university-based research and publications can keep up. This partnership between students and future teachers allows our college student candidates for teacher certification to engage in practices responsive to contemporary education, and it strengthens a foundation of collaboration between students and teachers that college students can take into their teaching practice.

Student perspectives and voices are essential to analyses and development of teacher–student relationships. When students' perspectives and voices are centered in the development of teacher–student relationships, it invites students to participate in their learning in a way that may influence students' conceptions of their value in a learning space. Disrupting hierarchical structures by inviting secondary students and college students to build relationships and engage in reciprocal partnerships begins the development of a practice that should be fundamental in education. This shift away from top-down or neutral (read professional distance) allows for humanizing connections. It provides teachers and students with the opportunity to see each other beyond the lenses of their perceived roles, and this may lead to a deeper sense of belonging and the extension of grace from teachers to students, between students and their peers, and from students to their teachers.

EXPLORING INTERSECTING VOICES THROUGH THE STUDENT VOICE RESEARCH FRAMEWORK

The intersecting voices approach TLT embraces offers an example of how to enact all four of the interrelated SVRF principles and strategies for engaging with youth in research. For intersubjectivity, we explain how this is a topic of ongoing conversation and a focus of ongoing negotiation as the project unfolds over the course of the semester. The kinds of voice preservice teachers, we as facilitators, secondary students, and school-based facilitators use as the project unfolds shift as we build relationships through dialogue. For reflexivity, we focus on our own lived experiences and the commitments derived from them and on how we identify student participants and structure conversation across perspectives, and how we all learn to engage in respectful dialogue across differences. Regarding power dynamics, we discuss how our coursework and the TLT project explores and revisits issues of power and how the four different institutional positions we occupy—secondary students, school-based educators, college students, and university-based educators—throw power dynamics into particularly stark relief. Finally, in terms of strategies congruent with students' contexts, cultures, experiences, perspectives, and knowledge, we discuss how students draw on their particular lived experiences and insights to offer sources of data, to be active respondents, and to act as co-researchers (Fielding, 2004).

Learning and taking up the idea that "we're all learning" is what makes this approach research and, in particular, what Paris (2011) calls *humanizing research*. Such research takes a methodological stance that requires inquiries to involve "dialogic consciousness-raising and the building of relationships of dignity and care for both researchers and participants" (Paris, 2011, p. 140). Committed to equity, this research approach endeavors to enact what Lauren calls for: "co-creating knowledge while prioritizing human connection, trust, care, and continued support."

Intersubjectivity

TLT is presented to college students and secondary students as composed of multiple spaces or venues through which individuals in both groups have various opportunities to use their own voices. Students see how their voices matter as they are structured into TLT's approach to teacher preparation. College-based educators, school-based educators, and college students are all looking to the secondary students as co-educators of our future teachers; these research relationships invite students' critical and authoritative voices.

Bragg (2007) argued that "what [students] say depends on what they are asked, how they are asked it, 'who' they are invited to [embody] in responding" (p. 31). There are at least three ways in which these questions are addressed in TLT. In the semester-long research project that is TLT, secondary students are asked in weekly email exchanges to address from their lived experiences and critical perspectives questions the college students explore in the college course, but they often move far beyond these basic areas of focus, depending on what each brings. In some cases, for instance, secondary students commiserate with college students as they study for exams, struggle with homework, or navigate a home/school balance. In other instances, secondary students share instances of racism they have experienced in their classrooms, seek advice about future steps, or share concerns about mental health and the need for self-care. In these questions, and others, college students work to listen deeply, demonstrate care, and in the context of the college seminar, seek support for how to best build relationships and learn. There is, of course, variation in the identities and attitudes both secondary students and college students bring, so no two exchanges are ever the same.

The one-on-one exchanges are triangulated by the full-group meetings of the secondary students facilitated by school-based educators, and here it is the school-based educators asking the students and the students asking and sharing with one another. This forum is complicated in terms of intersubjectivity, since the school-based educators and the secondary students might have various relationships, which might prompt the students to adopt a performative voice instead of sharing genuine insights (Cammarota & Fine, 2008; Conner, 2015; Johnson, 2018a), or to actively resist or work against the authority of the school-based educator. In recent semesters, college students and secondary students have supported the occurrence of secondary students facilitating their own full-group dialogue sessions at their school. This has allowed for the school-based educator to play a more observant role, thereby more fully taking up the position of learner, and afforded secondary students the opportunity to exercise their leadership capacity, enacting a teaching role. Further, this relinquishing of control on the school-based educator's part led to a new secondary student coordinator position. A secondary student who had participated in a previous year wished to return and suggested that she could serve in this role, essentially creating the position for herself. This student coordinator gives both the school-based and college-based educator feedback on topics selected for group discussion, develops discussion questions for the group, facilitates some group discussions, and supports new secondary student partners throughout TLT.

The one-on-one and group conversations are triangulated further through the full-group meetings of the college students facilitated by college-based educators, where the one-on-one exchanges and the audio recordings of the school-based meetings bring the secondary student voices into further dialogue with one another and with the theories the college students are exploring. The secondary student voices are treated as legitimate sources of knowledge alongside published research and the college students' own perceptions, understandings, and internalization of different ideologies. In these conversations, where multiple student voices are juxtaposed, the college students sometimes hear echoes and affirmations of what their own secondary student partners have articulated and sometimes learn of very different, sometimes contradictory, experiences and perspectives as those are shared by college students who are in dialogue with different secondary students. To support a generative reflective process, the university-based educator facilitates discussion in which theoretical arguments are positioned alongside divergent data from the student perspective—or examples where student perspectives are divergent themselves. College students discuss what might be contributing to these differences—what remains consistent; how context, identity, and perspective might be informing what we know/is known; and what questions remain. These consonances and complexities contribute to creating a context in which college students preparing to be teachers "dig deeper," to look for "hidden relationships" and "consider multiple possible interpretations (Fazey, 2010) in and of the voices they hear" (Cook-Sather & Curl, 2014, p. 101).

Reflexivity

As researchers and teacher educators, the three of us grew up under different circumstances, and each of us had childhood experiences that informed our ways of conceptualizing youth and facilitating the intersecting voices approach we take. Furthermore, because our approach has evolved over more than 25 years, the individual experiences, conceptualizations, and commitments each of us brings have played out in the context of different historical moments—in relation to student voice work in particular and active youth engagement more generally—as well as within a programmatic evolution toward partnership as an ethos. In this section we trace the evolution of TLT in relation to our own formative experiences and how the contexts in which TLT has evolved have informed college students' reflexive practice.

Chanelle, a Black woman, was raised by a single mother, who prioritized learning and created and seized *almost* every teachable moment. Chanelle's mother had a doctorate in Urban Education and was climbing the ranks in school administration; Chanelle was inspired by the relationships she witnessed her mother build with students and the attention her mother paid to their academic, social, and emotional needs. Her co-parenting father also valued learning, but through nontraditional methods. Both instilled the need to critique society and disrupt power structures for the benefit of the oppressed, and both argued that the only way to do this was through knowing, not simply performing in traditional classroom spaces, but engaging in deep self-designed inquiry and problem-based discovery. Being homeschooled for 7 years made this possible for Chanelle, and it presented a powerful contrast to the teaching and learning she experienced in public school. This upbringing informed Chanelle's future teaching practice and inclination to teach for equity, inspired her to invite student perspectives and voices in collaborative learning, and fostered her proclivity for prioritizing and building relationships.

Heather, a white woman, found school to be a refuge from a dysfunctional home, and through the support of an educational nonprofit meant to support "at risk youth who showed academic promise," she earned entry and a full scholarship to a nearby elite private high school. The first in her family to attend college, Heather learned through these educational experiences the strategy of "performance" and how to say and do what people—particularly teachers—wanted in order to get what she needed to ensure academic success. Later in graduate school, Heather worked (and continues to work many years later) to unlearn this practice, and she seeks authenticity in her educational experiences as student, teacher, professor, and researcher. She brought this appreciation for student voices *as they are* and an honoring of the insight all students bring to her work with TLT and notes how important it is that teachers become aware of the cultural and behavioral expectations they place on students, particularly when attempting to learn their perspective.

Alison, a white woman, grew up with significant socioeconomic privilege and attended well-resourced schools. This privilege intersected, however, with parental divorce and alcoholism, which created conditions that made her feel unseen and unheard. This confluence of access and inattention engendered an early awareness of the importance of knowing young people, of listening to their lives, which Alison carried into her practice as a secondary teacher and, ultimately, into the creation of TLT. Her commitment to listening came from not being listened to as a child. While her teachers may have listened more, her felt sense of not being listened to as a human being in the home permeated her childhood experience and informed her pedagogical and research practices.

These early lived experiences inform our conceptions not only of young people but of our responsibility in working with them through an intersecting voices approach to teacher education. While we experienced very different childhoods, we see a cross-cutting theme of standing with/for the oppressed, the "at risk," the ones needing refuge, the ones needing to be listened to. As former middle and secondary school teachers, each of us has worked in classrooms with young people. Our subsequent choice to work in teacher preparation reflects a longstanding commitment to be in learning and teaching partnerships with other learner-teachers. This commitment has taken the form of co-creating our courses in a variety of ways, from offering students choice in the more constrained circumstances of secondary schools to enacting antiracist pedagogy with students as co-teachers in our courses in higher education (Wilson & Cook-Sather, in press).

We do research with secondary students positioned as teacher educators and all participants positioned as co-learners because we recognize that all education is contextually, culturally, and personally specific; one cannot learn to teach in some abstract sense. Instead, one learns to teach— and teaches to learn—in relationship, and the most generative way to continue to teach and to learn is through relationship, reflection, and dialogue. Conceptualizing teacher education as partnership (Cook-Sather, 2021) as we do in our teacher preparation program leads us to structure opportunities for creating knowledge about teaching and learning as forms of research. All students are legitimate informants (Feuerverger & Richards, 2007) on the student experience, and as Yosso et al. (2004) have argued, we need to "look to the lived experiences of students of color . . . as valid, appropriate, and necessary forms of data" (p. 15) in particular—not in ways that "extract" knowledge but rather in ways that co-create, as our student Lauren calls for.

Power Dynamics

Consideration of power dynamics is a foundational component of TLT. The college students are required to engage in coursework throughout their time in the Education Program that destabilizes the traditional teacher–student power dynamics so often present in schooling and education. TLT then offers an explicit application of that framework, as each position—secondary students, college students, school-based educator, and university-based educator—serves as both teacher and learner. In addition to this structure, which actively challenges traditional power dynamics, the TLT program considers power dynamics in practice. Through building authentic relationships, valuing student knowledge, and making programmatic changes based on new contexts and student input, our project actively resists the persistent power dynamics that help to maintain hierarchical structures and privilege between student and teacher.

Building Authentic Relationships. Building authentic relationships is a foundation for engaging in student voice research, and explicit and intentional consideration of power dynamics is a central component of relationship building with young people. For this reason, TLT prioritizes 1:1 virtual engagement between college students and secondary students with the chance for each to actively build a relationship with at least one other person in the program. Each college student maintains a weekly communication with their secondary student partner throughout the full semester prior to student teaching. As the college students learn with and from the secondary students, they not only come to understand particulars of that student's identity and experiences but also develop a mindset that will keep them seeking such understanding. As one college student wrote:

> Listening to the student's perspective can be more than just listening to the student's perspective on school. I want to listen to my students' lives. I want to listen to what makes them unique individuals. I want to listen to their quirks, their rich personalities, and their heritages. I want to listen to their culture of one: the unique combination of their experiences that make them one of a kind, their humanity. (Cook-Sather & Curl, 2014, p. 85)

TLT also affords the chance to build and/or deepen authentic relationships between student and teacher. Secondary students are invited to share insights with the school-based educator who facilitates TLT. As relationships between students and the school-based educator deepen over the course of the academic year, students become more comfortable sharing areas for improvement for the school-based educator. Students are also encouraged to use any method of communication with which they are comfortable, for instance "standard," academic language in spoken or electronic exchanges is not required (Baker-Bell, 2020), and students are invited to share examples and insights in whatever way feels most comfortable. As one school-based educator explained, TLT "provides a whole different opportunity to engage in conversation with the students"—conversation both as research and as relationship building. This school-based educator, who perpetually conducts informal research in her classrooms, gathering student feedback and acting on it, noted that "what's different about [TLT] is that I get a much broader response and there are no repercussions for what the students say; they can be really honest about their experience" (Cook-Sather, 2007b, pp. 353–354). Another school-based educator concurred with these reflections and also explained that participating in TLT "had an interesting effect on the kids who were also my students. It changed my relationship with them: I felt much more connected with them, I got to know them better, and they saw me differently." Part of that different way the secondary students saw the teacher was as a researcher:

> Because we had the chance to have this conversation outside of class, outside of a grade, they saw me as a person who was inquiring and eager to hear what they had to say, and I think that changed the way they looked at me as a teacher. (Cook-Sather, 2007b, p. 354)

Empowering Students and Valuing Their Knowledge. TLT creates structures through which students empower themselves and recognize the power of the knowledge they hold. Contributing to that sense of empowerment, as the school-based educator notes above, is the fact that the students are not graded for this work. Secondary students are explicitly positioned as co-educators of the college students and both school- and university-based educators, and they are compensated, not graded, for their time and insight. As mentioned, the perspectives of students are also put in dialogue with theory and can sometimes be used to challenge a theory or consider it through an applied lens. In this way, college students draw on the experiences and opinions of secondary students as a source of their learning and in their writing for the course. Final learnings are also shared at the closing gathering of the semester where secondary and college students and university-based and school-based educators alike publicly share insights gained, which intentionally positions everyone as a learner. One college student articulated this very reciprocity in a final celebration: "Learning and teaching don't go in one direction. In [TLT] we [college students] learned from you [secondary students]." This college student did not see this learning coming to an end. She continued: "Learning from students doesn't stop. As teachers we're still learners and as students you are teachers in the sense that you are teaching us about yourselves and what matters to you" (Cook-Sather & Curl, 2014, p. 94).

Secondary and college students are also empowered as co-presenters at conferences, co-authors of publications, and presenters and authors in their own school context. One year, students, with the school-based facilitator, presented findings from their weekly dialogue as professional development during a faculty meeting. Another year, students authored an article in their school newspaper, which included varied perspectives on the role culture plays in the classroom based on discussion in their weekly dialogue. Furthermore, both secondary and college students co-authored chapters of a book on learning from the student's perspective (Cook-Sather, 2001). Recently, student partners have begun suggesting different topics to the college-based educator for college students to engage, which resulted in a revised syllabus and course schedule. For example, in the most recent semester, the new student coordinator of TLT felt it was important to discuss student mental health and emergency online remote learning. The college-based educator revised the scholarly texts that college students were assigned to respond to this request, and these were two of the more spirited discussions of the semester among all students, secondary and college students.

Rather than perpetuate the assumption that professors or those who hold a doctorate are the sole creators of knowledge, these practices—inviting students to contribute to and lead the construction and sharing of knowledge—challenge long-held power dynamics present in schools at every level. The knowledge that students possess is therefore valued programmatically and in the wider academic community as well. This approach supports a challenge to persistent power dynamics in academia as well as in K–12 schools.

Willingness to Change and Evolve. TLT has been led by three different university-based educators with four different school-based educators, in five different schools, over the last 25 years. The program is committed to evolving and being responsive to new contexts and realities, which offers a significant strategy that ensures power dynamics remain fluid, equitable, and challenged. As technology developed, so too did the method of exchange between secondary and college students (starting with handwritten letters, moving through email, and branching into texts, SnapChat, or video calls). With each new school-based educator, school site, and group of secondary and college students, new dynamics have emerged regarding who is taking up space, what students want to share, and how to best support their (and our) collective learning and teaching.

In recent years, students have begun to lead some weekly discussions and develop their own questions so that the dialogues could be more responsive to student interests and experiences. Previously, the school-based educator and college-based educator decided on the schedule of topics and discussion questions prior to the semester. Most recently, during the pandemic and coming off of a summer in which racial injustice and polarized politics were necessarily at the forefront of national discourse, changes needed to be made to the weekly dialogue to ensure that power dynamics recentered toward, and were responsive to, students. This created space for the school-based educator to actively learn from students and grow as a participant and learner, rather than only as a facilitator. Embedding this awareness of the need for change, the program has space to continue to evolve in a way that can address power dynamics that consistently show up in a hierarchical society.

Context

As noted above, TLT positions students as sources of data, active respondents, and co-researchers (Fielding, 2004). Through various methods, secondary students analyze and critique their educational experiences in process, while offering their insights to push the thinking of current and future educators. Attention to student culture is centered in the ways TLT is enacted. These interactions encourage secondary students and college students to consider their positionality as welcomed and valued. However, this also represents natural ways of engaging in learning, but traditional, Western, and white ways of conceptualizing research (Zuberi & Bonilla-Silva, 2008) may have socialized and trained these practices out of researchers. Without the humanizing elements we've discussed, that both our student Lauren and Paris (2011) call for, researchers can do real damage to young people, especially when culture and positionality are ignored, color-blind and identity-blind practices are adopted, and young people are framed as "damaged" (Tuck, 2009). As Lauren notes, these ways, which are often positively regarded as neutral, actually veer to a normalized base of white ways of knowing and doing, and what is commonly regarded as a sound practice of maintaining professional distance positions students as subjects of study, rather than whole human beings who can and should be co-partners in any research into their world.

In TLT, students are not asked to change who they are to participate. When in conversation with their college-student partners, and even in weekly dialogues, students are encouraged to set their own ways of communication. For example, students can use their own language (Baker-Bell, 2020; Jordan, 1988), meaning they are not reprimanded for speaking in nonstandardized American English. They are also free to provide their input without the burden of what some label "respectful dialogue," which actually censors students. Secondary students are encouraged to challenge, question, or critique traditional structures and practices. In consideration of the role of research, we advocate for more work to be done on the part of the researcher to adapt to the environment that students are in and have created. TLT strives to enact what Paris (2011) described in his work on humanizing research within a school community: he built relationships with students, invited students to speak in their own voices, and observed to consider how he needed to fit in the space with them, rather than assuming they needed to change to be in dialogue with him. This is especially important, particularly when the power dynamic is already complex, with researchers as outsiders who are socially perceived as authorities and experts. Over the 25 years that we have maintained TLT, in contexts from suburban public schools to urban charter schools, we have worked to build, through relationships and over time, spaces within which student voices were valued and recognized, and college students learned from them both in the context of their particular school and more generally regarding the ways they as future practicing teachers need to keep listening.

CONCLUSION

We have argued that engaging in humanizing and rights-centered student voice research involves attention to relationships and power through reflexivity, student empowerment, and reciprocal conceptions of teaching and learning. We argue that consideration of power and a welcoming of evolution are necessities and perpetual ways of being. Reciprocal and forward-moving teaching and learning means always changing in response to context, participant experience, and partners' contributions as those create the capacity to acknowledge and center equity. The longer we sustain the work described here, the better and more equitable interactions and outcomes can be. Power will always try to fall back into hierarchies, but over time, how to engage in and sustain such a project becomes clearer and the iterations not only build but deepen knowledge. This kind of project is not something you do just once and are done. Duration—sustained and sustainable engagement—and iterations matter. Practice matters. You don't get it right the first time. And you never get it right once and for all. The project we've described has been in the making for more than 25 years and we consider it forever in the making!

Furthermore, the context and what happens in the wider-world impact what happens in the project. As we discussed, in the mid- and late 1990s, there were not the same kinds of youth-led protests as in the last 10 years, or if there were, social media did not make them immediately accessible to all. This shift affects how college students perceive secondary students as authorities and those with voice and knowledge that count. Acknowledging students as authorities was the impulse behind creating TLT. The idea that future teachers can be prepared to teach without being in relationship with students and schools is absurd, so we urge teacher educators to consider how to integrate the components of the Student Voice Research Framework into their programs.

TLT has been responsive to the diverse ways students can engage, through various platforms and formats. This, in turn, increases students' participation in politics, social action, communication, and advocacy. Connections through digital media can lead to collaboration and mobilization, and these too have evolved with the program. The concept and the structure of the program, however, remain relevant, even as students and technology change. The structure is grounded and responsive; as change happens, the program responds. The theoretical underpinnings we have provided help ground the approach in current and relevant phenomena and movements. Here too we urge teacher educators to consider how components of the Student Voice Research Framework as we have discussed them here might inform their programs.

While research can be critiqued for being one-sided and serving only the university-based researcher, the intersecting-voices approach that informs TLT values the shared knowledge that all parties develop. For the secondary students, that includes self-knowledge used in subsequent classes, relationships with teachers and peers, and college and job applications, supporting students to view themselves as teachers as well as students. For college students preparing to be teachers, the knowledge includes self-knowledge as ongoing learners and insights as would-be teachers, as well as pedagogical approaches that are put into practice. Both school- and college-based educators gain the same knowledge as the students and college students, which informs our pedagogy. As college-based educators expected to publish, we also draw on this knowledge to inform our scholarship, and thereby the wider community of teacher education scholars (Cook-Sather, 2002a, 2002b, 2006b, 2009b; Cook-Sather & Curl, 2014, 2016; Cook-Sather & Youens, 2007; Wilson, under review). We also gain knowledge regarding how to perpetually revise this research- and relationship-centered approach to teacher preparation.

The Student Voice Research Framework presented in this text is enacted in our approach to teacher education as an ongoing, reciprocal process of systematic reflection on and enactment of teaching and learning. Through critically engaging reflexivity, intersubjectivity, power dynamics, and the use of research strategies grounded in student context and perspectives, we enact a radical form of teacher education. This is not only "radical collegiality" (Fielding, 1999a) among participants, although it is that; it is also that every participant—college students, university-based educators, secondary students, and school-based educators—is at once a learner, teacher, and researcher. We hope this chapter will contribute to other teacher educators conceptualizing their practice in this way.

Conclusion

The Past, Present, and Future of Student Voice Research

Joseph Levitan and Marc Brasof

The field of student voice research is filled with passionate folks who offer more than just insights into school change; they often are motivated by and design projects that enact the very changes we hope to see in a more just and equitable world. Educational institutions should behave like learning organizations and are well served when they destroy disempowering barriers and seek out the perspectives, solutions, and collaborative activities that will support learning for all. We believe that education should be uplifting, individualized, contextualized, and collective in nature. Student voice research can help to serve those goals, to elevate the most important voices impacted by education systems as a means to be empowering, but also to gain a deeper appreciation and understanding of the work of education, which is complex, challenging, and central to a healthy democracy.

A democracy that emphasizes collaboration throughout society with fair processes and space for voice distributes decision-making power equitably. Collaborations that name and more fully address injustice and oppression hold a lot of potential. We have seen social movements and many activist networks continue to influence the political sphere and find their way into education by challenging unproductive narratives in curriculum and other school policies and processes hindering a more peaceful and joyful co-existence. The lesson that continues to emerge is that wisdom can come from creating intentional, inclusive, and empathetic communities that aim to unleash the creative potential in everybody. Student voice research can name and elevate the various differences in our community that help us contextualize and individualize our system of practices while at the same time identify common ground to build an agreed upon set of aims and standards of expectations that strengthens and/or revises our social contract. We have yet to cross paths with an educational researcher in the student voice field that disagrees with these ideas. But, a belief in an idea alone does not change our shared realities, and in fact, without careful critical and reflexive approaches and methods, a belief in an idea can lead to problems.

Having a good and worthy mission can produce romanticized images of the work researchers are doing and misguide us—the field is not without its blind spots and challenges, and we are products of our socialization. As we point out in our opening chapters of this book, researchers bring a lot of past, present, and future mental images that have been learned. These can create misinterpretations or lead us down the wrong path as we seek to understand the contexts in which we raise youth. No one is immune to such (mis)judgments. What we have created here, then, is a synthesis of thinkers who have come before us and who are engaged in research now in the hope of supporting researchers who will emerge in student voice work in the future.

Ultimately, we hope this volume supports research projects that move us toward a more democratic and just society. A transparent map of how one might navigate the challenges of doing research with youth can bridge the gap between our aspirations and our practices—and as ours and others' work illustrate, there are real gaps to overcome. We need to keep our eyes on the known gaps and surface others because our present-day conditions—global climate change; economic, political, and cultural oppression—have manifested due to our belief systems and historic and current patterns of behavior and have created micro- and macro-structures that engender these problems and create a sense that they are unsolvable.

Underlining this point is that this book was written during the COVID-19 pandemic, a worldwide crisis that, for many, finally lifted that veil effectively hiding oppression and inequities (gaps in our social fabric) that have led to deep wounds in our society. We kept hearing the phrase in many circles, "we are not all in the same boat" as a very real recognition that inequitable distribution of resources is having dire impacts on the most vulnerable in society. Furthermore, this pandemic, and concurrent crises, has shown many of us the wounds that could very well lead us toward humanity's end if we do not find a way to work together—better—for the common good. It is even hard to write these words now in recognition of its truth, but we must. Whereas we are definitely scarred by these acute and chronic crises, we are also creating new potentials and possibilities in education and the wider ecosystem.

As researchers and educators, we have tools to help solve these chronic problems, but they need to be well directed. We cannot solve the systemic health, educational, and environmental problems in our society with surgical intervention. While intensive research on one specific topic has done some significant good in the past to move nuanced conversations forward and to create new and useful knowledge (though not all knowledge has to be useful to be valuable), it has also led us to compartmentalize issues that are actually interconnected—causing new harm and leaving the old systemic wounds still open. Now, more than ever, we need to look at the whole ecosystem. The pandemic has been a window into this thinking. Like a system, the pandemic was inserted into and exacerbated the many intertwined and long-standing political, cultural, economic, and technological problems— problems that a focused, surgical solution, like a vaccination, cannot cure. We need to uproot and reimagine these many systems through prolonged, healthy, and inclusive dialogue that cultivate collective responses to these issues. Student voice research can play an important part in this vision.

In education, we need to see schools as a microcosm of society, as an ecosystem that requires us to approach its challenges by avoiding surgical-like interventions, and instead link our tools of research to a deep commitment to democracy, intellectual discourse, and collective action that aims to heal wounds, strengthen its response systems, and cultivate a healthier whole. This will allow schools to contribute to the ongoing struggles that our society as a whole are facing. Students are not immune to the entrenched crises facing our society. In fact, they are highly affected by these ongoing social, health, and environmental issues. We need to make sure that they can speak back and speak to the problems they are living through and will be addressing throughout their lives. The student voice field strongly illustrates that youth not only have a stake in this mission but want to be active participants.

One important approach to healing systemic wounds with our current tools (adding the SVRF to that toolbox) is to recognize that we have more work to do in engaging and elevating the stories of a range of identities that youth occupy and the impact of these positionalities in learning settings. In this volume, we only began to touch on the intersectionality of student voice research and youth identities, and we encourage more scholarship that recognizes how researchers can approach the study of students' experiences in ways that acknowledge and honor all of their identities, including gender, religion, Indigeneity, ability, race, class, culture, sexual orientation, and language, along with the many more identites that exist. A major critique emerging in the student voice research community is the predominance of white, middle- and upper-class youth in student voice literature, yet there is a diverse population engaged in change efforts in many educational and community spaces across the world. Though we see more of that scholarship emerging in the YPAR literature, there is still a serious gap in the extant student voice literature on how to do research with individuals and groups experiencing marginalization.

Further thinking and work needs to be done on considerations of identity if we are to achieve our aforementioned aims. Core to student voice research is honoring the insights students offer, but sometimes those insights are limited because we may not be honoring and being responsive to the many identities youth and adults bring with them—particularly because the field is dominated by white researchers. The need to understand how identity influences relationships in student voice work is critical. How can we create new bridges in a divisive world if we exclude essential features of what makes a person? And as Lindsay Lyons, Ellen MacCannell, and Vanessa Gold argue in Chapter 5, the field is ready for the next leap in terms of testing the validity and reliability of the theory and practice of student voice for school and community improvement in order to hone models and support future transformational projects.

Our educational institutions can be ground zero for such research projects to cultivate the hope, knowledge, and power needed to transform our world (and maybe save humanity itself). But let us not mince words here; educational institutions are part of the system that needs changing. They are sites of social reproduction, while also being sites of potential transformation. The need for transformation has never been more urgent, but change does not happen by holding on to past notions, comforts, and our accustomed ways of being. We must not reproduce the social, political, cultural, and economic relationship patterns of our past and present because they further entrench oppression. Now, we need to reimagine what it means to learn together, what our common good is, and how we achieve it. Student voice researchers can investigate questions relevant to the specific ideas, concerns, and needs of our most marginalized students to improve educational policy and practice. Are we saying student voice research is the panacea? No, but we know it is a necessary component to democratizing schools by supporting self-expression and aggregating concerns that are so central to democratic discourse. And perhaps along the way, in the act of rethinking what it means to be educated for democracy, student voice research that engages with the principles highlighted in SVRF can create *a* pathway forward for society, of which we need many.

Already, we see the possibilities of how doing student voice scholarship helps us to uncover the complexity of the world. Creating spaces of sharing, dialogue, collaboration, and analysis reveals insights—contextual, timeless, and actionable—as demonstrated by the chapters in this volume. There *is* a diversity within the field of research methods, showing how unifying goals and diversity of methods and perspectives is not only possible, but also strengthens the work. The sample of key methods in this volume offer excellent starting points and considerations.

Nonetheless, the ways in which student voice research can be productively undertaken, and what is required to ensure quality in student voice research within this diversity, is an ongoing dialogue. Our interactions with student voice researchers and their research have reaffirmed that this community will continue to experiment with innovative strategies and question its place in the world. We must continue to explore ways in which we can build those intersubjective understandings that help us create a more nuanced and complete picture of our worlds, and how to collaborate to make the world better. How do we solve our most pressing problems if we do not understand each other? How do we get to that understanding without recognizing and addressing the power dynamics that disrupt the possibility of what can come from genuine and authentic co-creation? These are questions that are yet to be addressed in ways that lead to justice, democracy, and good lives for all. This is what we believe Michael Fielding was getting at over 20 years ago with his notion of "radical collegiality" in which schools need "a much more overt openness and reciprocity indicative of a much more flexible, dialogic form of democratic practice . . . to open up new understandings and insights. . . . These in turn generate a new and interesting sense of practical and hopeful possibilities that nurture a genuinely inclusive sense of community in which each cares for the other reciprocally" (2001b, pp. 130–131).

We know that more questions need to be addressed, and that this is an incomplete volume. The work is ongoing, and we continue to seek out and encourage discourse. Education is like an evolving organism, and we need adaptive researchers who can navigate the complexities of organizational life. With reflective and reflexive researchers and educators who have the tools and abilities to work with youth to ensure their voices are part of the democratic vision of education and society we hope for, we can all contribute to a more just, thriving, and joyful world. Our hope is that this volume is a jumping-off point for researchers to tackle the many pressing issues facing us all. Student voice researchers will continue to push for more justice, voice, and democracy, and we hope that more will join in this essential work.

References

Abell, N., Springer, D. W., & Kamata, A. (2009). *Developing and validating rapid assessment instruments*. Oxford University Press.

Abson, D. J., Fischer, J., Leventon, J., Newig, J., Schomerus, T., Vilsmaier, U., von Wehrden, H., Abernethy, P., Ives, C. D., Jager, N. W., & Lang, D. J. (2017). Leverage points for sustainability transformation. *Ambio, 46*(1), 30–39. https://doi.org/10.1007/s13280-016-0800-y

Adichie, C. N. (2009, July). *The danger of a single story* [Video]. TED Conferences. https://www.ted.com/talks/chimamanda_ngozi_adichie_the_danger_of_a_single_story

Alcoff, L. (1991). The problem of speaking for others. *Cultural Critique, 20*, 5–32. https://doi.org/10.2307/1354221

Alderson, P. (1995). *Listening to children: Children, ethics and social research*. Barnardo's.

Alderson, P. (2000). Children as researchers: The effects of participation rights on research methodology. In P. Christensen & A. James (Eds.), *Research with children: Perspectives and practices* (pp. 241–275). Falmer Press.

Altbach, P. G. (1966). Students and politics. *Comparative Education Review, 10*(2), 175–187.

Anderson, D., Graham, A., & Thomas, N. (2019). Assessing student participation at school: Developing a multi-dimensional scale. *International Journal of Student Voice, 2*(9). https://ijsv.psu.edu/?article=assessing-student-participation-at-school-developing-a-multidimensional-scale

Argyris, C., & Schon, D. A. (1974). *Theory in practice: Increasing professional effectiveness*. Jossey-Bass.

Arnot, M., McIntyre, D., Pedder, D., & Reay, D. (2003). *Consultation in the classroom: Pupil perspectives on teaching & learning*. Pearson Publishing.

Arnott, L. & Wall, K. (Eds.). (2021). *Research through play: Participatory methods in early childhood*. Sage.

Arnstein, S. R. (1969). A ladder of citizen participation. *Journal of the American Institute of planners, 35*(4), 216–224.

Ashton, R. (2008). Improving the transfer to secondary school: How every child's voice can matter. *Support for Learning, 23*(4), 176–182.

Avramides, A. (2020). Knowing others as persons. *Inquiry*, 1–23.

Baker, B., Farrie, D., & Sciarra, D. (2018, February). *Is school funding fair? A national report card, 7th edition*. Education Law Center. https://drive.google.com/file/d/1BTAjZuqOs8pEGWW6oUBotb6omVw1hUJI/view

Baker-Bell, A. (2020). *Linguistic justice: Black language, literacy, identity, and pedagogy*. Routledge.

Ball, J., & Janyst, P. (2008). Enacting research ethics in partnerships with Indigenous communities in Canada: "Do it in a good way." *Journal of Empirical Research on Human Research Ethics, 3*(2), 33–51.

Barnard-Dadds, T., & Conn, C. (2018). Challenges of listening to an autistic pupil in a person-centred planning meeting. *Journal of Research in Special Educational Needs, 18*, 15–24.

Baron, C. (2018). Surveys and scales. In A. E. Booysen, R. Bendl, & J. K. Pringle (Eds.), *Handbook of research methods in diversity management, equality and inclusion at work* (pp. 418–456). Edward Elgar Publishing.

Baumann, P., Millard, M., & Hamdorf, L. (2014). *State civic education policy framework*. Education Commission of the States and National Center for Learning and Civic Engagement.

Beauchamp, C., & Thomas, L. (2009). Understanding teacher identity: An overview of issues in the literature and implications for teacher education. *Cambridge Journal of Education, 39*(2), 175–189. https://doi.org/10.1080/03057640902902252

Berger, B. K. (2005). Power over, power with, and power to relations: Critical reflections on public relations, the dominant coalition, and activism. *Journal of Public Relations Research, 17*(1), 5–28.

Bergmark, U., & Kostenius, C. (2018). Students' experiences of meaningful situations in school. *Scandinavian Journal of Educational Research, 62*(4), 538–554.

Bernstein, I. H., & Nunnally, J. (1994). *Psychometric theory*. McGraw Hill.

Bertrand, M. (2014). Reciprocal dialogue between educational decision makers and students of color: Opportunities and obstacles. *Educational Administration Quarterly, 50*(5), 812–843.

Besteman, C. (2020). On ethnographic unknowability. *Writing Anthropology: Essays on Craft and Commitment*, 53.

Biddle, C. (2015). *Communities discovering what they care about: Youth and adults leading school reform together* (Publication No. 3715475) [Doctoral dissertation, The Pennsylvania State University]. ProQuest Dissertations & Theses Global.

Biddle, C., & Hufnagel, E. (2019). Navigating the "danger zone": Tone policing and the bounding of civility in the practice of student voice. *American Journal of Education, 125*(4), 487–520. https://doi.org/10.1086/704097

Biddulph, M. (2011). Articulating student voice and facilitating curriculum agency. *The Curriculum Journal, 22*(3), 381–399.

Biddulph, M. (2012). Young people's geographies and the school curriculum. *Geography, 97*, 155–162.

Biedenbach, T., & Jacobsson, M. (2016). The open secret of values: The roles of values and axiology in project research. *Project Management Journal, 47*(3), 139–155. https://doi.org/10.1177/875697281604700312

Blaisdell, C., Arnott, L., & Wall, K. (2018) Look who's talking: Using creative, playful arts-based methods in research with young children. *Journal of Early Childhood Research, 17*(1), 14–31.

Boomer, G., Lester, N., Onore, C., & Cook, J. (Eds.). (1992). *Negotiating the curriculum: Educating for the twenty-first century*. Falmer.

Borer, M. I., & Fontana, A. (2012). Postmodern trends: Expanding the horizons of interviewing practices and epistemologies. In J. F. Gubrium, J. A. Holstein,

K. D. Marvasti, & K. D. McKinney (Eds.), *Handbook of interview research: The complexity of the craft* (pp. 45–60). Sage.

Bourdieu, P. (1977). *Outline of a theory of practice.* Cambridge University Press.

Bourdieu, P. (1989). Social space and symbolic power. *Sociological Theory, 7*(1), 14–25.

Bourke, R., & Loveridge, J. (2016). Beyond the official language of learning: Teachers engaging with student voice research. *Teaching and Teacher Education, 57,* 59–66. https://doi.org/10.1016/j.tate.2016.03.008

Bower, L. L. (2003). Student reflection and critical thinking: A rhetorical analysis of 88 portfolio cover letters. *Journal of Basic Writing,* 47–66.

Boyatzis, R. E. (1998). *Transforming qualitative data: Thematic analysis and code development.* Sage.

Bragg, S. (2007). "Student voice" and governmentality: The production of enterprising subjects? *Discourse: Studies in the Cultural Politics of Education, 28*(3), 343–358. https://doi.org/10.1080/01596300701458905

Brasof, M. (2014). *Student voice in school reform: A case study of Madison high school's youth-adult governance model* (Publication No. 3623116) [Doctoral dissertation, Temple University]. ProQuest Dissertations & Theses Global.

Brasof, M. (2015). *Student voice and school governance: Distributing leadership to youth and adults.* Routledge.

Brasof, M. (2018). Using linkage theory to address the student voice organizational improvement paradox. *Journal of Ethical Educational Leadership, March,* 44–65.

Brasof, M. (2019). Meeting the discipline challenge: Capacity-building youth-adult leadership. *Journal of Educational Change, 20*(3), 1–24, 375–398.

Brasof, M., & Mansfield, K. (Eds.) (2018). Student voice and school leadership [Special issue]. *Journal of Ethical Educational Leadership, March*(1), 5–311.

Brasof, M., & Peterson, K. (2018). Creating procedural justice and legitimate authority within school discipline systems through youth court. *Psychology in the Schools, 55*(7), 832–849.

Brau, B. (2021). Constructivism. In R. Kimmons (Ed.), *Education research: Across multiple paradigms* (3.3). EdTech Books. https://edtechbooks.org/education_research/constructivismy

Bron, J., & Veugelers, W. (2014). Why we need to involve our students in curriculum design: Five arguments for student voice. *Curriculum and Teaching Dialogue, 16*(1/2), 125–139.

Bronfenbrenner, U. (1994). Ecological models of human development. *Readings on the Development of Children, 2*(1), 37–43.

Bucknall, S. (2014). Doing qualitative research with children and young people. In A. Clark, R. Flewitt, M. Hammersley, and M. Robb (Eds.), *Understanding research with children and young people* (pp. 69–84). Sage.

Bundick, M., Quaglia, R., Corso, M., & Haywood, D. (2014). Promoting student engagement in the classroom. *Teachers College Record, 116*(4) 1–34.

Cahill, H., & Dadvand, B. (2018). Re-conceptualising youth participation: A framework to inform action. *Children and Youth Services Review, 95*(December), 143–153.

Cahnmann-Taylor, M., & Siegesmund, R. (2018). *Arts-based research in education: Foundations for practice* (2nd ed.). Routledge.

Call-Cummings, M., & Ross, K. (2019). Re-positioning power and re-imagining reflexivity: Examining positionality and building validity through reconstructive horizon analysis. In K. K. Strunk & L. A. Locke (Eds.), *Research methods for social justice and equity in education* (pp. 3–14). Palgrave Macmillan.

Camangian, P. (2008). Untempered tongues: Teaching performance poetry for social justice. *English Teaching-Practice and Critique, 7*(2), 35–55.

Cambridge. (2021). Student. In *Cambridge Advanced Learner's Dictionary & Thesaurus.* https://dictionary.cambridge.org/dictionary/english/student?q=Student

Cammarota, J., & Fine, M. (2008). Youth participatory action research: A pedagogy for transformational resistance. In J. Cammarota & M. Fine (Eds.), *Revolutionizing education: Youth participatory action research in motion* (pp. 1–12). Routledge.

Capewell, C. (2016). Glue ear—A common but complicated childhood condition. *Journal of Research in Special Educational Needs, 16*(2), 122–131.

Carrington, S., Allen, K., & Osmolowski, D. (2007). Visual narrative: A technique to enhance secondary students' contribution to the development of inclusive, socially just school environments—Lessons from a box of crayons. *Journal of Research in Special Educational Needs, 7*(1), 8–15.

Cassidy, C. (2007). *Thinking Children.* Continuum.

Chadderton, C. (2011). Not capturing voices: A poststructural critique of the privileging of voice in research. In G. Czerniawski & W. Kidd (Eds.), *The student voice handbook: Bridging the academic/practitioner divide* (pp. 73–85). Emerald.

Charteris, J., & Smardon, D. (2019). The politics of student voice: Unravelling the multiple discourses articulated in schools. *Cambridge Journal of Education, 49*(1), 93–110.

Choudry, A., & Kapoor, D. (2010). Learning from the ground up: Global perspectives on social movements and knowledge production. In A. Choudry & D. Kapoor (Eds.), *Learning from the ground up* (pp. 1–13). Palgrave Macmillan.

Christians, C. G. (2018). Ethics and politics in qualitative research. In N. K. Denzin, & Y. S. Lincoln (Eds.), *The Sage handbook of qualitative research* (5th ed., pp. 66–82). Sage Publications.

Clark, A. (2005). Listening to and involving young children: A review of research and practice. *Early Child Development and Care, 175*(6), 489–505.

Clark, A. (2007). A hundred ways of listening: Gathering children's perspectives of their early childhood environment. *Young Children, 62*(3), 76–81.

Claxton, G., & Carr, M. (2004). A framework for teaching learning: The dynamics of disposition. *Early Years, 24*(1), 87–97.

Cleary, L. M. (1996). "I think I know what my teachers want now": Gender and writing motivation. *The English Journal, 85*(1), 50–57.

Coates, J., & Vickerman, P. (2008). Let the children have their say: Children with special educational needs and their experiences of physical education—A review. *Support for Learning, 23*(4), 168–175.

Cody, J., McGarry, L., Czerniawski, G., & Kidd, W. (2012). Small voices, big impact: Preparing students for learning and citizenship. *Management in Education, 26*(3), 150–152.

Comer, J. (2005) *Comer school development program. James Comer interview.* PBS. https://www.pbs.org/makingschoolswork/sbs/csp/jamescomer.html

Comesaña, J., & Klein, P. (2019). Skepticism. In E. D. Zalta (Ed.), *The Stanford Encyclopedia of Philosophy* (Winter). https://plato.stanford.edu/archives/win2019/entries/skepticism

Connell, R. W. (1993). *Schools and social justice*. Temple University Press.

Conner, J. (2015). Student voice: A field coming of age. *Youth Voice Journal*, 2056–2969.

Conner, J. (2016). Pawns or power players: The grounds on which adults dismiss or defend youth organizers in the USA. *Journal of Youth Studies*, 19(3), 403–420.

Conner, J., Brown, A., & Ober, C. N. (2016). The politics of paternalism: Adult and youth perspectives on youth voice in public policy. *Teachers College Record*, 118(8), 1–48.

Conner, J., Ebby-Rosin, R., & Brown, A. S. (Eds.) (2015). Speak up and speak out: Student voice in American educational policy. A National Society for the Study of Education Yearbook. Teachers College Record.

Cook-Sather, A. (2001). Between student and teacher: Learning to teach as translation. *Teaching Education*, 12(2), 177–190.

Cook-Sather, A. (2002a). Re(in)forming the conversations: Student position, power, and voice in teacher education. *Radical Teacher*, 64, 21–28.

Cook-Sather, A. (2002b). Authorizing students' perspectives: Toward trust, dialogue, and change in education. *Educational Researcher*, 31(4), 3–14.

Cook-Sather, A. (2006a). Sound, presence, and power: Exploring "student voice" in educational research and reform. *Curriculum Inquiry*, 36(4), 359–90.

Cook-Sather, A. (2006b). "Change based on what students say": Preparing teachers for a more paradoxical model of leadership. *International Journal of Leadership in Education*, 9(4), 345–358.

Cook-Sather, A. (2006c). The "constant changing of myself": Revising roles in undergraduate teacher preparation. *Teacher Educator*, 41(3), 187–206.

Cook-Sather, A. (2007a). Resisting the impositional potential of student voice work: Lessons for liberatory educational research from poststructuralist feminist critiques of critical pedagogy. *Discourse: Studies in the Cultural Politics of Education*, 28(3), 389–403.

Cook-Sather, A. (2007b). What would happen if we treated students as those with opinions that matter? The benefits to principals and teachers of supporting youth engagement in school. *NASSP Bulletin* 91(4), 343–362.

Cook-Sather, A. (2009a). From traditional accountability to shared responsibility: The benefits and challenges of student consultants gathering midcourse feedback in college classrooms. *Assessment & Evaluation in Higher Education*, 34(2), 231–241.

Cook-Sather, A. (2009b). "I am not afraid to listen": Prospective teachers learning from students to work in city schools. *Theory into Practice*, 48(3), 176–181.

Cook-Sather, A. (2015). Dialogue across differences of position, perspective, and identity: Reflective practice in/on a student-faculty pedagogical partnership program. *Teachers College Record*, 117(2) 1–42.

Cook-Sather, A. (2018a). Listening to equity-seeking perspectives: How students' experiences of pedagogical partnership can inform wider discussions of student success. *Higher Education Research and Development*, 37(5), 923–936.

Cook-Sather, A. (2018b). Tracing the evolution of student voice in educational research. In R. Bourke & J. Loveridge (Eds.), *Radical collegiality through student voice* (pp. 17–38). Springer.

Cook-Sather, A. (2020). Student voice and pedagogical partnership through and as disruption, revealing and challenging inequity. In M. A. Peters (Ed.), *Encyclopedia of teacher education* (pp. 1–5). Springer. https://link.springer.com/referencework/10.1007%2F978-981-13-1179-6

Cook-Sather, A. (2021). Living and learning partnerships in teacher education. In L. Shagrir & S. Bar-Tal (Eds.), *Exploring professional development opportunities for teacher educators: Promoting faculty-student partnerships*. Routledge.

Cook-Sather, A., & Curl, H. (2014). "I want to listen to my students' lives': Developing an ecological perspective in learning to teach. *Teacher Education Quarterly, 41*(1), 85–103.

Cook-Sather, A., & Curl, H. (2016). Positioning students as teacher educators: Preparing learners to transform schools. In A. Montgomery & I. Kehoe (Eds.), *Reimagining schools* (pp. 65–76). Springer.

Cook-Sather, A., & Youens, B. (2007). Repositioning students in initial teacher preparation: A comparative case study of learning to teach for social justice in the United States and in England. *Journal of Teacher Education, 58*(1), 62–75.

Coronel, J. M., & Pascual, I. R. (2013). Let me put it another way: Methodological considerations on the use of participatory photography based on an experiment with teenagers in secondary schools. *Qualitative Research in Education, 2*(2), 98–129.

Costello, J., Toles, M., Spielberger, J., & Wynn, J. (1997). History, ideology and structure shape the organizations that shape youth. *Youth Development: Issues, Challenges and Directions*, 185–232.

Costello, J., Toles, M., Spielberger, J., & Wynn, J. (2001). How history, ideology, and structure shape the organizations that shape youth. In P. L. Benson & K. J. Pittman (Eds.), *Trends in Youth Development* (pp. 191–229). Springer Science.

Cox, S., & Robinson-Pant, A. (2006). Enhancing participation in primary school and class councils through visual communication. *Cambridge Journal of Education, 36*(4), 515–532. https://doi.org/10.1080/03057640601048431

Crenshaw, K. (1991). Mapping the margins: Intersectionality, identity politics, and violence against women of color. *Stanford Law Review, 43*(6), 1241–1299.

Crenshaw, K. (2015). *On intersectionality: The essential writings of Kimberle Crenshaw*. New Press.

Creswell, J. W., & Plano Clark, V. L. (2011). *Designing and conducting mixed methods research* (2nd ed.). Sage.

Criado, T. S., & Estalella, A. (2018). Introduction. In A. Estalella & T. S. Criado (Eds.), *Experimental collaborations. Ethnography through fieldwork devices* (pp. 1–30). Berghahn.

Curl, H., Cook-Sather, A. (2021). "Teaching and learning together": One model of rights-centred secondary teacher preparation in the United States. In J. Gillett-Swan & N. Thelander (Eds.), *Children's rights from international educational perspectives: Wicked problems for children's education rights* (Transdisciplinary perspectives in educational research, vol 2, pp. 27–38). Springer. https://doi.org/10.1007/978-3-030-80861-7_3

Czerniawski, G., & Garlick, S. (2011). Trust, contextual sensitivity and student voice. In G. Czerniawski & W. Kidd (Eds.), *The student voice handbook: Bridging the academic/practitioner divide* (pp. 277–294). Emerald Group Publishing

Czerniawski, G., & Kidd, W. (Eds.). (2011). *Student voice handbook: Bridging the academic/practitioner divide*. Emerald Group Publishing.

Czerniawski, G., & Kidd, W. (2012). Repositioning trust: A challenge to inauthentic neoliberal uses of pupil voice. *Management in Education, 26*(3), 130–139.

Dalton, G., & Devitt, A. (2016). Irish in a 3D world: Engaging primary school children. *Language Learning & Technology, 20*(1), 21–33.

Dare, L., Nowicki, E. A., & Smith, S. (2019). On deciding to accelerate: High-ability students identify key considerations. *Gifted Child Quarterly, 63*(3), 159–171.

Darling-Hammond, L. (2010). Teacher education and the American future. *Journal of Teacher Education, 6*(102), 35–47.

Darling-Hammond, L., & Oakes, J. (2021). *Preparing teachers for deeper learning.* Harvard Education Press.

Davies, P., Popescu, A., & Gunter, H. (2011). Student participation in school ICT policy-making: A case of students as researchers. *Management in Education, 25*(2), 71–77.

Delamont, S. (1976). *Interaction in the classroom.* Methuen.

Deleuze, G. (1988). *Spinoza: Practical philosophy* (R. Hurley, Trans.). City Lights Books.

Deleuze, G. (1992). *Expressionism in philosophy: Spinoza.* Zone Books.

Delpit, L. (2006). *Other people's children: Cultural conflict in the classroom.* New Press.

Demerath, P. (2002). Perspective-taking in the practice-research gap: Using ethnography to help schools see themselves. In B. A. U. Levinson, S. L. Cade, A. Padawer, & A. P. Elvir (Eds.), *Ethnography and education policy across the Americas* (pp. 143–154). Praeger.

Denzin, N. K. (2001). The reflexive interview and a performative social science. *Qualitative Research, 1*(1), 23–46.

Department of Health and Human Services, 45 C.F.R. 46 Subpart D, §46.402 (a), §46.408 (2018).

Department of Health, Education, and Welfare. (1979, April 18). *The Belmont Report.* https://www.hhs.gov/ohrp/sites/default/files/the-belmont-report-508c_FINAL.pdf

DeVellis, R. F. (2017). *Scale development: Theory and applications* [Kindle edition]. Sage.

Dewey, J. (1902). *The child and the curriculum.* University of Chicago Press.

Dewey, J. (2008). *The child and the curriculum including the school and society.* Cosimo, Inc.

Dockney, J., & Tomaselli, K. G. (2009). Fit for the small(er) screen: Films, mobile TV and the new individual television experience. *Journal of African Cinema, 1*(1), 126–132.

Donaldson, M. (1987). *Children's minds.* Fontana Press.

Drydyk, J. (2012). A capability approach to justice as a virtue. *Ethical Theory and Moral Practice, 15*(1), 23–38.

Earle, J., & Kruse, S. D. (1999). *Organizational literacy for educators.* Routledge.

Edmondson, A. C., & McManus, S. E. (2007). Methodological fit in management field research. *Academy of Management Review, 32*(4), 1246–1264.

Edwards, S., & Brown, C. (2020). Close-to-practice research: The need for student voice and the strange case of Academy X. *London Review of Education, 18*(3), 480–494. https://doi.org/10.14324/LRE.18.3.11

Eisenberg, N. (1986). *Altruistic emotion, cognition, and behavior*. Erlbaum.

Ellsworth, E. (1989). Why doesn't this feel empowering? Working through the repressive myths of critical pedagogy. *Harvard Educational Review, 59*(3), 297–324. https://doi.org/10.17763/haer.59.3.058342114k266250

Enright, E., & O'Sullivan, M. (2013). "Now, I'm a magazine detective the whole time": Listening and responding to young people's complex experiences of popular physical culture. *Journal of Teaching in Physical Education, 32*(4), 394–418.

Estalella, A., & Criado, T. S. (2019). DIY anthropology. Disciplinary knowledge in crisis. *Anuac, 8*(2), 143–165.

Faircloth, S. C., & Tippeconnic, J. W. (2004). Utilizing research methods that respect and empower indigenous knowledge. *Tribal College Journal, 16*(2), 24–27.

Faldet, A. C., & Nes, K. (2021). Valuing vulnerable children's voices in educational research. *International Journal of Inclusive Education*, 1–16. https://doi.org/10.1080/13603116.2021.1956602

Fazey, I. (2010). Resilience and higher order thinking. *Ecology & Society, 15*(3), Article 9. https://www.jstor.org/stable/26268183?seq=1

Feuerverger, G., & Richards, E. (2007). Finding their way: ESL immigrant and refugee students in a Toronto high school. In D. Thiessen & A. Cook-Sather (Eds.), *International handbook of student experience in elementary and secondary school* (pp. 555–575). Springer.

Fielding, M. (1999a). Radical collegiality: Affirming teaching as an inclusive professional practice. *The Australian Educational Researcher, 26*, 1–34.

Fielding, M. (1999b). Target setting, policy pathology and student perspectives: Learning to labour in new times. *Cambridge Journal of Education, 29*(2), 277–287.

Fielding, M. (2001a). Beyond the rhetoric of student voice: New departures or new constraints in twenty first century schooling? *Forum, 43*(2), 100–110.

Fielding, M. (2001b). Students as radical agents of change. *Journal of Educational Change, 2*(2), 123–141. https://doi.org/10.1023/A:1017949213447

Fielding, M. (2004). Transformative approaches to student voice: Theoretical underpinnings, recalcitrant realities. *British educational research journal, 30*(2), 295–311.

Fielding, M. (2006). Leadership, radical student engagement and the necessity of person-centred education. *International Journal of Leadership in Education, 9*(4), 299–313.

Fielding, M. (2011). Student voice and the possibility of radical democratic education: Re-narrating forgotten histories, developing alternative futures. In W. Kidd, & G. Czerniawski (Eds.), *The student voice handbook: Bridging the academic/practitioner divide* (pp. 3–17). Emerald Group Publishing Ltd.

Fielding, M., & Bragg, S. (2003). *Students as researchers: Making a difference*. Pearson.

Fine, M. (1992). *Disruptive voices. The possibilities of feminist research*. University of Michigan Press.

Finneran, R., Mayes, E., & Black, R. (2021). Pride and privilege: The affective dissonance of student voice. *Pedagogy, Culture & Society*, 1–16. https://doi.org/10.1080/14681366.2021.1876158

Fletcher, A. (2021). *Ladder of meaningful student involvement*. Sound Out. https://soundout.org/2015/02/02/ladder-of-student-involvement

Foley, D. (2002). Aboriginal standpoint theory. *Journal of Australian Indigenous Studies, 5*(3), 3–13.

Foucault, M. (1978). *The history of sexuality. Volume I: An introduction*. (R. Hurley, Trans.). Pantheon Books. (Original work published 1976)

Fowler, F. (2004). *Policy studies for educational leaders. An introduction* (2nd ed.). Pearson.

Fowler, F. (2009). *Policy studies for educational leaders*. (3rd ed.). Pearson.

Freire, P. (2000). *Pedagogy of the oppressed* (20th-anniversary ed.). Continuum.

Freire, P. (1998). *Pedagogy of freedom: Ethics, democracy, and civic courage*. Rowman & Littlefield.

Fricker, M. (2007). *Epistemic injustice: Power and the ethics of knowing*. Oxford University Press.

Garman, N. (1994). Qualitative inquiry: Meaning and menace for educational researchers. *Mini Conference on Qualitative Approaches in Educational Research* [Paper presentation], Adelaide, Australia.

Gehlbach, H., & Brinkworth, M. E. (2011). Measure twice, cut down error: A process for enhancing the validity of survey scales. *Review of General Psychology, 15*(4), 380–387. https://dx.doi.org/10.1037/a0025704

Ginwright, S., Noguera, P., & Commarota, J. (Eds.). (2006). *Beyond resistance: Youth activism and community change. New democratic possibilities for policy and practice for America's youth*. Routledge.

Giroux, H., & Purple, D. (1983). *The hidden curriculum: Education Illusion or Insight*. McCutchan.

Goncu, A. (1998). Development of intersubjectivity in social pretend play. In D. Faulkner, K. Littleton & M. Woodhead, (Eds.), *Cultural worlds of early childhood* (pp. 185–198). Routledge.

Gonzales, N., Moll, L., & Amanti, C. (2005). *Funds of knowledge*. Lawrence Erlbaum.

Goodman, P. (2011). *Growing up absurd: Problems of youth in the organized society*. New York Review of Books.

Graham, A., & Phelps, R. (2003). 'Being a teacher': Developing teacher identity and enhancing practice through metacognitive and reflective learning processes. *Australian Journal of Teacher Education, 27*(2). https://ro.ecu.edu.au/ajte/vol27/iss2/2/

Gramsci, A. (1973). *Letters from prison*. (L. Lawner, Trans.). Harper & Row. (Original work published 1947)

Greene, M. (1977). Toward wide-awakeness: An argument for the arts and humanities in education. *Teachers College Record, 79*(1), 119–125.

Grosz, E. (2008). *Chaos, territory, art: Deleuze and the framing of the earth*. Columbia University Press.

Groundwater-Smith, S., Dockett, S., & Bottrell, D. (2014). *Participatory research with children and young people*. Sage.

Groundwater-Smith, S., Mayes, E., & Arya-Pinatyh, K. (2014). A bridge over troubling waters in education: The complexity of a students as co-researchers project. *Curriculum Matters, 10*, 213–231. http://www.nzcer.org.nz/nzcerpress/curriculum-matters/articles/bridge-over-troubling-waters-education-complexity-students-com

Guinness. (2021). *Guinness world records*. https://www.guinnessworldrecords.com

Gullion, J. S. (2016). *Writing ethnography*. Sense Publishers.

Gullo, G. L., Capatosto, K., & Staats, C. (2018). *Implicit bias in schools: A practitioner's guide*. Routledge.

Gunter, H., & Thomson, P. (2007a). But, where are the children? *Management in Education, 21*(1), 23–28.

Gunter, H., & Thomson, P. (2007b). Learning about student voice. *Support for Learning, 22*(4), 181–188.

Habermas, J. (1987). *The theory of communicative action* (Vol. 2). Beacon.

Hadfield, M., & Haw, K. (2001). 'Voice', young people and action research. *Educational Action Research, 9*(3), 485–502.

Hahl, K., & Mikulec, E. (2018). Student reflections on teacher identity development in a year-long secondary teacher preparation program. *Australian Journal of Teacher Education, 43*(12). http://dx.doi.org/10.14221/ajte.2018v43n12.4

Hajisoteriou, C., Karousiou, C., & Angelides, P. (2018). Successful components of school improvement in culturally diverse schools. *School Effectiveness and School Improvement, 29*(1), 91–112.

Hall, C., & Thomson, P. (2021). Making the most of arts education partnerships in schools. *Curriculum Perspectives, 41*(1), 101–106.

Haraway, D. (2016). *Staying with the trouble.* Duke University Press.

Harcourt, D., Perry, B., & Waller, T. (Eds.). (2011). *Researching young children's perspectives: Debating the ethics and dilemmas of educational research with children.* Routledge.

Harding, S. (Ed.) (2004). *The feminist standpoint theory reader.* Routledge.

Harro, B. (2000). The cycle of socialization. In M. Adams, W. J. Blumenfeld, R. Castaneda, H.W. Hackman, M. L. Peters, & X. Zuniga (Eds.), *Readings for diversity and social justice* (pp. 15–20). Routledge.

Hart, R. A. (1992). *Children's participation: From tokenism to citizenship.* UNICEF International Child Development Centre.

Hart, R. A. (1997). *Children's participation. The theory and practice of involving young citizens in community development and environmental care.* Earthscan Publications & UNICEF.

Hart, R. A. (2008). Stepping back from 'The Ladder': reflecting on a model of participatory work with children. In A. Reid, J. Bjarne-Bruun, J. Nikel, & V. Simobska (Eds.), *Participation and learning: Developing perspectives in education and the environment, health and sustainability* (pp. 19–31). Springer.

Hazlett, A. (2015). The civic virtues of skepticism, intellectual humility, and intellectual criticism. In J. Baehr (Ed.), *Intellectual virtues and education: Essays in applied virtue epistemology* (pp. 71–92). Routledge.

Heshusius, L. (1995). Listening to children: "What could we possibly have in common?" From concerns with self to participatory consciousness. *Theory into practice, 34*(2), 117–123.

Hickey-Moody, A., Horn, C., & Willcox, M. (2019). Steam education, art/science and quiet activism. In P. Burnard & C.-G. Laura (Eds.), *Why science and art creativities matter: (Re-)configuring STEAM for future-making education* (pp. 200–228). Brill.

Hinkin, T. R. (1998). A brief tutorial on the development of measures for use in survey questionnaires. *Organizational Research Methods, 1*(1), 104–121. https://dx.doi.org:10.1177/109442819800100106

Hinman, L. M. (2013). *Ethics: A pluralistic approach to moral theory* (5th ed.). Wadsworth.

Hodgkinson, C. (1991). *Educational leadership: The moral art*. SUNY Press.

Holdsworth, R. (2000). Schools that create real roles of value for young people. *Prospects, 115*(3), 349–362.

Holdsworth, R., Stafford, J., Stokes, H., & Tyler, D. (2001). *Student action teams—An evaluation: 1999–2000. Working Paper 21*. Australian Youth Research Centre.

Hollins, K., Gunter, H., & Thomson, P. (2006). Living improvement: A case study of a school in England. *Improving Schools, 9*(2), 141–152.

Holquist, S. (2019). Student Voice in Education Policy: Understanding student participation in state-level K-12 education policy making. http://hdl.handle.net/11299/206658

Honkasilta, J., Vehkakoski, T., & Vehmas, S. (2016). 'The teacher almost made me cry': Narrative analysis of teachers' reactive classroom management strategies as reported by students diagnosed with ADHD. *Teaching and Teacher Education, 55*, 100–109.

Hopson, R. K. (2009). Reclaiming knowledge on the margins: Culturally responsive evaluation in the current evaluation moment. In K. E. Ryan, & J. B. Cousins (Eds.), *The Sage international handbook of educational evaluation* (pp. 429–446). Sage Publications.

Hornberger, N. H., & De Korne, H. (2018). Is revitalization through education possible? In L. Hinton, L.M. Huss, & G. Roche (Eds.) *The Routledge handbook of language revitalization* (pp. 94–103). Routledge.

House, R. J., & Howell, J. M. (1992). Personality and charismatic leadership. *Leadership Quarterly, 3*(2), 81–108.

Hurlbert, M., & Gupta, J. (2015). The split ladder of participation: A diagnostic, strategic and evaluation tool to assess when participation is necessary. *Environment Science & Policy, 50*(June), 100–133.

Hurworth, R. (2004). Photo-interviewing. *Qualitative Research Journal, 4*(1), 73.

Ivinson, G., & Renold, E. (2020). Moving with the folds of time and place: Exploring gut reactions in speculative transdisciplinary research with teen girls' in a post-industrial community. In C. A. Taylor, J. B. Ulmer, & C. Hughes (Eds.), *Transdisciplinary feminist research: Innovations in theory, method and practice* (pp. 168–183). Routledge.

Jakobsen, G. (1995). *When education for cooperation leads to development in cooperatives: A study of educational processes*. Centre for Development Research.

James, W. (2007). *The principles of psychology* (Vol. 1). Cosimo, Inc.

Johnson, K. M. (2017). *"Finding yourself in a foreign country": The subjective learning experiences of students in an embedded short-term study abroad program* (Publication No. 13918120) [Doctoral dissertation, The Pennsylvania State University]. ProQuest Dissertations Publishing.

Johnson, K. M. (2018a). Deliberate (mis)representations: A case study of teacher influence on student authenticity and voice in study abroad assessment. *International Journal of Student Voice, 3*(4).

Johnson, K. M. (2018b). " You learn how to experience yourself": A photo-cued investigation of empowerment in study abroad. *Journal of Comparative and International Higher Education, 10*(2), 2–13.

Johnson, K. M. (2020). Hotdog as metaphor: (Co)Developing stories of learning through photo-cued interviewing. *Teachers College Record, 122*(9), 1–38.

Johnson, K. M., & Levitan, J. (2020). Identity, culture, and iterative curriculum development: Collaborating with girls from Indigenous communities to Improve education. *International Journal of Student Voice, 7,* 1–30.

Johnson, K. M., & Levitan, J. (2021). *Exploring the identities and experiences of rural first-generation indigenous students using photo-cued interviewing.* Sage Publications.

Johnson, K. M., & Levitan, J. (2022). Rural indigenous students in Peruvian urban higher education: interweaving ecological systems of coloniality, community, barriers, and opportunities. *Diaspora, Indigenous, and Minority Education, 16*(1), 21–42.

Johnson, R. B., & Onwuegbuzie, A. J. (2004). Mixed methods research: A research paradigm whose time has come. *Educational Researcher, 33*(7), 14–26. https://dx.doi.org:10.3102/0013189X033007014

Jones, K. R., & Perkins, D. F. (2005). Determining the quality of youth-adult relationships within community-based youth programs. *Journal of Extension, 43*(5).

Jordan, J. (1988). Nobody mean more to me than you and the future life of Willie Jordan. *Harvard Educational Review, 58*(3), 363–375. https://doi.org/10.17763/haer.58.3.d171833kp7v732j1

Kegan, R. (1994). *In over our heads: The mental demands of modern life.* Harvard University Press.

Kegan, R. (2001). Competencies and working epistemologies: Ways we want adults to know. In D. S. Rychen & L. H. Salganik (Eds.), *Defining and selecting key competencies* (pp. 192–204). Hogrefe & Huber Publishers.

Kellett, M. (2010). Small shoes, big steps! Empowering children as active researchers. *American Journal of Community Psychology, 46*(1–2), 195–203.

Kelty, C. M. (2019). *The participant: A century of participation in four stories.* University of Chicago Press.

Kohan, W. O. (2020). Paulo Freire and the childhood of a philosophical and educational life. In W.O. Kohan & B. Weber (Eds.), *Thinking, childhood, and time* (pp. 131–144). Lexington Books.

Komulainen, S. (2007). The ambiguity of the child's 'voice' in social research. *Childhood 14*(1), 11–28.

Koomen, M. H. (2016). Inclusive science education: Learning from wizard. *Cultural Studies of Science Education, 11*(2), 293–325.

Krauss, S., Kornbluh, M., & Zeldin, S. (2017). Community predictors of school engagement: The role of families and youth-adult partnership in Malaysia. *Children and Youth Services Review, 73,* 328–337.

Lahman, M. K. (2008). Always othered: Ethical research with children. *Journal of Early Childhood Research, 6*(3), 281–300.

Leavy, P. (2017). *Research design: Quantitative, qualitative, mixed methods, arts-based, community-based, participatory research approaches.* Guilford Press.

LeBar, M. (2020, August 7). *Justice as a virtue.* Stanford Encyclopedia of Philosophy. https://plato.stanford.edu/entries/justice-virtue

Lee, C., & Johnston-Wilder, S. (2013). Learning mathematics—Letting the pupils have their say. *Educational Studies in Mathematics, 83*(2), 163–180.

Lee, L., & Zimmerman, M. (2001). Passion, action and a new vision for student voice: Learning from the Manitoba School improvement program. Manitoba School Improvement Program.

Lee, M. (2006). *Cree (Nehiyawak) teaching*. Four Directions Teachings. http://fourdirectionsteachings.com/transcripts/cree.pdf

Lee, N. (2001). *Childhood and society: Growing up in an age of uncertainty*. Open University Press.

Levitan, J. (2015). More than access: Overcoming barriers to girls' secondary education in the Peruvian Andes. In S.L. Stacki & S. Bailey (Eds.), *Educating adolescent girls around the globe* (pp. 80–96). Routledge.

Levitan, J. (2018). The danger of a single theory: Understanding students' voices and social justice in the Peruvian Andes. *Teachers College Record, 120*(2), 1–36.

Levitan, J. (2019a). Ethical relationship building in action research: Getting out of Western norms to foster equitable collaboration. *Canadian Journal of Action Research, 20*(1), 10–29.

Levitan, J. (2019b). The role of reflexivity in performing collaborative student voice research. In I. R., Berson, C. Gray, & M. J. Berson (Eds.), *Participatory methodologies to elevate children's voice and agency* (pp. 73–92). Information Age Publishing Inc.

Levitan, J., & Carr-Chellman, D. (2018). Learning, selfhood, and pragmatic identity theory. *The Journal of Educational Thought (JET)/Revue de la Pensée Éducative, 51*(2), 140–161.

Levitan, J., & Johnson, K. M. (2020). Salir adelante: Collaboratively developing culturally grounded curriculum with marginalized communities. *American Journal of Education, 126*(2), 195–230.

Levitan, J., & Post, D. (2017). Indigenous student learning outcomes and education policies in Peru and Ecuador. In R. Cortina (Ed.), *Indigenous education policy, equity, and intercultural understanding in Latin America* (pp. 27–49). Palgrave Macmillan.

Levitan, J., Carr-Chellman, D., & Carr-Chellman, A. (2020). Accidental ethnography: A method for practitioner-based education research. *Action Research, 18*(3), 336–352.

Levitan, J., Mahfouz, J., & Schussler, D. L. (2018). Pragmatic identity analysis as a qualitative interview technique. *Forum: Qualitative Social Research 19*(3), 218–239.

Levy, B. (2016). Advising a model United Nations club: A scaffolded youth-adult partnership to foster active participation and political engagement. *Teaching and Teacher Education, 59*, 13–27.

Lincoln, Y. S. (1995). Emerging criteria for quality in qualitative and interpretive research. *Qualitative Inquiry, 1*(3), 275–289.

Lincoln, Y. S., & Guba, E. G. (1985). *Naturalistic inquiry*. Sage Publications.

Lodge, C. (2005). From hearing voices to engaging in dialogue: Problematising student participation in school improvement. *Journal of Educational Change, 6*(2), 125–146. https://doi.org/10.1007/s10833-005-1299-3

Loewenstein, E. A. (1994). Dissolving the myth of the unified self: The fate of the subject in Freudian analysis. *Psychoanalytic Quarterly, 63*(4), 715–732.

Luke, C., & Gore, J. M. (Eds.). (1992). *Feminisms and critical pedagogy*. Routledge.

Lundy, L. (2007). 'Voice' is not enough: Conceptualising article 12 of the United Nations convention on the rights of the child. *British Educational Research Journal, 33*(6), 927–942.

Lundy, L. (2018). In defence of tokenism? Implementing children's right to participate in collective decision-making. *Childhood, 25*(3), 105–122.

Lundy, L., & Cook-Sather, A. (2016). Children's rights and student voice: Their intersections and the implications for curriculum and pedagogy. In D. Wyse, L. Hayward, & J. Pandya (Eds.), *The SAGE handbook of curriculum, pedagogy and assessment* (pp. 263–277). Sage.

Lynch, M. P., Johnson, C. R., Sheff, N., & Gunn, H. (2016, September 6). *Intellectual humility in public discourse*. IHPD literature review. Humility & Conviction in Public Life. Humanities Institute, University of Connecticut.

Lyons, L. B. (2018). *Fostering leadership in high school: Development and validation of student leadership capacity building scales* (Publication No. 449) [Doctoral dissertation, Antioch University]. Antioch University Repository and Archive. https://aura.antioch.edu/etds/449

Lyons, L., Brasof, M., & Baron, C. (2020). *Measuring mechanisms of student voice: Development and validation of student leadership capacity building scales*. AERA Open.

Mackey, H. J. (2018). Contemporary decolonization: Dismantling policy barriers to systemic equity and self-determination. In R. Papa & S. W. J. Armfield (Eds.), *The Wiley handbook of educational policy* (pp. 267–287). Wiley.

MacLure, M. (2013). The wonder of data. *Cultural Studies ↔ Critical Methodologies, 13*(4), 228–232. https://doi.org/10.1177/1532708613487863

Malaguzzi, L. (1996). *The hundred languages of children: The Reggio Emilia approach to early childhood education*. Ablex Publishing Corporation.

Mansfield, K. C. (2014a). Creating smooth spaces in striated places: Toward a global theory for examining social justice leadership in schools. In I. Bogotch & C. Shields (Eds.), *The international handbook on social [in]justice and educational leadership* (pp. 37–50). Springer.

Mansfield, K. C. (2014b). How listening to student voices informs and strengthens social justice research and practice. *Educational Administration Quarterly, 50*(3), 392–430.

Mansfield, K. C., Fowler, B., & Rainbolt, S. (2018). The potential of restorative practices to ameliorate discipline gaps: The story of one high school's leadership team. *Educational Administration Quarterly, 54*(2), 303–323.

Mansfield, K. C., Welton, A., & Halx, M. (2012). Listening to student voice: Toward a more inclusive theory for research and practice. In C. Boske & S. Diem (Eds.), *Global leadership for social justice: Taking it from the field to practice* (pp. 21–42). Emerald Group Publishing Limited.

Margolis, E., & Zunjarwad, R. (2018). Visual research. In N. K. Denzin & Y. S. Lincoln (Eds.), *The SAGE handbook of qualitative research* (5th ed.) (pp. 600–626). Sage.

Massumi, B., & McKim, J. (2009). Micropolitics: Exploring ethico-aesthetics. *Inflexions: A Journal for Research-Creation, 3*(Oct), 1–20.

Matthews, G. B. (1994). *The philosophy of childhood*. Harvard University Press.

Maxwell, J. A. (1996). *Qualitative research design: An interpretive approach*. Applied Social Research Methods Series, Vol. 41. Sage Publications.

Maxwell, T. (2006). Researching into some primary school children's views about school: Using personal construct psychology in practice with children on the special needs register. *Pastoral Care in Education, 24*(1), 20–26.

Mayes, E. (2016a). *The lines of the voice: An ethnography of the ambivalent affects of student voice* [Unpublished doctoral dissertation]. University of Sydney. http://hdl.handle.net/2123/15274

Mayes, E. (2016b). Shifting research methods with a becoming-child ontology: Co-theorising puppet production with high school students. *Childhood, 23*(1), 105–122. https://doi.org/10.1177/0907568215576526

Mayes, E. (2019). Reconceptualizing the presence of students on school governance councils: The a/effects of spatial positioning. *Policy Futures in Education, 17*(4), 503–519.

Mayes, E. (2020). Student voice in school reform? Desiring simultaneous critique and affirmation. *Discourse: Studies in the Cultural Politics of Education, 41*(3), 454–470. https://doi.org/10.1080/01596306.2018.1492517

Mayes. E., Bakhshi, S., Wasner, V., Cook-Sather, A., Mohammad, M., Bishop, D. C., Groundwater-Smith, S., Prior, M., Nelson, E., McGregor, J., Carson, K., Webb, R., Flashman, L., McLaughlin, C., & Cowley, E. (2017). What can a conception of power do? Theories and images of power in student voice work. *International Journal of Student Voice, 2*(1). https://ijsv.psu.edu/?article=what-can-a-conception-of-power-do-theories-and-images-of-power-in-student-voice-work

Mayes, E., Davis, B., Towers, I., Arya-Pinatyh, K., & Groundwater-Smith, S. (2013). Students researching curriculum development: Sharing our voices on education. *Connect, 204*, 14–21. http://research.acer.edu.au/cgi/viewcontent.cgi?article=1213&context=connect

Mayes, E., Finneran, R., & Black, R. (2018). *Victorian student representative council (VicSRC) primary school engagement (PSE) evaluation.* https://drive.google.com/file/d/15Rk2kmkMH4f9NSJAdV8Me2odXXufoN0o/view

Mayes, E., Finneran, R., & Black, R. (2019). The challenges of student voice in primary schools: Students 'having a voice' and 'speaking for' others. *Australian Journal of Education, 63*(2), 157–172. https://doi.org/10.1177/0004944119859445

Mayes, E., & Kelly, M. (forthcoming). Students researching 'inequality': Perplexities and potentialities of arts-informed research methods for students as researchers. In D. Price, B. MacGill, & J. Carter (Eds.), *Arts-based practices with young people at the edge.* Palgrave Macmillan.

McIntosh, P. (1988). White privilege: Unpacking the invisible knapsack. *Peace and Freedom, 49*(4), 10–12.

McLeod, J. (2011). Student voice and the politics of listening in higher education. *Critical Studies in Education, 52*(2), 179–189.

McNae, R. E. (2018). Sharing their wor[l]ds: Appreciating student's voices in strength-based youth leadership development. *Journal of Ethical Educational Leadership,* (Special Issue), 137–153.

Mertens, D. M. (2003). Mixed methods and the politics of human research: The transformative-emancipatory perspective. In A. Tashakkori & C. Teddlie (Eds.), *Handbook of mixed methods in social and behavioral research* (pp. 135–164). Sage.

Mirra, N., Garcia, A., & Morrell, E. (2015). *Doing youth participatory action research: Transforming inquiry with researchers, educators, and students.* Routledge.

Mirra, N., Garcia, A., & Morrell, E. (2018). *Doing youth participatory action research.* Routledge.

Mitchell, C., De Lange, N., & Moletsane, R. (2018). *Participatory visual methodologies: Social change, community and policy.* Sage.

Mitchell, C., & Moletsane, R. (Eds.) (2018). *Disrupting shameful legacies: Girls and young women speak back through the arts to address sexual violence.* Brill/Sense.

Mitchell, M., Readman, K., Henderson, A. J., Lovell, G., Glencross, S., & Chambers, K. (2017). *Students as partners: Raising the student voice in the evaluation of learning and teaching.* University of the Sunshine Coast, Queensland.

Mitchell, C., & Sackney, L. (2011). *Profound improvement: Building learning-community capacity on living-systems principles* (2nd ed.). Routledge.

Mitra, D. (2004). The significance of students: Can increasing "student voice" in schools lead to gains in youth development? *Teachers College Record, 106*(4), 651–688.

Mitra, D. (2005). Adults advising youth: Leading while getting out of the way. *Educational Administration Quarterly, 41*(3), 520–553.

Mitra, D. (2006). Increasing student voice and moving toward youth leadership. *The Prevention Researcher, 13*(1), 7–10.

Mitra, D. (2006). Student voice or empowerment? Examining the role of school-based youth-adult partnerships as an avenue toward focusing on social justice. *International Electronic Journal for Leadership in Learning, 10*(22), 1–17.

Mitra, D. (2007a). The role of administrators in enabling youth-adult partnerships in schools. *NASSP Bulletin, 91*(3), 237–256.

Mitra, D. (2007b). Student voice in school reform: From listening to leadership. In D. Thiessen & A. Cook-Sather (Eds.), *International handbook of student experience in elementary and secondary school* (pp. 727–744). Springer.

Mitra, D. (2008a). Balancing power in communities of practice: An examination of increasing student voice through school-based youth–adult partnerships. *Journal of Educational Change, 9*(3), 221–242.

Mitra, D. (2008b). *Student voice in school reform: Building youth-adult partnerships that strengthen schools and empower youth.* State University of New York Press.

Mitra, D. L., Frick, W. C., & Crawford, E. R. (2011). The ethical dimensions of student voice activities in the United States. In G. Czerniawski, & W. Kidd (Eds.), *The student voice handbook: Bridging the academic/practitioner divide* (pp. 367–378). Emerald Group Publishing.

Mitra, D. L., & Gross, S. J. (2009). Increasing student voice in high school reform: Building partnerships, improving outcomes. *Educational Management Administration & Leadership, 37*(4), 522–543.

Mitra, D. L., & Kirshner, B. (2012). Insiders versus outsiders: Examining variability in student voice initiatives and their consequences for school change. In B. J. McMahon, & J. P. Portelli (Eds.), *Student engagement in urban schools: Beyond neoliberal discourses* (pp. 49–72). Information Age Publishing Inc.

Mitra, D., Lewis, T., & Sanders, F. (2013). Architects, captains, and dreamers: Creating advisor roles that foster youth-adult partnerships. *Journal of Educational Change, 14*(2), 177–201.

Mitra, D., Serriere, S., & Stoicovy, D. (2012). The role of leaders in enabling student voice. *Management in Education, 26*(3), 104–112.

Møller, J. (2006). Democratic schooling in Norway: Implications for leadership in practice. *Leadership & Policy in Schools, 5*(1), 53–69.

Montessori, M. (1982). El Niño, el secreto de la infancia (6ª reimp.). *Diana. (Obra original publicada en 1958).*

Montessori, M. (2009*). The secret of childhood.* Ballantine Books. (Original work published 1936)

Montessori, M. (1912). *The Montessori method: Scientific pedagogy as applied to child education in the children's houses* (Anne E. George, Trans.). Stokes.

Morell, L. (2008). Contributions of middle grade students to the validation process of a national science assessment study. *Middle Grades Research Journal, 3*(1).

Morgan, A. E., & Kennewell, S. E. (2006). Initial teacher education students' views on play as a medium for learning—a divergence of personal philosophy and practice. *Technology, Pedagogy and Education, 15*(3), 307–320.

Morgan, G. (2011). Reflections on images of organization and its implications for organization and environment. *Organization & Environment, 24*(4), 459–478.

Morgan, P. L. (2006). Increasing task engagement using preference or choice-making: Some behavioral and methodological factors affecting their efficacy as classroom interventions. *Remedial and Special Education, 27*(3), 176–187.

Murris, K. (2020). Posthuman child: Deconstructing western notions of child agency. In W. O. Kohan & B. Weber (Eds.), *Thinking, childhood, and time* (pp. 161–178). Lexington Books.

Nelson, E. (2015). Student voice as regimes of truth: Troubling authenticity. *Middle Grades Review, 1*(2), Article 3. http://scholarworks.uvm.edu/mgreview/vol1/iss2/3

Nelson, E. (2017). Re-thinking power in student voice as games of truth: Dealing/ playing your hand. *Pedagogy, Culture & Society, 25*(2), 181–194. http://dx.doi .org/10.1080/14681366.2016.1238839

Niccolini, A. D., Zarabadi, S., & Ringrose, J. (2018). Spinning yarns: Affective kin-shipping as posthuman pedagogy. *Parallax, 24*(3), 324–343. https://doi.org/10 .1080/13534645.2018.1496582

Nind, M. (2011). Participatory data analysis. A step too far? *Qualitative Research 11*(4), 349–363.

Nunnally, J. (1978). *Psychometric theory*. McGraw-Hill.

O'Connell, K. M. (2007). Art, nature, and education: Rabindranath Tagore's holistic approach to learning. In D. T. Hansen (Ed.), *Ethical visions of education: Philosophies in practice* (pp. 126–140). Teachers College Press.

O'Grady, K. (2006). The development of beliefs and values in early adolescence: A case study through religious education pedagogy. *International Journal of Children's Spirituality, 11*(3), 315–327.

Olson, M. M., & Raffanti, M. A. (2006). Leverage points, paradigms, and grounded action: Intervening in educational systems. *World Futures, 62*(7), 533–541.

Orner, M. (1992). Interrupting the calls for student voice in "liberatory" education: A feminist poststructuralist perspective. In C. Luke & J. Gore (Eds.), *Feminisms and critical pedagogy* (pp. 74–89). Routledge.

Ozer, E. J., & Wright, D. (2012). Beyond school spirit: The effects of youth-led participatory action research in two urban high schools. *Journal of Research on Adolescence, 22*(2), 267–283. https://doi.org/10.1111/j.1532-7795.2012.00780.x

Page, T. (2018). Teaching and learning with matter. *Arts, 7*(4), 82–93. https://doi.org /10.3390/arts7040082

Paris, D. (2011). "A friend who understand fully": Notes on humanizing research in a multiethnic youth community. *International Journal of Qualitative Studies in Education, 24*(2), 137–149. https://doi.org/10.1080/09518398.2010.495091

Parker, P. S. (2020). *Ella Baker's catalytic leadership: A primer on community engagement and communication for social justice*. University of California Press.

Parnell, R., & Procter, L. (2011). Flexibility and placemaking for autonomy in learning. *Educational & Child Psychology, 28*(1), 77–88.

Parr, J., & Hawe, E. (2020). Student pedagogic voice in the literacy classroom: A review. *Research Papers in Education*, 1–24. https://doi.org/10.1080/02671522.2020.1864769

Parson, L. (2019). Considering positionality: The ethics of conducting research with marginalized groups. In K. K. Strunk & L. A. Locke (Eds.), *Research methods for social justice and equity in education* (pp. 15–32). Palgrave Macmillan.

Patton, M. Q. (1990). *Qualitative evaluation and research methods* (2nd ed.). Sage Publications.

Pautsch, C. A. (2010). *Leadership to support student voice: The role of school leaders in supporting meaningful student government and voice* (Doctoral dissertation). University of Wisconsin–Madison, Madison, WI.

Pazey, B. L., & DeMatthews, D. (2019). Student voice from a turnaround urban high school: An account of students with and without dis/abilities leading resistance against accountability reform. *Urban Education, 54*(7), 919–956.

Peterson, C., & Seligman, M. E. P. (2004). *Character strengths and virtues. A handbook and classification.* Oxford University Press.

Petrie, P. (2011). *Communication skills for working with children and young people: Introducing social pedagogy* (3rd ed.). Jessica Kingsley publishers.

Pinar, W. (2011). *The character of curriculum studies: Bildung, currere, and the recurring question of the subject.* Springer.

Pomar, M. I., & Pinya, C. (2017). Learning to live together. The contribution of school. *Curriculum Journal, 28*(2), 176–189.

Popkin, R. (2013). *The history of scepticism from Erasmus to Descartes.* Oxford University Press.

Powell, M. A., Graham, A., Fitzgerald, R., Thomas, N., & White, N. E. (2018). Well-being in schools: What do students tell us?. *The Australian Educational Researcher, 45*(4), 515–531.

Practical Ethics Center. (2003). *Online Research Ethics Course.* University of Montana. Office of Research Integrity. https://ori.hhs.gov/education/products/montana_round1/research_ethics.html

Psychology Wiki. *Reflexivity (social theory).* https://psychology.wikia.org/wiki/Reflexivity_(social_theory)

Quijano, A. (2014). "Bien vivir:" Entre "desarrollo" y la des/colonialidad del poder. In A. Quijano (Ed.), *Cuestiones y horizontes: de la dependencia histórico-estructural a la colonialidad/descolonialidad del poder* (pp. 847–859). CLACSO.

Quinn, S., & Owen, S. (2016). Digging deeper: Understanding the power of 'student voice.' *Australian Journal of Education, 60*(1), 60–72.

Redmond, S. (2013). *An explorative study on the connection between leadership skills, resilience and social support among youth* (Publication No. 10458) [Doctoral dissertation, National University of Ireland, Galway]. NUI Galway.

Reeder, L. G. (1972). The patient-client as a consumer: Some observations on the changing professional-client relationship. *Journal of Health and Social Behavior 13*(4), 406–412.

Reichert, F., Chen, J., & Torney-Purta, J. (2018). Profiles of adolescents' perceptions of democratic classroom climate and students' influence: The effect of school and community contexts. *Journal of Youth and Adolescence, 47*(6), 1279–1298.

Reflexivity (social theory). Psychology Wiki. https://psychology.fandom.com/wiki/Reflexivity_(social_theory)

Renold, E. (2018). 'Feel what I feel': Making da(r)ta with teen girls for creative activisms on how sexual violence matters. *Journal of Gender Studies, 27*(1), 37–55. https://doi.org/10.1080/09589236.2017.1296352

Renold, E., & Ringrose, J. (2019). JARring: Making phEmaterialist research practices matter. *MAI: Feminism and Visual Culture, Spring*. https://maifeminism.com/introducing-phematerialism-feminist-posthuman-and-new-materialist-research-methodologies-in-education

Reyes, C. C. (2019). An English learner as a cultural broker for youth interviews. *The Qualitative Report, 24*(3), 532–549.

Roberts, A., & Nason, R. (2011). Nobody says no: Student self-censorship in a collaborative knowledge building activity. *Journal of Learning Design, 4*(4), 56–68.

Roberts, H. (2000). Listening to children: And hearing them. In P. Christensen & A. James (Eds.), *Research with children: Perspectives and practices* (pp. 142–159). Falmer Press.

Robinson, C. (2011). Children's rights in student voice projects: Where does the power lie? *Education Inquiry, 2*(3), 437–451.

Robinson, C., & Taylor, C. (2007). Theorizing student voice: Values and perspectives. *Improving schools, 10*(1), 5–17.

Robinson, C., & Taylor. (2013). Student voice as a contested practice: Power and participation in two student voice projects. *Improving Schools, 16*(1), 32–46.

Rodgers, C. (2018). Descriptive feedback: Student voice in K-5 classrooms. *Australian Educational Researcher, 45*(1), 87–102.

Rogoff, B., Chavajay, P., & Matusov, E. (1993). Questioning assumptions about culture and individuals. *Behavioral and Brain Sciences, 16*(3), 533–534.

Rose, R., & Shevlin, M. (2004). Encouraging voices: Listening to young people who have been marginalised. *Support for Learning, 19*(4), 155–161.

Rubin, B., & Jones, M. (2007). Student action research: Reaping the benefits for students and school leaders. *NASSP Bulletin, 91*(4), 363–378.

Rudduck, J. (2007). Student voice, student engagement, and school reform. In D. Thiessen & A. Cook-Sather (Eds.), *International handbook of student experience in elementary and secondary school* (pp. 711–726). Springer.

Rudduck, J., & Demetriou, H. (2003). Student perspectives and teacher practices: The transformational potential. *McGill Journal of Education, 38*(2), 274–288.

Rudduck, J., & Fielding, M. (2006). Student voice and the perils of popularity. *Educational Review, 58*(2), 219–231.

Rudduck, J., & McIntyre, D. (2007). *Improving learning through consulting pupils*. Routledge.

Russell, L. (2007). Mentoring is not for you!: Mentee voices on managing their mentoring experience. *Improving Schools, 10*(1), 41–52.

Saeed, S., & Zyngier, D. (2012). How motivation influences student engagement: A qualitative case study. *Journal of Education and Learning, 1*(2), 252–267.

Saggers, B., Campbell, M., Dillon-Wallace, J., Ashburner, J., Hwang, Y. S., Carrington, S., & Tones, M. (2017). Understandings and experiences of bullying: Impact on students on the autism spectrum. *Australasian Journal of Special Education, 41*(2), 123–140.

San Pedro, T., & Kinloch, V. (2017). Toward projects in humanization: research on co-creating and sustaining dialogic relationships. *American Educational Research Journal, 54*(1), 737–394. https://doi.org/10.3102/0002831216671210

Schäfer, N., & Yarwood, R. (2008). Involving young people as researchers: Uncovering multiple power relations among youths. *Children's Geographies, 6*(2), 121–135. https://doi.org/10.1080/14733280801963003

Schussler, D. L. (2006). Defining dispositions: Wading through murky waters. *Teacher Educator, 41*(4), 251–268.

Schwandt, T. A. (2015). *The Sage dictionary of qualitative inquiry* (4th ed.). Sage Publications.

Sclater, M., & Lally, V. (2013). Virtual voices: Exploring creative practices to support life skills development among young people working in a virtual world community. *International Journal of Art & Design Education, 32*(3), 331–344.

Seltzer-Kelly, D., Westwood, S. J., & Peña-Guzman, D. M. (2012). A methodological self-study of quantitizing: Negotiating meaning and revealing multiplicity. *Journal of Mixed Methods Research, 6*(4), 258–274.

Shay, M. (2019). Extending the yarning yarn: Collaborative yarning methodology for ethical Indigenist education research. *Australian Journal of Indigenous Education, 1–9.*

Sheehan, M., & Johnson, D. (2012). Philosophical and methodological beliefs of instructional design faculty and professionals. *Educational Technology Research and Development, 60*(1), 131–153. https://doi.org/10.1007/s11423-011-9220-7

Sherif, V. (2018). Practices of youth leadership development in rural high school context: Findings from a qualitative secondary analysis. *Journal of Ethical Educational Leadership (1),* 276–294.

Shier, H. (2001). Pathways to participation: Openings, opportunities and obligations. *Children & Society, 15*(2), 107–117.

Shosh, J. (2019). Democratizing knowledge of teaching and learning through student leadership projects. *Educational Action Research, 27*(3), 396–413.

Silva, E. (2001). Squeaky wheels and flat tires: A case study of students as reform participants. *Forum, 43*(2), 95–99.

Simmons, C., Graham, A., & Thomas, N. (2015). Imagining an ideal school for well-being: Locating student voice. *Journal of Educational Change, 16*(2), 129–144.

Smith, A. B. (2016). *Children's rights: Towards social justice.* Momentum Press Health.

Smith, D. (1987). *The everyday world as problematic: A feminist sociology.* Northeastern University Press.

Smith, D. (1990). *The conceptual practices of power.* Northeastern University Press.

Smith, H., & Haslett, S. (2017). Children's rights in education research: From aims to outcomes. *Cambridge Journal of Education, 47*(3), 413–438.

Smith, L. T. (1999). *Decolonizing methodologies: Research and indigenous peoples.* Zed Books.

Smith, L. T. (2005). On tricky ground: Researching the Native in the age of uncertainty. In N. K. Denzin & Y. S. Lincoln (Eds.), *The Sage handbook of qualitative research* (3rd ed., pp. 85–107). Sage Publications.

Smyth, J. (2006). 'When students have power': Student engagement, student voice, and the possibilities for school reform around 'dropping out' of school. *International Journal of Leadership in Education, 9*(4), 285–298.

Smyth, J. (2007). Toward the pedagogically engaged school: Listening to student voice as a positive response to disengagement and 'dropping out'? In D. Thiessen & A. Cook-Sather (Eds.), *International handbook of student experience in elementary and secondary school* (pp. 635–658). Springer.

Smyth, J. (2012). Doing research on student voice in Australia. *Management in Education, 26*(3), 153–154.

Smyth, J., & Hattam, R. (2001). 'Voiced' research as a sociology for understanding 'dropping out' of school. *British Journal of Sociology of Education, 22*(3), 401–415.

Snow, K. C., Hays, D. G., Caliwagan, G., Ford, D. J., Jr., Mariotti, D., Mwendwa, J. M., & Scott, W. E. (2016). Guiding principles for indigenous research practices. *Action Research, 14*(4), 357–375.

Solnit, R. (2020). *Reflections of my nonexistence*. Viking Press.

Spector, P. E. (1992). *Summated rating scale construction: An introduction*. Sage.

Spence, J. (2003). *Cultural sniping*. Routledge.

Spivak, G. C. (1988). Can the subaltern speak?. In C. Nelson & L. Grossberg (Eds.), *Marxism and the interpretation of culture* (pp. 271–313). University of Illinois Press.

Starratt, R. J. (2004). *Ethical leadership* (vol. 8). Jossey-Bass.

Steup, M. (2020). Epistemic duty, justified belief, and voluntary control. In K. McCain & S. Stapleford (Eds.), *Epistemic duties* (pp. 7–28). Routledge.

Stewart, K. (2007). *Ordinary affects*. Duke University Press.

Sumida Huaman, E. (2020). Mink'a methodologies: Quechua research in the Peruvian Andes. In E. Sumida Huaman & N. D. Martin (Eds.), *Indigenous knowledge systems and research methodologies: local solutions and global opportunities* (pp. 252–271). Canadian Scholars.

Tangen, R. (2009). Listening to children's voices in educational research: Some theoretical and methodological problems. *European Journal of Special Needs Education, 23*(2), 157–166.

Taylor, C., & Robinson, C. (2009). Student voice: Theorising power and participation. *Pedagogy, Culture and Society, 17*(2), 161–175. https://doi.org/10.1080/14681360902934392

Taylor, M. (2010). *Twenty-first century enlightenment*. Royal Society of Arts. https://www.thersa.org/globalassets/pdfs/reports/rsa_21centuryenlightenment_essay1_matthewtaylor.pdf

Thompson, J., Mitchell, C., & Starr, L. J. (2019). *Cellphilming: A tool for addressing gender equality. A facilitators guide*. CODE.

Thomson, P. (2007). Making it real: Engaging students in active citizenship projects. In D. Thiessen & A. Cook-Sather (Eds.), *International handbook of student experience in elementary and secondary school* (pp. 775–804). Springer.

Thomson, P. (2011). Coming to terms with 'voice.' In G. Czerniawski & W. Kidd (Eds.), *The international handbook of student voice* (pp. 19–30). Emerald.

Thomson, P., & Gunter, H. (2006). From 'consulting pupils' to 'pupils as 'researchers': A situated case narrative. *British Educational Research Journal, 32*(6), 839–856.

Thomson, P., & Gunter, H. (2007). The methodology of students-as-researchers: Valuing and using experience and expertise to develop methods. *Discourse, 28*(3), 327–342.

Thomson, P., & Gunter, H. (2008). Researching bullying with students: A lens on everyday life in a reforming high school. *International Journal of Inclusive Education, 12*(2), 185–200.

Thomson, P., & Gunter, H. (2011). Inside, outside, upside down: The fluidity of academic researcher 'identity' in working with/in school. *International Journal of Research & Method in Education, 34*(1), 17–30.

Thomson, P., & Hall, C. (2020). Beyond civics: Art and design education and the making of active/activist citizens. In L. Burgess & N. Addison (Eds.), *Debates in arts and design education* (2nd ed., pp. 31–44). Routledge.

Thomson, P., & Hall, C. (2021). 'You just feel more relaxed': An Investigation of Art Room Atmosphere. *International Journal of Art & Design Education, 40*(3), 599–614.

Thomson, P., Hall, C., Earl, L., & Geppert, C. (2018). *Time to listen: Evidence from the tracking arts learning and engagement (TALE) Project.* https://researchtale .files.wordpress.com/2019/07/time-to-listen-tale-project-final-report.pdf

Thomson, P., Hall, C., Earl, L., & Geppert, C. (2019a). The pedagogical logics of arts-rich schools: a Bourdieusian analysis. *British Journal of Sociology of Education, 40*(2), 239–253.

Thomson, P., Hall, C., Earl, L., & Geppert, C. (2019b). Subject choice as everyday accommodation/resistance: Why students in England (still) choose the arts. *Critical Studies in Education, 61*(5). https://doi.org/10.1080/17508487.2018.1525754

Thomson, P., Hall, C., Earl, L., & Geppert, C. (2019c). *Tracking arts learning and engagement (Final report).* University of Nottingham School of Education.

Thomson, P., Hall, C., Earl, L., & Geppert, C. (2020). Towards an arts education for cultural citizenship. In S. Riddle & M. Apple (Eds.), *Reimagining education for democracy* (pp. 1–13). Routledge.

Thomson, P., & Holdsworth, R. (2003). Theorising change in the educational 'field': Re-readings of' student participation' projects. *International Journal of Leadership in Education, 6*(4), 371–391.

Thomson, P., McQuade, V., & Rochford, K. (2005). "My little special house": Reforming the risky geographies of middle school girls at Clifftop College. In G. Lloyd (Ed.), *Problem girls; Understanding and supporting troubled and troublesome girls and young women* (pp. 172–189). Routledge Falmer.

Thorndike, E. (1931). Human learning. Elliot, R.M. (Ed) *The century psychology series*. The Century Co.

Thurston, W. E., Cove, L., & Meadows, L. M. (2008). Methodological congruence in complex and collaborative mixed method studies. *International Journal of Multiple Research Approaches, 2*(1), 2–14. https://doi.org/10.5172/mra.455.2.1.2

Treseder, P. (1997). *Empowering children & young people: Training manual.* Save the Children.

Tuana, N. (2007). Conceptualizing moral literacy. *Journal of Educational Administration, 45*(4), 364–378.

Tuck, E. (2009). Suspending damage: A letter to communities. *Harvard Educational Review, 79*(3), 409–428.

Tyack, D. B., & Cuban, L. (1995). *Tinkering toward utopia: A century of public school reform.* Harvard University Press.

UNESCO Youth Programme. (2021). *By youth, for youth, with youth.* https://en .unesco.org/youth

United Nations. (1989). *United Nations Convention on the Rights of the Child.* https://www.ohchr.org/en/professionalinterest/pages/crc.aspx

van Manen, M. (2016). *Researching lived experience: Human science for an action sensitive pedagogy.* Routledge.

VicSRC. (2021). Victorian Student Representative Council. https://www.vicsrc.org.au

Wall, K. (2017). Exploring the ethical issues related to visual methodology when including young children's voice in wider research samples. *International Journal of Inclusive Education, 21*(3), 316–331.

Wall, K. (2021). Productive parallels between young children's voice and practitioner voice. In M. A. Peters (Ed.) *Encyclopaedia of teacher education.* Springer. https://doi.org/10.1007/978-981-13-1179-6_435-1

Wall, K., Cassidy, C., Robinson, C., Hall, E., Beaton, M., Kanyal, M. & Mitra, D. (2019). Look who's talking: Factors for considering the facilitation of very young children's voices. *Journal of Early Childhood Research, 17*(4), 263–278.

Wang, C. C. (1999). Photovoice: A participatory action research strategy applied to women's health. *Journal of Women's Health, 8*(2), 185–192.

Wernick, L. J., Woodford, M. R., & Kulick, A. (2014). LGBTQQ youth using participatory action research and theater to effect change: Moving adult decision-makers to create youth-centered change. *Journal of Community Practice, 22*(1–2), 47–66.

Whitty, G., & Wisby, E. (2007). Whose voice? An exploration of the current policy interest in pupil involvement in school decision-making. *International Studies in Sociology of Education, 17*(3), 303–319. https://doi.org/10.1080/09620210701543957

Widlok, T. (2018). Learning how to share. In M. LeBar (Ed.), *Justice* (pp. 93–177). Oxford University Press.

Wilson, C. (under review). "That's my Black students grown up": Revolutionizing teacher education through critical race inquiry.

Wilson, C., & Cook-Sather, A. (in press). Rippling the patterns of power: Enacting anti-racist pedagogy with students as co-teachers. In J. Neuhaus (Ed.), *Picture a professor: Intersectional teaching strategies for interrupting bias about faculty and increasing student learning.* West Virginia University Press.

Wisby, E. (2011). Student voice and new models of teacher professionalism. In G. Czerniawski & W. Kidd (Eds.), *The student voice handbook: Bridging the academic/practitioner divide* (pp. 31–44). Emerald Group Publishing

Wong, N., Zimmerman, M., & Parker, E. (2010). A typology of youth participation and empowerment for child and adolescent health promotion. *American Journal of Community Psychology, 46*(1), 100–114.

Woods, P. (2005). *Democratic leadership in education.* Paul Chapman.

Worthington, R. L., & Whittaker, T. A. (2006). Scale development research: A content analysis and recommendations for best practices. *The Counseling Psychologist, 34*(6), 806–838. https://dx.doi.org:10.1177/0011000006288127

Yonezawa, S., & Jones, M. (2007). Student co-researchers: How principals can recruit, train, and enlist the help of students to examine what works and does not work in their schools. *NASSP Bulletin, 91*(4), 322–342.

Yosso, T. J., Parker, L., Solórzano, D. G., & Lynn, M. (2004). From Jim Crow to affirmative action and back again: A critical race discussion of racialized rationales and access to higher education. *Review of Research in Education, 28*, 1–25. http://www.jstor.org/stable/3568134

Zarabadi, S., & Ringrose, J. (2018). Re-mattering media affects: Pedagogical inter-ference into pre-emptive counter-terrorism culture. In A. Baroutsis, S. Riddell, & P. Thomson (Eds.), *Education research and the media: Challenges and pos-sibilities* (pp. 66–79). Routledge.

Zeldin, S., Krauss, S. E., Collura, J., Lucchesi, M., & Sulaiman, A. H. (2014). Con-ceptualizing and measuring youth–adult partnership in community programs: A cross national study. *American Journal of Community Psychology, 54*(3–4), 337–347

Zeldin, S., Krauss, S. E., Kim, T., Collura, J., & Abdullah, H. (2016). Pathways to youth empowerment and community connectedness: A study of youth–adult partnership in Malaysian after-school, co-curricular programs. *Journal of Youth and Adolescence, 45*(8), 1638–1651.

Zuberi, T., & Bonilla-Silva, E. (Eds.). (2008). *White logic, white methods: Racism and methodology.* Rowman & Littlefield Publishers.

About the Editors and Contributors

Marc Brasof is an associate professor of education in the School of Education at Arcadia University and has taught for over 22 years in public schools as a social studies teacher and at the academy in teacher education and educational leadership. Dr. Brasof was the Rosemary and Walter Blankley Endowed Chair, in which he developed the Social Action and Justice Education Fellowship to help diversify the teacher workforce and shift teacher education towards more critical educational practices. Dr. Brasof's research examines school change from the perspective of student voice, organizational learning, civic education, and equity.

Joseph Levitan, PhD, is an assistant professor in the Department of Integrated Studies in Education at McGill University. He has worked as a teacher and educational leader for over 14 years. He has also founded two community-based education centers in the Andes. His research and publications are in the areas of student voice methodologies for socially just school change; community-based participatory action research; and the intersections of identity, wellbeing, educational policy, and social justice. He is currently undertaking a large community-based research project (funded by the Social Science and Humanities Research Council of Canada) to understand how to co-construct more culturally grounded curriculum with Quechua-speaking youth.

Lorna Arnott is a senior lecturer and director of early years in the School of Education, University of Strathclyde. Lorna's main area of interest is in children's early play experiences, particularly in relation to technologies, social, and creative play. She also has a keen interest in research methodologies, with a specialist focus on consulting with children and methods derived from pedagogy. Lorna is the convener for the Digital Childhoods, STEM and Multimodality Special Interest Group as part of the European Early Childhood Educational Research Association and is the deputy editor for the *International Journal of Early Years Education* and assistant editor for the *Journal of Early Childhood Research*.

Mhairi C. Beaton is a professor at Carnegie School of Education at Leeds Beckett University. Her research interests focus on the interface of teacher education, student voice, and inclusion. Formerly a primary teacher, Mhairi's work is characterized by a partnership approach with and for educational practitioners and young people as they collectively examine how educational provision might be re-visioned to be fully inclusive of all.

Claire Cassidy is a professor of education at the University of Strathclyde. Her research interests coalesce around three main and, for her, interrelated themes: practical philosophy with children and young people, children's human rights and human rights education, and childhood studies. Through her work she aims to raise children's status and support them to participate more fully in society, particularly through philosophical dialogue, for which she trains practitioners nationally and internationally.

Alison Cook-Sather is Mary Katharine Woodworth Professor of Education at Bryn Mawr College and director of the Teaching and Learning Institute at Bryn Mawr and Haverford Colleges in the United States. A former secondary English teacher and co-creator of the secondary teacher certification program at Bryn Mawr and Haverford Colleges, Alison has developed internationally recognized programs that position students and teachers as pedagogical partners, published over 100 articles and book chapters and eight books, and spoken or consulted on partnership work in 13 countries. Learn more about Alison's work at https://www.alisoncooksather.com.

Heather Curl is core faculty at Antioch University in Seattle and chair of the master's in education program. She has served as a middle and high school teacher of English and social studies; an elementary and secondary teacher educator in the United States, Zambia, and China; and a consultant and board member to nonprofits focused on supporting a strengths-based approach to social mobility through education. Dr. Curl's current scholarship focuses on social mobility, student voice, and antiracist social studies education.

William C. Frick, PhD, is the Rainbolt Family Endowed Presidential Professor of Educational Leadership and Policy Studies in the Jeannine Rainbolt College of Education at the University of Oklahoma. He is the founding director of the Center for Leadership Ethics and Change. A PhD graduate of the Pennsylvania State University, his research interests include the philosophy of administrative leadership, school system reform within urban municipality revitalization efforts, and broader cultural studies exploring the intersection of identity and schooling.

Vanessa Gold is a doctoral student in the Department of Integrated Studies of Education at McGill University, studying pedagogical change processes in secondary schools. The research areas informing her work include student voice, educational leadership, and action research. Her PhD research has been funded by The Social Sciences and Humanities Research Council of Canada through the Canada Graduate Scholarships Program.

Elaine Hall is professor of legal education at Northumbria University. Previously a primary school teacher, psychotherapist, and historian, she writes, researches, and worries about learning across the life span, the implications for our data of how and why we choose particular research methods, and what we (think we) mean when we say we want to increase representation and voice.

Kayla Johnson is an assistant professor in the Department of Educational Policy Studies and Evaluation and director of Graduate Global Learning Initiatives in the College of Education at the University of Kentucky. She uses visual, participatory, and student voice methods to improve access to and progression through higher education as well as learning in education-abroad programming.

Lindsay Lyons (she/her) is an educational justice coach who works with teachers and school leaders to inspire educational innovation for racial and gender justice, design curricula grounded in student voice, and build capacity for shared leadership. Lindsay taught in NYC public schools, holds a PhD in leadership and change, and is the founder of the educational blog and podcast, *Time for Teachership*.

Ellen MacCannell is a doctoral student in the Department of Integrated Studies of Education at McGill University studying pedagogical change processes in secondary schools. Her research interests include secondary school change initiatives, educational leadership, student voice, and sustainability in change processes.

Eve Mayes (she/her) is a senior research fellow at Deakin University in the School of Education (research for educational impact). She lives and works on unceded Wadawurrung Country. Her publications and research interests are in the areas of student voice and activism, climate justice education, affective methodologies, and participatory research. Eve is currently undertaking the Australian Research Council (ARC) Discovery Early Career Fellowship (DECRA) project: Striking voices: Australian school-aged climate justice activism (2022–2025).

Carol Robinson is a professor of children's rights at Edge Hill University. Her research interests combine theoretical and empirical work focusing on the voices, experiences, rights, and empowerment of children and young people.

A major focus of Carol's work has been around developing insights into issues relating to children's human rights education. Carol has previously taught in secondary schools and pupil referral units for children who have been excluded from their mainstream school.

Lisa J. Starr is a well-respected and collegial educational leader in the field of education. Currently she is an associate professor and chair of the Department of Integrated Studies in Education at McGill University. She is the past director of the Internships and Student Affairs Office for the Faculty of Education and past president of the Canadian Association for the Study of Women and Education (CASWE). She completed her doctoral degree in the Department of Curriculum and Instruction at the University of Victoria. Her current SSHRC-funded research, *NEXTschool: An Innovative Approach to High School Education*, is a study of three Quebec high schools engaging in the process of educational reform.

Pat Thomson is professor of education in the School of Education, The University of Nottingham. She is a fellow of the Academy of Social Science (UK) and the Royal Society of Arts, and a former school principal of disadvantaged schools in South Australia.

Kate Wall is professor of education at the University of Strathclyde. A primary teacher by background, her work is characterized by inquiry-based partnership with children and practitioners of all ages and stages. She is interested in methodologies for gathering learner perspectives on experience, curriculum, and metacognition, and she is recognized for her work on how visual approaches with pedagogic orientations can facilitate this kind of dialogue. Kate's work aims to generate knowledge of ethical practice for eliciting voice within a democratic community, and to do this, particularly with young children, she has needed to look to more creative methods and practices for supporting the level of participation and ensuring authentic voice.

Chanelle Wilson is an assistant professor of education in the Bryn Mawr and Haverford Colleges education program, and the director of Africana Studies at Bryn Mawr College. She has served as a public school practitioner, teaching secondary education students in the United States and around the world. Dr. Wilson's current scholarship focuses on race and antiracism in education and anticolonial practices in education.

Index